ACCLAIM for
The Silence of Morning

BY D.A. HICKMAN

"In *The Silence of Morning*, the author gives us an insightful and candid memoir after the suicide of her son at age 27. 'Grief was at the wheel' in this telling, but so are wisdom and discovery. At its center lies heartfelt candor in a lyrical voice in praise of life."

—MARY L. TABOR, AUTHOR OF *WHO BY FIRE*

"Most pass through life slightly oblivious to the impact of devastating grief—that is, until we experience it firsthand. In *The Silence of Morning*, I cried as I followed the author along her path, a spiritual journey in which she survived her darkest moments. Ultimately, illumination follows: about life, loss, spirituality. No one will avoid great, heartrending loss, but Hickman's memoir offers caring and friendship to anyone navigating such perilous waters. A book to treasure."

—LYNNE MORGAN SPREEN, AUTHOR OF *DAKOTA BLUES*

"After the author's son—bright, caring, but battling drug addiction—takes his life, Hickman enters the bewildering realm of grief: 'the world's teacher in disguise.' As her quest for solace and insight unfolds in *The Silence of Morning*, we see her loss and the world's: the boy with the fishing pole and paper route, the struggling young man devouring books while incarcerated … yet searching for life purpose and meaning, the hopeful farm hand in jeans, scuffed boots. All of us are made of loss, and how we respond—or choose not to—is as personal as a fingerprint. Keenly aware of the world's preference for mindlessness, its impatience with the sick and the dying, its notable indifference toward death, Hickman reads widely, reflects on time, lives in the now. And draws nearer to her essential self. This story conveys a distilled wisdom: the gift of a spiritual seeker's brave inquiry."

—RICHARD GILBERT, AUTHOR OF *SHEPHERD: A MEMOIR*

"As Hickman gently takes us on a harrowing yet deeply inspiring journey of growing spiritual awareness, a wise, compassionate companion emerges. In *The Silence of Morning* the author—insightful, sublime—shines a strong light on a viable path to wholeness."

—CATHRYN WELLNER, AUTHOR, PHOTOGRAPHER

Also by the Author

Always Returning: The Wisdom of Place
(Capturing Morning Press, 2014, second edition, *Heart Resides*)

Where the Heart Resides: Timeless Wisdom of the American Prairie
(William Morrow, Eagle Brook, 1999, first edition)

*I am drawn to Hickman's eloquent, inspirational
writing ... the way she pulls her reader away
from the chaos into a place of quiet reflection.*
—KATHLEEN POOLER, MEMOIRIST

The Silence of Morning

I truly hope my memoir speaks to loss and grief, but to other societal issues as well. I tried to capture our culture, its addictive tendencies, and the troubling implications that follow. The spiritual component is here, as well. I will always be a student of society looking for the deeper story and the universal message to derive a better understanding of the human condition.

—D.A. HICKMAN

Capturing
Morning
press

The Silence of Morning

A MEMOIR OF TIME UNDONE

D. A. HICKMAN

Capturing Morning Press

Published by
Capturing Morning Press

Print ISBN-13: 978-0-9908423-6-1
E-book ISBN-13: 978-0-9908423-1-6

Produced in the United States of America

First Edition

capturingmorningpress.com

CMP@capturingmorningpress.com

Logo design © EKM, 2014

"Sunbeam Dance" by D.A. Hickman, first published fall
2011 *Pasque Petals*, South Dakota State Poetry Society

This book, heartfelt, hopefully inspiring and engaging, is not intended as a substitute for professional help or advice. Readers should seek such services, as needed, and whenever required or recommended.

Copyright © 2015 artist Paul C. Jackson
"Silence of Morning" watercolor
pauljacksonart@gmail.com • Columbia, Missouri

Book & cover design
Michele DeFilippo @ 1106Design.com • Phoenix, Arizona

~

Text set in Adobe Caslon Pro, a popular serif typeface originally designed around 1722 by William Caslon (1692–1766).

We went down into the silent garden. Dawn is the time when nothing breathes, the hour of silence. Everything is transfixed, only the light moves.

—LEONORA CARRINGTON (1917–2011)

For Matthew—his presence and love, his place in the world of time, his eternal spirit.

SUNBEAM DANCE

BY D.A. HICKMAN

Never works to
go to bed early
when needing to
rise before dawn,
so instead of
subscribing to
a magic formula
grown musty, I
read poetry by
Tennyson until
daybreak, knowing
words on a page
will guide me to
the morning light.

Life is more than an ending.
—from THE SILENCE OF MORNING

Matthew: 2006 (Thanksgiving, Christmas) and 2007 (fishing).

Sorrow and silence are strong, and patient endurance is godlike.
—HENRY WADSWORTH LONGFELLOW

Contents

Part II
What Time Reveals

The Silence of Morning

My religion consists of a humble admiration of the illimitable superior spirit who reveals himself in the slight details we are able to perceive with our frail and feeble mind.

—ALBERT EINSTEIN

Preface

This isn't a book about Buddhism, Catholicism, or any other category of religious belief. Rather, it's about a journey of growing spiritual awareness that tapped into many schools of thought to uncover the "peace of God which passeth all understanding." A willingness to question everything, in fact, is what sustained my commitment to spiritual growth.

Sometimes such questioning is spontaneous, or a profound catalyst may offer a push. A powerful push. Sensing an infinite number of paths leading to spiritual realization—as many as experience and intuition can inform—I embraced this catalyst as an opportunity to push beyond dogma (ancient belief systems) too often created, sustained by history, power, ego. Stereotypes and superficial judgments that suggest nothing more than pre-packaged definitions of reality. Some, curiously popular. My ardent desire to transcend the anguish that arrived with my son's loss also fueled my questioning—slowly taking me somewhere *new* in the spiritual sense.

John Lennon said, "I believe in God, but not as one thing, not as an old man in the sky. I believe that what people call God is something in all of us. I believe that what Jesus and Mohammed and Buddha and all the rest said was right. It's just that the translations have gone wrong." *Something* in all of us, indeed. I love Lennon's choice of words. He leads us in a fruitful direction, suggesting we look internally for what we're too often led to believe is an external discovery. Consider the problems of our world that stem from an excessive external focus. The enormous suffering generated as we search endlessly for a "special" life purpose, when discovering our essential self—*that something within*—and learning to fully live from that place, is our actual, and irreplaceable, mission.

We're much more than surface impressions suggest, but possessing faith in the human experience, no matter how confusing, stark, or challenging, is what finally leads us to our spiritual center. Yet, that's where we tend to get sidetracked. Doubting life experience, its vagueness and fleeting nature, its sorrows and mysteries, almost by default, we assimilate popularized, mainstream values that take us far, far afield.

Usually (with luck), something happens that pushes us to question what we believe or were taught to think, and finally, we are forced to acknowledge our deep weariness with the world: unfathomable suffering caused by destructive societal patterns, habitual ways of judging and perceiving, attachment to the dullness (sameness) of the conditioned mind. Then true change occurs. That's when I began to see, ever more deeply, what was merely hidden by a frenzied, conflict-ridden world following an antiquated, generic map.

Life is much simpler than we presume, but our gaze must shift: eyes turning within, consistently, patiently. Mythologist Joseph Campbell told us, "The goal of life is to make your heartbeat match the beat of the universe, to match your nature with Nature."

Oh, how that resonates. We need a plethora of such voices flowing from everywhere, anywhere, even if once resisted. Voices that challenge us to know ourselves deeply.

Navigating the dimensions of grief, I sought the wisest, most engaging voices I could find regardless of origin. Lao Tzu, for one. Lacking a survival map or bread crumbs to follow, a few of his words became a spiritual guide. As a creative beacon in my search for understanding, if I stayed true to the process—listened to my intuition—I hoped to find *the way of heaven, the way of the sage.* Nothing less felt adequate.

As a quiet, steady reminder, I close each chapter with Lao Tzu's insightful message. Like a bell chiming, it's a consistent and gentle imperative to look within. A comforting message against the grimness—*the necessary isolation*—of the journey. Inviting the bell, as opposed to ringing it, is a mindfulness practice used in meditation; since each chapter represents a determined push through the maze of time, I invite the bell 24 times.

Lao Tzu, a Chinese philosopher, was revered as a great master during the sixth century (604 B.C.–531 B.C.). He wrote the *Tao Te Ching,* or *The Book of the Way.*

Given the countless number of enlightened voices (deceased and living) in the world, I could have selected words of guidance, of comfort, from many sources. Whether popular, obscure, or discovered quite by accident, the key, I found, was opening without prejudice or expectation to what I didn't know I needed, wanted, to know.

A persistent willingness to explore the deepest mysteries illuminated a path of renewal that felt like a winding set of days, months, and years, without beginning or end. Mind and heart will try very hard to grasp the unthinkable, but the hard ground of loss must be worked, *surrendered to*, on the level of soul to deeply transform us. To rouse us from our sleep.

God's finger touched him and he slept.
—LORD ALFRED TENNYSON

An Austere Garden
An Introduction

*F*lash frozen, a defenseless cod yanked from a rumbling, fertile sea, I no longer felt real, and knew only that my will to live was being tested. Hiding from the world in my writing study, a compact sunny nook turned slate gray as though drained of all signs of life, I felt a piercing void. Emptiness overwhelmed. Time stood uncomfortably still.

Scanning the west-facing room, its white walls and beige curtains, I looked around for *something* comforting. Gazing blankly at whatever was perched on my shelves—pictures, books, a few mementos—the futility of my search exaggerated my disbelief, my muddled thoughts. That I couldn't possibly know *what* to look for, given the circumstances, didn't occur to me for a very long time.

Grief has many universal qualities, but only as an individual did I come to understand its blinding power—its unique role in my life. And only as an individual did I learn the life-changing lessons that flowed well beyond the person, the relationship, I grieved for—my son Matt, or Matthew, and the 27-year history that seemed lost forever.

Admittedly, this potent insight didn't arrive like a new pair of dress shoes, delicately concealed by white tissue in the perfect-size box. Discovering the formidable lessons of loss took tremendous patience. Had to be discovered, teased out, like the pale flicker of dawn that refuses anything more until the allotted time has elapsed. Because of his sheer absence, I *knew* my son had disappeared from our lives without warning, but an academic understanding—an intellectual awareness—is virtually useless in this grievous context.

Matthew's death left me spiritually challenged. Powerful questions pushed me to the other side of the world and beyond. The essence of grief, in fact, how it must be known firsthand to be known at all, was slow to come into focus. Emotional exhaustion clouded my vision; riveting sadness burrowed into my soul. Grief, it seemed, was the worst kind of intruder—a foreign presence my entire being tried to reject, as if optional or somehow less than monumental. Forced to confront something vast, supremely powerful, and well beyond my frame of reference, 52 years of life experience suddenly held no significance.

Extreme sounding, perhaps, yet death—especially from suicide—is also at the far end of the spectrum: the very edge of human understanding. A faint whisper in the night. And knowing, from a shaky place within, how ill-prepared I was to cope with the gravity of a family tragedy—its nameless, staggering ache, its uncertain aftermath—I feared I would fold. Only the feeble question of *when* remained.

Telling myself that many had known such despair, that something called shock would insulate me from devastating pain for a time, was pointless. Understanding that death can occur anytime, anyplace, and often when *least* expected, didn't help either. Only, much later, when drawn to the wisdom of Zen, did I discover a mirror image. Feeling stuck in a rock garden, for instance, resonated with me. Stark, too, had its place. Empty spaces felt real. In a thin book about Zen rock gardening, I learned that sitting with stones could lead me to a "still point" within, one to help me grapple with fierce challenges.

So I sat with my grief—allowing its intense, unyielding nature—to study every rock, every shadow, that came into view, to watch rays of piercing sunshine that danced like spotlights, guiding me to moments where I might pause more deeply on aspects of Matthew's journey. Somehow, while I experienced the past, present, and future in a confusing but oddly revealing blur, more than eight years elapsed, and after seven years of work, surprisingly, I finished writing this book. But in the spiritual sense, I'm still sitting in that rock garden.

The barest essentials reveal the greatest insights, and the conditioned mind, created by the fury of endless expectations flowing from countless directions—a conformist society, those who depend on the status quo, the "you" they are comfortable with, the "you" they are unwilling to release—tends to cause suffering. But hard times require us to sit with a distressing reality until we truly open to the deeper aspects of ourselves.

Matthew's death delivered this kind of impact but, eventually, a different day dawned: well after the hopeful garden I'd so patiently nurtured vanished in a furious flash. When everything turned black and white, and only jagged stones remained. But learning to sit comfortably amongst them until they smoothed, finally aligning myself with their subtle energy, took such a long time. Even longer, until I sensed something peaceful, almost pleasing, within this austere garden of rock arranged just so.

En route, I was forced to turn back countless times, retreating further and further until I'd bravely walked, once more, through the magical doors of childhood. Significant loss yanks you up, shakes you like a helpless rag doll, and drops you back at the beginning of your remembered history. Once there, I felt driven to understand the reserved young girl who was uncommonly content to keep company with her grandmother.

In hindsight, our time together resembled an informal spiritual retreat, with Anna, the calm, centered Zen master. Actually a devout Roman Catholic, she manifested her lovely spiritual dimension in causal, commonplace ways she likely wasn't aware of, but when seeking her vibrant memory, I invariably encounter a timeless wisdom. The kind shared in my first book, *Where the Heart Resides—Timeless Wisdom of the American Prairie*. Written nine years before Matthew's death, I explored the organic wisdom of people and place at the turn of the century, and later revisited the book in 2014, in a 15th anniversary edition, as *Always Returning: The Wisdom of Place*.

Of course now I understand more clearly how my physical roots had informed a deep awareness of my spiritual roots, helping me to feel inspired and nurtured by a rugged but stunningly beautiful geography, and by a culture easily misunderstood or ridiculed when stereotypical frameworks lacking depth and nuance are utilized.

Huddled like old friends in a sunny breakfast nook, my grandmother and I sipped hot tea with honey. I asked questions (the best I could muster). Anna answered. Sometimes with just a smile, or a kind expression, and then there was the solitude of a comfortable silence. Quietly, I admired her book of poetry by Tennyson. Noticed how she conveyed her love of music, nature, life. An impressionable youngster in awe of her grandmother's peaceful spirit. But what else was there, besides a beautiful experience, a beneficial and loving relationship?

Because of grief, the extended periods of contemplation it provoked, I came to know Anna's memory more deeply, appreciating anew the lessons I'd unknowingly absorbed. But renewing this critical connection from my earliest days gave me something else: an emotional courage I wasn't at all sure I possessed.

I knew little about suicide when Matthew died. Yet, if nearly one million (statistics vary significantly) people make an attempt every year, it's not exactly a rare phenomenon. But, after believing for years in my son's struggle, how had he become just another statistic—another young man overcome by insurmountable issues, the formidable tides of life?

Hopefully the revealing edges of this wrenching experience will shine a light on the perplexing human condition. We can condemn others—look down on those with serious challenges—or we can evolve into a more humane world by finally accepting our shared humanity, and the quest to survive on a planet with increasingly limited resources.

Most would agree, after all, that sustaining life is quite an endeavor.

Curiously, however, we busy ourselves with nonsensical comparisons, insisting some life situations are "better" or "best." Of course the ego craves superiority, so the insidious illusion of separateness is born, renewed, and born again. Yet, we *know* there isn't a "best way" to live—no ordained path boasting the *Good Housekeeping* seal of approval. Even when lives appear paradisiacal, invariably, it's a surface impression or merely temporary circumstances that can't reflect long-term reality. Daily life is never perfect or painless.

As the well-known Zen proverb keenly instructs: "The obstacle is the path." So, I hope this book offers reasonable challenges of its own: Narrative layers shaped by experience, persistent curiosity, research, and serendipity that only become apparent as chapters shift and sway but, finally, like grief itself, give way to something more; chapters offering levity or emanating a dark gravity, and sometimes both. My intuition, not the imagined expectations of others, set the pace. What one likes, even loves, the next finds disastrous. J.R.R. Tolkien once said about *The Lord of the Rings*, "Some who have read the book, or at any rate have reviewed it, have found it boring, absurd, or contemptible; and I have no cause to complain, since I have similar opinions of their works, or of the kinds of writing that they evidently prefer."

Life is unpredictable and short, and conformity rarely produces works of art—in any medium, in any form. As da Vinci believed, "The painter will produce pictures of little merit if he takes the works of others as his standard." And so it is that I paint with words, with the humility of knowing nothing can be *fully* explained (truth is always a matter of context and state of consciousness, never absolute), but also with a deepening awareness: an inner peace increasingly independent of external events, mental projections, or surface interpretation. Thus, I am inspired to capture this powerful experience as a whole—not its most dramatic details, necessarily, but its riveting essence.

Not easy. Perhaps impossible. Nonetheless, I decided to try. Opting for a minimum of loosely structured scenes, I avoided writing dialogue I had no way to recall precisely, and dug deeper. Writing sparely (Zen-like approach), I stitched together chapters with a light touch, artistic pacing. Anchored in the physical world, more often, the spiritual, I wanted the hollowness of days that felt endless to resonate fully before moving on.

Sharing, unduly so, the privacy of my family wasn't necessary. Do we really need yet *another* diversion: a fantastical, soap-opera-like window into harried lives, a jazzed-up storyline? Something to help us encounter a timeless, sacred, inner world sounds promising though.

Part one ("What Time Conceals") is about Matthew's sudden absence in a time-based world: the intense questioning his death ignites. Time, spinning a thick web around many of my perceptions, fosters a skewed sense of reality that exacerbates my suffering. *Time lost, time stolen, time endured.* Almost imperceptibly, though, an internal shift begins: I grasp, more clearly, how time tends to conceal the expansive, comforting world of spirit. In part two ("What Time Reveals"), I probe its well-kept secrets and, while exploring its para-doxical contours—time conceals, but also reveals—realize how, as a mechanism for life, time also provides an opportunity, *and a reason*, to consider the mysteries of existence.

One begets the other. So focusing even less on chronology as the book evolves, viewing life and death less literally—absent a linear framework, one-dimensional definitions that I (like most) grew up with—I inch my way past the deafening drumbeat of calendar dates, numbers on a clock, logical-sounding timelines, and sequential thinking.

To my relief, as I try to transcend our cultural obsession with time, that rigid dividing line between life and loss (an agonizing separation that fuels pain, frustration, and even stymied spiritual growth) fades. Leaning deeply into my insights, I reject the contentious dance between living and dying that begs the question of mortal existence. And, finally, I come to accept that a deep, abiding peace is dependent on my willingness to *become* the twining of life and loss. Only then am I free to experience life on a deeper level, beyond the heavily personalized sense of self we are taught to cultivate, to believe in.

While loss may be intrinsic to each breath, Rumi consoles, "Goodbyes are only for those who love with their eyes. Because for those who love with heart and soul there is no such thing as separation."

The Silence
of Morning

Part I
What Time Conceals

But there was no need to be ashamed of tears, for tears bore witness that a man had the greatest of courage, the courage to suffer.

—VIKTOR E. FRANKL,

MAN'S SEARCH FOR MEANING

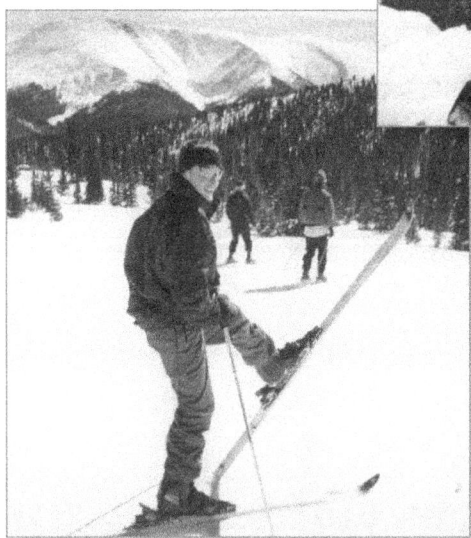

Heaven and earth and I are of the same root,
The ten-thousand things and I are of one substance.
—ZEN MASTER SOJO (384–414 A.D.)

Slamming Doors

here was no returning to "normal" this time. Nothing as gradual as picking up speed after a sudden stop when the driver in front slams on his brakes in heavy, fast-moving traffic. This time, the highway itself had disappeared. Only a trifle of dust left swirling in the air. Had I imagined it all in the first place, believed in the predictability of a life path I had no reason to claim as mine—like many, traveling through time partially aware, in a shadowy kind of trance, while senselessly convinced of a better, brighter day? And now, what was Joan Didion's popular memoir, *The Year of Magical Thinking*, doing in my hands?

Curiously, the paperback, with its impressive National Book Award Winner seal, had made a quick round trip, landing back in my Carmel, Indiana, mailbox and, apparently, it was for me. Still standing in our driveway, I'd opened the mailer, read the enclosed note. The message was brief, but the familiar handwriting was graceful, steady, and even conveyed a certain warmth. Inattentively turning pages, I considered how few absolutes there were: rare moments when mortality and the banality of existence come into exquisite focus. Death is one of those moments—its overwhelming impact, sweeping.

Ironically, I'd sent Didion's memoir (about first-year survival after losing a spouse while also having her only child in the ICU) to a good friend of mine only weeks before our own family tragedy struck. June's husband, Quay, after a close marriage of 50 years, had died of complications from the flu; I knew she would appreciate Didion's plight. But as soon as she heard about Matthew's death, thinking the book was newly relevant to me, she put it right back in the mail. Though grateful, after walking inside, I set the book aside.

Confident it was a touching memoir—what a befitting title—I also sensed that losing a son, of 27, to shocking circumstances, might deliver a different, possibly sharper, blow. In private, we anticipate burying our grandparents, parents, or *possibly* even a spouse, but sons and daughters fall in a far different category. Except in sad, twisted stories, we love them fearlessly, from the core of our being. An ineffable dynamic, really.

When I later learned that Didion's daughter also passed away a couple of years after her husband's fatal heart attack, I felt a deeper kinship. But, of course, loss is loss, always excruciating, and when I finally read her memoir, I appreciated this haunting, verifiable observation: once grief arrives, it's something *other* than our expectations.

The Crash of Death

Leaving Indianapolis early in the morning, we drove to Kirksville, Missouri, on a warm summer day with a hazy feeling of disbelief and shock permeating the car. The totality of our existence had shifted, and I dreaded facing Matt's empty, silent house: his activities, framed, much as he'd left them. Later, I learned law enforcement and a girlfriend of brief duration had combed through his house before our arrival but, otherwise, Matt's worldly belongings seemed to be precisely where he'd left them: a life, in sum, on a mortal plane. As we traveled, I wondered how it would feel to stand on the ground where my son spent his final moments, us looking out on a changed world—one that no longer included him.

Could I trace his steps—alter the scenario, cajole him back somehow?

Would I feel his presence, or merely collapse with emotional exhaustion, my head a vast blur of nothing?

Mostly, though, as the miles passed unnoticed, my thoughts were jumbled, incoherent. Trying to catch my mind, I hoped to prevent it from spinning off wildly into outer space, never returning. *Please God*, wasn't there some way for life to resume its predictable course of shelter, cars, and green beans—the simple, necessary things—with our family still intact, with the son who smiled readily: the one with the kind, trusting eyes?

Staring at an empty stretch of highway, I attempted to imagine days ahead by peeking at them from afar, from around an invisible corner. Terrified to face them head-on, it was as close as I could get. Never interested in watching violent movies, now this extreme act in our very midst. What degree of intense suffering, mental torment, anguish, had led to such an overpowering feeling of despair: rational, irrational, or largely induced by a controlled substance and painful withdrawal from unsustainable highs?

Questions stampeded through the gates of my awareness, but I sat motionless—lost in a debilitating haze of confusion, sorrow, and worry.

Grateful for my 29-year-old daughter, my heart broke for Erin's loss: an only sibling, a younger brother, a best friend and trusted confidant. Where would I find the emotional strength to support her through this wilderness? What kind of superhuman strength would it require?

Although a strong young woman, Erin was in the midst of her own personal transition. Could she cope with additional stress: the pulverizing strain of a loss I prayed she would never have to endure? But, realistically, I was powerless to spare her, myself, or anyone, this unexpected good-bye. I also considered my husband's pain. Married when Matt was a ninth grader, they had already known one another for several years. The love and respect between John and Matt was apparent.

Choosing the quaint, historic town of Deadwood—home to Wild Bill Hickok, Poker Alice, Calamity Jane, and the beautiful Black Hills—we hosted, in 1995, a casual, mid-December wedding. A fun time of year to get our families together, during our road trip we stopped in eastern South Dakota for a night. Still early, we decided to try out the hotel pool. Immediately, the whirlpool caught Matt's attention and, before long, we joined him. Sitting on the sidelines, my feet dangling in the water, I noticed Matt gazing at the metal steps in the bubbling water. Moments later with a proud smile, he proclaimed, that soon, John would be his "step-ladder."

We laughed—what beautiful creativity—but the affection in Matt's voice was clear. He was not only offering John his seal of approval, he was also saying, in his own way, that he appreciated having him in his life.

There are an abundance of wonderful men out there, but marrying one my children didn't value, or vice versa, wasn't for me and, fortunately, Matt and John had common interests. Both loved to snow ski. And movies with a humorous bent were high on their list. They played cards and pool, went camping or boating, and John taught Matt how to water ski. Sometimes they spent time in the kitchen making simple dishes like spaghetti or meatloaf, frying walleye or whipping up a delicious chocolate cake with thick frosting. More serious projects came into focus too: homework, science projects, constructing bat houses for those who understood the mosquito-catching prowess of those funny night-swooping creatures, snow shoveling, yard or garden work, or maybe painting something. The usual stuff.

But now, only the whir of tires against asphalt—a flat, lifeless sound—surrounded me. Gazing aimlessly through my car window, glimpses of the past roared to life. There was Matt: his tentative efforts to steady himself in the water that bright summer day. Catching on quickly, he dropped the second ski with ease. Snow skiing also came easily. He loved ski trips and camping with his friends who often joined us for weekends at Lake Oahe or LaFramboise Island near my hometown. But catching a string of walleye on the Missouri was too quiet, too slow, for Matt.

Dangling fishing line in deep river water, "doing nothing" while waiting for a nibble, didn't intrigue him in the slightest. Not then, anyway.

Leaving Indiana and headed to Danville, Illinois, with each passing mile, we were ever closer to Missouri. An undesirable destination, the highway stretching ahead of us like an endless black runway. Charles, Matt's biological father, came to mind.

Was he also shattered by the crash of death? Not married since Matt's boyhood, biological parents rarely stop loving their children just because of distance, living arrangements, or marital status. And, fortunately, for the most part, we maintained a reasonably cooperative relationship. Still, parenting is a subjective science, and I asked myself if we had done all we could for our two beautiful children—then again, what was enough? Or too much? Knowing there were no definitive answers to such questions was useless.

A Bumpy Ride

Matt began to struggle more noticeably in grade school—minor infractions that drove school personnel mad with frustration because, in that era, they were fixated on paddling. Yet a wise heart intuits that it doesn't benefit a child (or an adult, for that matter) to suffer a lack of emotional and physical control at the hands of someone unwilling (or unable) to communicate in a constructive, mature fashion. It shouldn't surprise us, however, that an unenlightened world justifies, *tries to normalize*, a culture of violence: counterproductive behavior turned to for entertainment or when deemed acceptable or necessary.

Yet blame without deeper understanding—a degree of wisdom—can be self-serving: a quick-fix habit, an excuse, a way to avoid the complexity of a situation or limited options. In fact, such painful, possibly fictional, conjecture is a stumbling block when it comes to discovering creative, life-enhancing answers and empowered solutions.

Many who didn't especially like classrooms still contributed to the world in profound and creative ways: Rabindranath Tagore, Albert Einstein, George Bernard Shaw, Mark Twain, H. L. Mencken, Margaret Mead, Winston Churchill, John Updike, Woody Allen,

Eckhart Tolle, and J.K. Rowling. That's barely a handful, though, when millions have known this frustrating reality.

Matt also disliked educational settings.

Smart enough, I was told with a sigh, but disinterested.

Attention-deficit issues were possible, but Matt also seemed happy to ignore many traditional subjects. As though vacillating between boredom or the need for a more interactive, engaging, upbeat academic environment, Matt definitely managed to annoy more than one teacher. But, curiously, when I helped him with projects or assignments, he seemed to put more energy into them, as though benefiting from patient, persistent interaction: caring and steady intellectual and emotional support. Relying solely on internal resources was a much bigger challenge for him. And, yes, it was the '80s.

Attention deficit hypertension disorder (ADHD) wasn't a topic in mainstream conversation, nor was it commonplace to whisk children and parents off to expensive therapy sessions. Having done my graduate work in sociology, I presumed this was another "era of labeling"— when schools, society, tossed kids with annoying difficulties under a rather large bus labeled "bad." Strong, fear-based reactions tend to frame challenging issues as character flaws—permanent, immovable shortcomings—instead of as areas of potential personal growth.

Loretta LaRoche, international consultant, suggests a different approach: "To rid yourself of a problem, stop looking at it as a problem. It's an opportunity to be alive. You have to stop making it wrong to have problems." What a great idea! Kids and challenges go hand in hand; it's up to the adults to bring a little creativity, a little wisdom, to the table, isn't it?

The miles ticked by like darts seeking an unwelcome target.

I thought about Matt's personality; he liked being part of the decision-making process. *We all do.* Yet, in nearly every context, even as we stress the "proper" words, how often do we touch the dazzling stars above, putting such constructive concepts into practice in fruitful (and satisfying) ways: cooperation, coordination, teamwork, open dialogue, joint and creative problem-solving, transparency, or collaboration? Rarely, I would wager.

Still, I offered Matt safe choices whenever possible. I wanted him to be a participant in life, not a blind "yes-man." Maybe this contributed to his inability to apply himself at school, to invest his energies academically. School, in many ways, is a narrow path of tradition and rules that is about mastering conformity and hiding one's individuality, not about learning how to weigh options or make constructive, proactive decisions.

We've all been there. Even with learning and discovery as the stated mission, what is the larger reality in some classrooms? Overly authoritarian teachers had limited success with Matt. When willing to give a little, however—encouraging student involvement—they were more likely to engage him: to gain his cooperation, his respect. Those teachers, in fact, liked Matt; he liked them. Alas, such insightful and gifted teachers aren't found in every classroom, but he had some along the way. Men and women I admired.

I loved school, regardless of environment, subject, or day of the week, so I was worried and mystified by Matt's disinterest—his endless struggle to find meaning and purpose in a mandatory system he mostly rejected. With all the valuable research done in the past 25 years, it's not inconceivable that Matt had a mild-to-moderate learning disability, even a neurological condition that was undiagnosed or misunderstood. But I'm hesitant to make assumptions or apply labels that give the illusion of truth when so many students simply dislike academic environments.

Eckhart Tolle, an extremely influential author and spiritual leader on a global scale, was permitted, for instance, to quit school at 13 while living in Germany with his mother. From there, the young Tolle, his parents, no longer together, went to live with his father in Spain. But, on his own initiative apparently, he studied literature, languages, and other subjects at home, only returning to a formal educational setting in his late teens. At a later date, Tolle opted to discontinue his Ph.D. program, one he no longer found relevant.

There are other plausible explanations for Matt's educational resistance.

Dietary factors, for instance, are considered in relation to ADHD in *Grain Brain: The Surprising Truth About Wheat, Carbs, and Sugar.* A neurologist, Dr. David Perlmutter thinks wheat could be as addictive as cocaine, and also points out that we need to know more about gluten sensitivity.

While lasting answers are typically elusive, I hope parents and school systems will see greater merit in creating educational choices, instead of assuming that student difficulties are beyond positive intervention. A curious, exploratory approach in many situations may reveal better solutions. Perhaps, more creative testing or in-depth evaluations could help. Issues stem from myriad sources—emotional, physical, intellectual, spiritual, cultural—so isn't it a mistake to *assume* we know exactly what troubles our children, youth?

Digging deeper takes time and energy—resources, I know, are spread thin in public schools—but, realistically, assuming a student merely doesn't want to comply may create more (or worse) problems. Imposing negativity on symptoms alone makes little sense, as life-saving doors slam shut when we fail to seriously consider creative options. Students aren't robots. We *know* this, yet, our behavior seldom reflects this fact. What children or youth present on the surface can be explored with an open mind, a caring approach, but, too often, we are satisfied with less, grabbing easy opportunities to label and tag: rushing to negate those who don't seem to measure up or fit in.

Unfortunately, the downward spiral regressive attitudes generate is largely inevitable.

I believe Matt was as confused by his reaction to some expectations—what most would consider average, normal, or acceptable—as anyone. Paradoxically, he was remarkably ordinary at times, just like any other kid: he had close friends, avoided popularity cliques. Later in life Matt told me he'd wanted lots of friends, but had felt too shy, even picked on by kids who, today, might qualify as bullies. Was he overly sensitive, or just a convenient target because he didn't play the "tough guy" role, so he appeared more vulnerable?

Fortunately, I didn't know how many similar questions I would encounter in the days and years ahead. Like facing bleak, unpleasant wallpaper in a hot, dry room, impossible questions framed my "new reality." Unanswerable, but always there—as though waiting to lure me down a slippery path littered with "maybe," "what if," or "if only."

We must have hit a bump in the road or something, because I jumped, realized I was still staring out the window, as though trying to distance myself (an impossible task) from the anguish that pinned me to the car seat. Slowly scanning the roadside and well beyond, I finally glanced upward, but my eyes landed on a plaintive-looking sky.

Projected emotions. The day, in truth, was bright, welcoming, warm—a contrast that nearly overwhelmed me. Summer, its generous, blue-sky days, when there was nothing comfortable or carefree about a seven-hour road trip to meet the clever hand of death. Fiddling with the radio, I imagined finding a "decent station," but had no idea what that would sound like in the vacuum of sudden absence. Giving up, I turned it off, lapsed back into a distracted, blank mood. John, still driving, was lost in emotions of his own.

During his grade school years, Matt sometimes surprised me with his strong opinions. He played soccer, was pretty good, but when he encountered teams with girls, refused to participate. Was having an older sister that annoying or had he been unduly influenced by male-female stereotypes—the kind portrayed on television or discussed with friends? Was he simply too shy?

I'll never know.

Matt never could (or would?) articulate why he didn't enjoy playing soccer with girls. A puzzle unto himself, perhaps, but once he discovered the exhilarating power of drugs to alleviate discomfort and pressure, to let him soar beyond frustration, doubt, and angst, it must have elicited a rare, otherworldly feeling, because that's when he charted his course with determination. Then … Matt knew exactly what he wanted.

Three C's

Nearing Kirksville, I gazed at open fields that flew by my window. The world appeared calm, settled, known: as if nothing had changed. Cattle grazed, birds swirled and soared in flight. Life and time, strolled along together, inextricably, and it seemed they were one incredible entity, vast and totally beyond reach.

Admittedly, I didn't understand the demands of time at all—its unmistakable unity with every aspect of life, its curious control of mortal existence. And how it insistently pressured me for *something* more without ever sharing the full story—explanations and key details that I needed to make better sense of our mysterious existence. How, for one thing, are we supposed to create meaning or lasting purpose within a shaky framework of limited duration?

But maybe I didn't understand my son either. Isn't it largely impossible to understand ourselves or another person? As his mother, though, I had patience for him—compassion, when those who didn't love (or like) Matt seemed to need easy compliance, mostly, and for him to be problem-free, predictably average, orderly, and invisible. Aren't those some of the implicit messages many adults seem to send us as we try to learn our way in the world?

Still, it was connection and support that helped Matt sustain an interest in activities; otherwise, he stalled out, muttering something about being unable to do it. Whatever *it* was. Sometimes he rushed to complete assignments, not caring how he scored, because he simply wanted to be done. Apparently his young mind buzzed with "what's next," as restless behavior patterns emerged, took root. Maybe a mind that was slightly too quick for some environments—a curious mind that wanted to explore, rush ahead, and engage.

More than a few suggested he would outgrow such issues.

"Slow to mature, that's all."

I shivered at the useless simplicity of this notion; wished Matt's life might have been so plain and ordinary, so grandly uncomplicated.

I spotted the small town ahead. Buildings, streets, traffic. Nothing I wanted to see or experience; nothing that could change my son's death. Already mid-afternoon when we crossed the city limits, I closed my eyes, resorted to the three C's from Alcoholics Anonymous: "You didn't cause it, you can't control it, you can't cure it."

Yet, like most of you reading this, I grew up in a high-pressure culture that prescribes perseverance and ingenuity for nearly everything so, understandably, I would have loved even *one more day* with my son. Another 24 hours to help him overcome a choice, a disease, a problem, or a lifestyle that ended his life, prematurely, and possibly, without his rational consent. Wouldn't you, if he were your son, your daughter?

But uncertainty—that relentless swirl of dark, futile questions—prevails in this funny world of life and time, merged like a flimsy marriage of precarious design, unknown origin.

Keeper of Many Secrets

Arriving at a Holiday Inn on the southern edge of Kirksville, I immediately noticed the bouquet of flowers that graced our room. The array of colors, a welcome contrast to the sterile feel of hotel decor. A younger sister's name on the card. She, her family, the most likely to send this thoughtful gesture of support since her oldest son, James, was lost to a fatal car accident some eight years prior. The terrain of loss also well known: a promising college student, a trip home an unforgettable day in May that resulted in tragedy.

"Hey, Aunt Daisy," he'd say in his energetic, eager voice, one now embedded within the very fabric of the cosmos. A voice I loved, and could never forget.

Studying the hopeful flowers arranged with obvious skill—blues, greens, whites, and pinks—I managed a deep, slow breath.

Would their warmth—the silent purity of nature—rescue me from the absolute terror of the moment: free me from an airless tunnel of death and time, forever entangled, like thick vines on a summer trellis? But moments later, I silently wished them away, along with a flood of sympathy cards I anticipated receiving as word spread through networks of family, friends. Flowers and cards only confirmed the cause of my wrenching pain. Grief torments, agitates, and turns well-meaning people into ungrateful, guilt-filled, perfectly awful human beings who are unable to appreciate acts of kindness bestowed on them. Yet, it's entirely understandable.

Would *doing nothing* better convey our compassion? Might it capture the unspeakable sting of death—sharing love, empathy via deep stillness: a spiritual stillness like Eckhart Tolle eloquently described in *Stillness Speaks*. "Your innermost sense of self, of who you are, is inseparable from stillness. This is the *I Am* that is deeper than name and form."

But lacking even a shred of mental clarity, this puzzle, like the others, simply hovered in the air. Revolving doors had entered my life with the presence of grief; straight lines of utter conviction swept away as if struck down by a mighty and imperfect storm. And then people began tapping lightly on our door. It seemed they wanted to hug us, talk to us, sit with us. Some, it seemed, merely wanted to stare at us, *at me*. Their irrational disbelief of death channeled in my direction, in Matthew's. I tolerated it, but had no true desire to talk to anyone. Was it supposed to comfort me, comfort them, or was it just a nervous noise?

Looking back, the need for conversation is probably intrinsic to the painful pairing of life and loss: what we resort to when the pinch of endings generates confusion, crippling bewilderment. Maybe familiar voices are supposed to soothe brittle nerves taut with fear.

Eventually, though, our room grew quiet. People left, stopped coming by. Relieved, I looked for my bag, unzipped it, but decided sleep would be an impossible mission. After propping pillows against the headboard to lean on, I sat and stared, for time unknown, into an uncompromising darkness. An unsettling mix of random voices, stray noises drifted in from the hall, adjacent rooms, outside. Looking for a blanket, the air conditioner still on high, I had no energy to lower it and, thankfully, John was asleep.

I didn't want to talk. Words had lost all meaning.

I wanted to sit like a stone and wonder why I would ever have to get up, move around, as if I had some idea where I was going or what I was doing. Why couldn't I sit alone in the cold dark until hell froze over? Because, like everyone, I was trapped by the pressure, the brashness, of time. Tomorrow would come. Dawn would arrive, an insistent light edging in around long beige drapes. I would be expected to rise—dress appropriately, function normally.

Performance measures at times like this ... nonsense. Perhaps fabricated by strangers from history, outlined by poorly informed souls sharing what they imagined to be factual. Funny yardsticks that create waves of discontent and unknown suffering.

What should we value, strive for; are we supposed to lead such largely predetermined lives? Something tells me, with so many lives careening off track, that we begin, at a very young age, to chase the wrong rainbows. Reliable statistics vary source to source, year to year, but Mental Health America reported that depression is a chronic illness exacting a significant toll on health, productivity. Impacting at least 21 million adults and children annually, it's a leading cause of disability (ages 15 to 44). Cited as the principal cause of the 38,364 suicides (the tenth leading cause of death) in 2010, approximately every 12.8 minutes, in 2013, someone in the United States reportedly died by suicide.

Yet, depression is an extremely complicated subject, one bound to enter every life one way or another. Professionals, some wiser than others, offer divergent opinions, point to competing treatment philosophies. But clearly, depression impacted Matt's life, and now, sitting motionless in an inhospitable hotel room trying to escape time and perky flowers, I felt its dim face creeping about. And I was its target. Not as a debilitating force, nor as clinical depression requiring therapy or medication, but as a new fact of life.

Of course grief empowers depression, brings its somber face to the fore and, with this realization, I knew I was no longer in the driver's seat. Grief was at the wheel. Now I was a reluctant passenger in my own life—the one hiding in the far back, cringing, half numb, asking impossible questions, suggesting a vastly different route. Begging for a smoother ride to an unknown destination. But grief, I would learn, was also the keeper of fearsome secrets: what death means, how profound sorrow invades every aspect of each day, how to survive its uncompromising intensity.

Would I be forced to embrace what seemed unbearable, since what we resist persists?

Finding solace in this lofty concept sounded like the purview of enlightened monks: those tucked away from mainstream worries, the pedantic slices of life. So I had no choice but to refuse grief's embrace. Who could convince me otherwise?

There was nothing to look to except the faint whispers of those who had trod before me—heads tucked low, saying little.

A door slammed in the parking lot. I jumped. Why so loud, disturbing? Another symbol of loss, the proverbial door closing so a window could open? Not in the mood for generic symbolism, even as I heard another slamming door, I would wait for the real God to show up, the one to get me through this. I *believed*, but also *questioned*, and this time, I wanted the details—in-depth explanations, consolation, and evidence of *something*.

Dawn arrived as a fuzzy continuum of then and now. Vague resistance was all I could manage, as harsh, unrelenting circumstances penetrated my awareness. Walls, draped in shadows, the cave I never wanted to emerge from. And, across the room, fragile flowers. Their colors sadly depleted. An unspoken mission—to console, to soothe— laid bare by this glaring day of black and white. The silence of morning, a cavernous, mocking echo revealed all of this, and more. Viscerally, I felt its cold, eerie precision: its force. Merciless. Absolute.

Inviting the Bell

"The Way of Heaven is to benefit others and not to injure. The Way of the sage is to act but not to compete."

—LAO TZU

Light Years Away

I've been drawn to the sun since childhood. My mother, so the story goes, took us to visit a kind woman in Denver who once had provided day care for me. I have no concrete memory of her, but after the usual round of greetings, the women, coffee in hand, sat down to talk—reportedly uttering kind, generous things about me.

Such a "good child." Happy to adhere to rules, easy to please.

In the meantime, still young and probably bored with adult conversation, I wandered around the house, landed in a room painted white, and after spotting empty walls, open, beckoning, came across a bright yellow crayon. Somewhere. And by the time they came looking for me—just imagine the look on their faces—I'd drawn, *on the wall*, a bunch of wavy lines extending from a rather large, lopsided circumference.

"It's the sun," I apparently explained with a shy smile, a shrug of the shoulders. Didn't that bare wall cry out for a touch of color? But, no, they were mostly aghast, not terribly impressed with my lively display of spirit.

What did move me—*inspire me*—that day?

Feelings of loneliness, sadness; a sudden creative impulse; a powerful urge to communicate something bright, cheerful—at the far end of the spectrum, a curious message in code from a spiritual plane. Whatever prompted me, my mother, now in her mid-eighties, smiles when reflecting on this popular family story, as though still amused or enchanted by my antics—how I'd dared to step out of character with a certain amount of charm, joy.

I also love this story because there are so many possibilities to consider. Did I want to signal an independent side, announce that I was growing up, able to entertain myself? Of course I'm unable to recall the incident directly or point to my exact motivation—having fun with color and shapes, sharing happiness, imagining warmth on a cool, cloudy day—but the sun story reminds me of my deep fondness for a young girl who may have already understood something of the "Love that moves the sun and the other stars," as Dante, the great Italian poet (1265–1321) once wrote.

Possibly, I was mostly curious about the giant yellow ball in the sky. Energetic colors like cheerful-yellow might have danced before my eyes like jelly beans in a fetching jar. Perhaps a yellow crayon was all I could find on that long-ago day. I would love to know the impetus behind the art. Sounds intriguing, doesn't it, to peer inside an impressionable young mind for its inner workings?

Did I want to leave my "signature" behind in a place I'd enjoyed, offer this nice woman, who once cared for me, a small gift—something for her to remember me by (I'm *sure* she did)? Alas, it's impossible to know the heart of that inquisitive girl with long, dark, wavy hair, the one I am allowed to see and know only from afar: fading pictures, incomplete stories, sketchy memories, and vague silly notions.

Randy Pausch, computer science professor at Carnegie Mellon, wrote about achieving his dreams in *The Last Lecture*. He died, sadly, from pancreatic cancer, but told us in his book that he was allowed, actually encouraged as a child, to draw on his bedroom walls. Raising his children likewise, to imagine, record their dreams for others to see and share, Pausch was an award-winning teacher and researcher. Even after his fatal diagnosis, he chose to inspire people by espousing the art of living wisely and well: no matter what. Maybe his parents had it right; maybe Randy did, too.

The rocket drawing on his book cover was from his bedroom wall. I would love to have a picture of my sun, but regardless of how I frame this humorous incident, I sense a wonderful mystery underlying this fleeting artistic impulse. A Picasso moment, an innocent urge that pointed to something more, a girl nursing sketchy, nascent dreams of becoming an artist—had I, in fact, been one in a former life? All I know is that, at the age of four or five, I'd noticed the sun. Huge, bright, warm—faraway, mysterious. I'd probably heard people say, "Sun's out, beautiful day," or "sure wish the sun was out today."

How could any of us, even as children, miss the world's love affair with the sun?

Historically, the sun has been tucked into legends and religions and stories. Science and the sun also walk hand in hand, and how many poems have been written about the fireball in the sky?

Perhaps, through my wall drawing, I was merely acknowledging my world as a young girl: the environment I was learning about, growing up with, via planet Earth. More interesting, perhaps, is the distinct possibility that I haven't changed much at all since those distant years. In obvious, commonplace ways, yes, but perhaps not in the more fundamental ways.

As a point of conjecture, I'm briefly exploring that possibility here because it could point to a deeper spiritual essence that is unchanging (and remains unchanged) during a lifetime. So infrequently do we truly take note of such things, digging purposefully into a hunch, an unproven perception. Rather, we become followers: sightless passengers on a spinning globe. And though we try to navigate wisely, even creatively, through the fields of time, we are tossed hither and yon, remaining curiously unaware and largely unrefined.

Yet Kahlil Gibran tells us, "The timeless in you is aware of life's timelessness. And knows that yesterday is but today's memory and tomorrow is today's dream."

Prairie Lilacs

If something needed to be done, I usually thought, *why not?* Our family built a house in the country—seven miles from the city limits—in the late '60s, the home I lived in during my junior, senior high school years. The oldest in a blended family of five, I was used to helping out, seldom questioned the need to act responsibly.

During those years, someone gave us 50 tiny lilac bushes for spring planting; I was game.

Lilacs smell divine. Their blooms, like delicate clusters of stars in purple or white, are prairie favorites. Growing up in Pierre, South Dakota, nearly everyone had lilacs in their yard. Lost in the beauty of the end result, I happily overlooked our hot, dry summers that would mean frequent watering until the young plants took root. The dogged prairie wind, blowing at gale force for back-to-back days, also dried things out quickly. But if others could grow lilacs, so could I. It couldn't be that difficult, could it? Digging 50 small holes in ground that was likely rock hard didn't deter me either.

If I wanted to arrive somewhere new, I assumed the journey might be taxing, and a sweet-smelling lilac bush to brighten a rough, unfinished yard just north of the Missouri River was difficult to resist. Besides, glorious spring—warm, alive, and greenish—had arrived. After enduring a long dreary stretch of winter, growing *something* felt natural. And worthwhile. A little manual labor, some moisture (spring showers would help), and abundant sunshine—that's all it would take for my bucket of pencil-thin bushes soaking eager roots in cool water to take off and, one fine day, explode with color.

Shovel in hand, I closely surveyed our yard for the best location. A u-shaped driveway lined with prairie stubble, thistle, and weeds, surrounded what we jokingly called a lawn. Somehow, though, I imagined a whimsical border of deep purple. Nature's art, a vibrant display after an endlessly cold, snowy winter. A spring bonanza.

Like the bare white wall that begged for some color, our country yard was too plain: usually brown, dry, lonely-looking, except for a small section by the front door. The only part that resembled a lawn, it was a rectangle we weeded, watered, and possibly even fertilized. Against this rustic backdrop I envisioned tender lilacs stretching skyward, so a prairie breeze could transport their aroma through open windows literally yearning to inhale their sweet fragrance.

Who could resist such a picture?

I started planting—along the u-shaped drive, and within it. The ground cried out for attention, for something green and encouraging, and even though this project may sound like a silly youthful pursuit, it felt rather inspired. I was already aware of an inner light, of a strong connection to vast unseen origins—the universe, a higher power, God, the source, the beloved—that fueled the journey. That kept me looking skyward.

I don't know when I began to know this for what it was, but my spirituality—my contemplative curious side—manifested as optimism, determination, or a hopeful nature, has been a consistent driving force. The origin of personal goals; the source of motivation to do what is right (or important) even if difficult or daunting; the creative and powerful link to feelings of urgency and purpose. And, most definitely, the fruitful roots of my intuition: the knowing voice within.

I doubt, however, that I could have articulated this with such clarity before Matthew's death. "Why not" is a reasonable response; I've asked myself the same question. My best guess is that, like many, I'd absorbed generic cultural definitions of religion, and didn't believe profound spiritual journeys were for the average among us. I can't recall anyone in my inner circle referring to such concepts during my childhood or youth.

Raised Catholic, I assumed the operative word was religion—following rules, learning scripture, obeying commandments, honoring holy days—as opposed to dynamic, spiritual orientations like living from the light within. And since I'd never been strongly drawn to "organized faith"—popular customs, worn-out labels, literal biblical translations, beliefs too often distorted, misapplied—my son's absence was the impetus to sort through these unwieldy issues. To dig deeper in search of an evolving, expanding sense of spirit.

I *knew* there was a life-giving force entirely beyond my limited mortal framework; but I also *knew* there was more to this story. Regardless of words, the endless, demoralizing fury they cause, I was certain an unseen dimension operated within me, and beyond me. Instinctively, my grandmother had led me to my spirituality by making me deeply aware of nature, peaceful relationships, music, poetry, and prayer, when I was only a girl. With her guidance, I'd grown accustomed to the power of silence, and even though we didn't talk about an inner light per se, or delve into eloquent or mystifying spiritual terms, I felt the sacred nature of life in her presence.

Doesn't it seem like most of us could benefit from learning about our innate, spiritual selves when still young, floundering about? Not in abstract terms mostly meaningless to children, but in ways that touch our souls?

If relying exclusively on external structures and divisive concepts (overtly religious pronouncements) to teach spirituality, it's way too easy to get drawn into the politics and drama of various religions (which religion is *truth*, for instance) instead of also learning to tap into the inherent wisdom of our inner worlds. Then, sadly, we may

never summon the courage, the motivation, to reach beyond dogma
in ways that feel right, or real.

When turned off by religious zealots, fire-and-brimstone preachers—I was—or when the world of spirit sounds vague, ethereal, and
a bit like wishful thinking, it's not difficult to get stuck. Religions,
in all their extremes and guises, are various things, depending on
our needs, beliefs, and assumptions, but feeling perplexed by massive
crowds taken in by a solitary voice on a stage isn't unusual. One day,
though, something—an experience, a friend, a book, an intuitive
nudge—may invite a deeper perspective, and we see through *all of it*
like never before. Breathing deeply, we look with new eyes, with new
intention. It felt, to me, like awakening to a wondrous, yet fundamental
process: one meant to be.

Religions can be powerful starting points, but the impetus to
truly live from a spiritual dimension seems to come from within. Joan
Chittister, a Catholic nun for 60-plus years and author of more than
50 books, writes eloquently about the God that isn't "Catholic" or any
religion, per se. Don't most doctrines point to similar (all-inclusive)
destinations? But I wouldn't discover her work, or the impressive
studies of Father Richard Rohr, until the spring of 2015. Catching
him in an interview with Oprah, I loved his authentic style.

Religion, he explained, is actually one of the safest places to hide
from God; even Jesus warned of the dangers of religion without dis-
missing it entirely. Rohr, a Franciscan priest for 44 years and author
of 30 books, founded the Center for Action and Contemplation in
Albuquerque. As we get to the level of spirituality, he explained, we
are finally moving beyond beliefs—and finding our way there because
of direct experience.

Although useful in many ways, I too felt that religions had their share of blind alleys. Hearing his comments felt like confirmation of everything I'd lived through and come to believe. I appreciated this insightful Rohr quote: "Sin happens whenever we refuse to keep growing" (*Falling Upward: A Spirituality for the Two Halves of Life*).

About the same time, I also discovered the work of Jiddu Krishnamurti—specifically, his last journal before his death in 1986. Born in British India, living in Ojai, California, he wrote about the "immensity of the mind and heart" that has little to do with organized religion. "Where there is division there must be conflict." *Precisely.*

He also points to the "true religious spirit" that "goes far beyond knowledge." Reading Krishnamurti, I discovered another kindred spirit: his teachings resonating with common sense, grace, and integrity. Philosophically, I saw the inherent wisdom of his expansive, enlightened perspective. God, I was certain, wasn't petty: wedded to mortal delineations. But *first*, we return to my younger days, to the multitude of steps between then and now, to the mysterious dance of life—a universal, effervescent story of love and loss.

Another Project

Planting lilacs preceded another big project I took on one summer. Still in high school, I decided to paint our house. No one else was interested, and even though I might not be able to do it all, I could do more than nothing. Brush, paint can in hand—an olive green, if memory serves—I considered where to begin. Shade would be good. I also wanted to choose an area that didn't require a ladder. Surely someone taller, more experienced, would volunteer to catch the high sections, apply the second coat.

Again, my high-energy nature, envisioning progress, looking past excuses, negativity, procrastination, pushed me to tackle the house project. True to form, I'd also seen a great deal of potential in my son. Believed in him, encouraged him to do what was needed even if others wanted to shrug off a project as too difficult, too steep, *too something*. That trait, however, must have been genetic—or somehow linked to my prairie heritage—because Matt often took a more relaxed, playful approach to things.

Maybe he grasped the impermanence of life at an early age; perhaps he believed that not-so-interesting projects were cooked up by adults to keep kids busy. It's also possible he struggled to generate the emotional and intellectual stamina to focus on work he found boring, because when doing something he loved—exploring ski slopes in search of black diamond runs—Matt was engaged.

Then the activity was worthy of his energy, time, and passion.

Both styles have value and worth, along with limitations and strengths.

With elements of yin and yang in everything, what one approach affords and nurtures, the next may detract from, thus generating the invisible but undeniable harmony of our incredible universe. Unfortunately, cultures are predictably narrow in labeling behavior and lifestyle as appropriate, productive, or sensible. Power and economics often prevail (and corrupt).

Still, on a cautiously hopeful note, as civilizations evolve, as our global society matures, unique opportunities may arise to facilitate greater freedom of expression. Now, though, I shudder to imagine the extensive suffering the world has known (*will know*) because of limited expectations built around biased, unrealistic standards of conformity.

As things turned out, my house painting project afforded a sense of accomplishment—an opportunity to improve something, to create a speck of beauty for myself and others—that I relished. Quite honestly, though, I was relieved when help arrived. It wasn't a small house. My arms ached; my enthusiasm sagged. And I no longer liked olive green.

Had I ever liked it? Too dark, right?

In case you're wondering why I'm sharing this brief autobiographical sketch in this early chapter, when I read a book, I want to know something about the author. Not a two-line bio, but something about her early days. It offers perspective, makes the big picture more salient. As complex human beings, a brief "about the author" section at the back of a book rarely provides meaningful illumination. I also felt it was important to share the personal context for this book—a story of grief, renewal, spiritual realization—early on. Lacking context, aren't we all merely stumbling around in the dark?

Grieg's Concerto

When I was a senior in high school, the beauty/talent show rolled around. Not sure how I became a contestant—class nomination?—I clearly recall my resistance. I enjoyed many extracurricular activities, but was wary of a Miss Something agenda. I played the piano somewhat, but parading down a makeshift runway in the school gymnasium in a formal gown after enduring an interview by a panel of strangers called judges about who knows what sounded uncomfortable and artificial.

Finally, though, I accepted my fate. I would have to participate in a curious display of senior girls—most, my good friends. In my usual fashion, when I knew there was no way out, I threw myself into the experience, *almost* wholeheartedly. But some 40 years later, my discomfort and trepidation are as memorable as the latent rebellion that stirred inside me. Like wearing ill-fitting shoes, I squirmed and whined my way through it. I'd been a serious debater—winning a few trophies around the state with my good friend and debate partner— had also pushed myself to join "declam" (or declamation) to defeat my irrational fear of public speaking, was a class officer and the first female vice-mayor of the student body, worked on the high school yearbook, was a member of the Honor Society, Quill and Scroll, and as a sophomore, spent one very awkward year as a cheerleader.

Though capable and willing, I had zero interest in uncomfortable gowns, or pretense. When I ran for vice-mayor, few of the 750 students in our high school took me seriously, however. *A girl*, but why? I'm not sure, but a classmate who was running for mayor was willing to add me to his ticket. I liked most everyone, including teachers, and must have believed I had some good ideas, or a few leadership skills, perhaps. Maybe I just wanted to shatter an outdated barrier for the other female students, even though I wasn't exactly an extrovert. But when we actually won, I was shocked. I'd kept my nerves under wrap long enough to address voters (the student body) in school assemblies, and we'd had fun coming up with campaign slogans, a party platform, and signs to hang in the cafeteria and halls, but when a "girl" became vice-mayor, I was as surprised as everyone else.

Given the march of time (1972 to now) this all sounds a bit trite, but back then, it felt sort of amazing. One of our proudest moments, for instance, was convincing the school board to permit outdoor graduation at Hollister Field. It was fun tying white balloons to rows of folding chairs, releasing them as a group to commemorate a milestone etched in stone. Bobbing in a spring breeze, they resembled daring halos that hopeful day in May.

What I'm trying to explain is that serving as vice-mayor suited me much more than competing with my good friends in a poise and beauty pageant. I shunned that kind of attention, didn't want *that* light shining my way. Forced from my comfort zone, I was cornered by the wishes of others and tradition—prevailing cultural, societal norms. On the plus side, I'd been playing the piano for some 12 years by then, so that's where I channeled my energy. When practicing, I even indulged myself in blissful childhood memories of sitting next to my grandmother while she stroked the pearly keys.

I was never passionate about the piano (small hands, short fingers, too worried about hitting the wrong notes to master such a lovely instrument), but could handle reasonably difficult music and survived the dreaded recitals. I also liked to play at night, after everyone else had gone to bed. Relaxing, soothing. Sitting down at the keyboard when the house was quiet, I'd get happily lost in the melody—the rhythm, the emotions of the piece—until someone applauded from a distant bedroom. Abruptly, my private reverie ceased. Then, the day, the hour, the setting, would zoom into focus, and a smile would cross my face. Someone liked the music, or wanted me to call it a night.

But what could I perform on a stage; what was competition-worthy?

Sorting through my sheet music, advanced lesson books, I hoped a piece would jump out at me like a bowl of chocolate ice cream on a hot summer day, because I had no idea what to play. Edvard Grieg's Concerto in A minor looked interesting. Scanning the notes, I put my fingers on the smooth-feeling keys to play a few bars—to evaluate difficulty, assess the melody—and loved the music immediately.

Slightly beyond my ability, I chose it anyway. If participation was mandatory, I would find a way to put substance into the experience. Although, I see that aspect of things more clearly in retrospect.

At my next piano lesson, I asked my teacher to help me learn the notes. She gazed at me with questioning eyes. Grieg's concerto was a serious piece of music, and since I was reserved and quiet, she seemed surprised. But I wouldn't be deterred, and due to a minor miracle the night of the competition, hit the notes with unusual dexterity. Pure adrenalin. Written in 1868 while Grieg was visiting Denmark as a 24-year-old from Norway, the stirring music was dramatic, memorable, soaring, and revised many times—the only concerto he would ever write. Whenever I hear the familiar melody, vivid memories rush to the surface.

When the results were announced, I'd won the talent contest, but not the overall title, and later that evening, once out of the phony dress and comfortably back at home, tears erupted. Relief? Partially. But I was also emotionally exhausted from playing a social role that felt alien, painfully artificial. Photographs from the event, a smile that looked forced, hesitant, confirmed my sentiments. My family, assuming I was upset because of the results, tried to comfort me, but they didn't understand.

Genuinely happy for the winner (we are still close friends), the truth was that I had felt terribly uncomfortable parading around in front of teachers, friends, and parents like a reluctant Barbie doll when I wanted nothing more than to be reading a good book in a pair of blue jeans.

I rarely played the piano after high school graduation.

Do I like knowing I can strike a few notes if the spirit moves me? I suppose, but I'm also content to let my musical skills lie dormant. It seemed strange, at first, not to play, but once I got to college, new interests beckoned. Eager to delve into classes, I wanted to leave the distraction of clubs, special projects, and extracurricular activities behind. High school, a hectic blur. I'd done too much, joined and participated whenever asked. Time to step back, assess my interests. Leaving the protective nest of my small and secluded hometown, venturing beyond everything known and loved, I also sought change.

And now I see how giving myself permission to chart a new course also helped me to develop a stronger sense of priorities once I was a freshman at Stephens, my mother's alma mater, in Columbia, Missouri. A two-year college when she was there, a four-year degree was the norm when I enrolled. (Stephens is still dedicated to the educational needs of women.)

A Sense of Self

Never quite sure why I believed in my own sense of direction, my spirituality must have played a role. The light within usually felt stronger, brighter, and truer than the pull of external circumstances, and I trusted a calm, inner voice even when the world around me was chaotic, or at odds. But self-trust also pushed me to question the heavy, puzzling demands of a conformist society.

Fortunately, this perspective gave me a viable lifeline to my son, because Matt had almost no interest in conformity for the sake of conformity.

In my first book, I wrote about the merits of a pioneer spirit: the inherent wisdom of embracing a life of adventure that doesn't have to be anything more than an attitude of personal growth, openness to learning, and the persistence to envision creative realities. I also see it as an ability—a desire—to distrust surface issues, faulty assumptions, and the (convenient) collective judgment of public opinion and mainstream culture.

In Matthew's life and loss, I've rediscovered myself time and time again, reclaiming what has always been there, but knowing it more fully each time. Rarely, do we see these things in the moment, however. We make it more complicated: high-pressure, painful, confusing. But I can envision a world where children are told upfront their life journey is only a deepening of everything they are born with: the poetic, insistent, illumination of intuition over time. Imagine how liberating (and practical) this would be, conceivably preventing an endless, tiring search for *whatever* may help us to understand ourselves. Traveling through time, before awakening in the spiritual sense, I would have loved to have possessed the wisdom of our spiritual reality here on Earth.

Awakening is nearly always a gradual process, for some it never seems to happen, but when it does, life steps—past, present, future— are newly illuminated.

What do I mean by awakening?

Sounds vague and abstract, but it's pretty straightforward. For me (a multitude of definitions exist), it's understanding that my personalized (conditioned) self isn't who I am at my spiritual core. That's a temporary self the world of time created, not my actual self—the soul, the spirit, the timeless aspect of being—that necessarily arises beyond external conditions, personal circumstances and, yes, time. Once we *know* this, the world shifts. More intent on living from an enlightened perspective, one avoiding drama, useless conflict, and the contentious (predictable) polarities of the mind, the "who done it" mindset often featured in movies, on television, and in many books, begins to feel boring, irrelevant, shallow. An abiding peace takes hold.

Naturally, and unavoidably, however, it seems we need substantial life experience to facilitate our own awakening and enlightenment.

A Frozen Lake

Besides lilac bushes, for as long as I remember, I gravitated toward growing things in any context or situation. Children, relationships, pets, projects, organizations, and abilities. I see, without even trying, possibilities everywhere. If I invest in someone or something, I take it seriously. Personal growth, also a lifelong priority, means staying open to learning. I want to be a student until my last earthly breath—want to feel my spirituality deepening, expanding into all parts of my life, as I continue to trust an invisible process.

In a classroom, if extra credit came up, I wasn't burdened with a sense of entitlement, was willing to *earn* the teacher's respect, and from the start, seemed to looked for ways—major, minor, serious, lighthearted—to engender a wiser, more caring world.

Could I grow a garden with flowers nice enough to share with someone? Write a poem that expressed the inexpressible; hammer out a more effective paragraph; track down a special gift for someone I admired, or support a cause I believed in?

Most of all, could I offer encouragement to others when things looked bleak?

Seemingly born with the desire to contribute in whatever circumstance I found myself in, you might say I was blessed with a touch of confidence, and wanted to use that sense of personal power in ways that embraced everything good in the world. Naturally, I was drawn to the pressing needs of nonprofit organizations. An inspiring niche where values, strengths, and professional abilities readily merged, the hopeful missions of nonprofits captured my heart, soul, and intellect by offering a viable opportunity to work from my spiritual core. Believing, apparently from youth, that life on Earth could be improved by striving to help others in need, by noticing what others seemed oblivious to, *by caring*, I also enjoyed working in human resources.

I believed in training staff; helping employees to develop their potential. I wanted the workplace to be fair, constructive, and progressive. Not every situation can be (or should be) salvaged—there is wisdom in knowing when employers and employees are a toxic pairing—but someone once told me I could spot the tiniest flower in the thickest patch of weeds. And, good or bad, I also have a penchant for detecting seeds that haven't sprouted.

Not yet, anyway.

What doesn't begin somewhere, in a lesser, unseen condition?

A prolific and wise poet, living between 1875 and 1926, Rainer Maria Rilke, points to another potent truth, however: "The purpose of life is to be defeated by greater and greater things." Matthew's loss was part of that purpose, perhaps. For nothing short of a lifetime, I had managed to grow things: building something out of nothing, creating contentment or joy out of pain, suffering, or confusion, and had resolutely found my way on the darkest, most inhospitable days. Supported the faintest heartbeat in whomever I loved.

But I could *not* save my son; I'd been defeated by something far greater.

And, yes, perhaps loss is life's greatest and *only* lesson. Even with repetition we never "get used to it." No matter what the situation, we feel blindsided by death; we take flight, shredded by pain. Doctors can warn us. Our intuition can alert us. But our emotional and mental capabilities are such that we can't truly prepare for death, or really comprehend it when it happens—unless we are a Buddha. Instead, we are stunned; shock waves traverse our frail spirits like violent currents of electricity. Wincing in pain, the next breath seems like a miracle. Yet, the unseen kernel of loss is within all of us, seemingly dormant until the appointed time and, reluctantly, I've come to believe we are meant to embrace our unavoidable mortal and spiritual transition from day one.

Imagine a world where there is less fear, regret, apprehension, around the inevitable. If we could somehow "relax" about death, about endings, maybe we could live with greater ease, self-awareness, and present-time contentment. Conceivably, we could quit running from the throes of mortality at the speed of sound.

Increasingly, I am interested in "being," permitting "doing" to take second place to a deepening awareness of spiritual realities. As I've heard others say, we are human *beings*, not human *doings*. Presence is what matters, especially when a higher level of consciousness (David Hawkins, M.D., Ph.D., wrote extensively about this) is accessed and shared.

Still, nothing is as straightforward as it sounds in a moment of gentle clarity.

Ralph Waldo Emerson suggested, "For everything you have missed, you have gained something else, and for everything you gain, you lose something else." Though pragmatically true, it's also safe to say that most countries and cultures emphasize and reward visible achievements, as opposed to mindful, peaceful, enlightened lifestyles. I wonder how many have paid a dear price for this limiting, superficial definition of life purpose. As curious as it may sound, the rare ability to simply sit down, joyfully and completely, is also important. Very important.

I once read about a man who does *zazen* (meditative sitting) in the winter on a frozen lake in Minnesota; he hoped, as I did, that it might catch on someday.

If not on a lake, then *somewhere*.

But the world of time conceals and denies truth; we strain against beneficial change. We even strain against enlightenment because we don't understand what it means, so we associate it with whatever we fear—whatever we label as "out there" or "weird" or "New Age propaganda." The reality is, however, that when naïvely planting lilacs in dry, inhospitable ground, struggling to paint a house on a hot summer day, practicing for my piano lessons, or fearlessly drawing a lopsided sun on a snow white wall, I, like all of us, was *already* enlightened. Light years would pass before this dawned on me, however.

Yet, D. H. Lawrence told us, "Life is a traveling to the edge of knowledge, then a leap taken." And perhaps that deep, formidable well within is hidden to us until deep suffering energizes our path, until our best efforts include an unwavering commitment to grappling with existential mysteries.

Inviting the Bell

"The Way of Heaven is to
benefit others and not to injure.
The Way of the sage is to act
but not to compete."
—LAO TZU

My heart has spread its sails to the idle winds
for the shadowy island of Anywhere.
—RABINDRANATH TAGORE, *STRAY BIRDS* (218)

A Piercing Sound

The mortal sense of self I'd built brick by brick, question by question and breath by breath vanished from my internal radar like a plane shot from the sky that ordinary day in June. Why had I *ever* believed I was resourceful, or resilient, when I could have been a child's stuffed animal, a plastic toy buried in an old-fashioned Cracker Jack box—*any inanimate object, really*—when that merciless moment descended?

On paper, and linked to nearly every memory, there was convincing evidence of love, hard work, and accomplishment. I held a master's degree—studied decision-making and complex organization in graduate school—and had a certain amount of expertise in org development after working with nonprofits over the years. Most organizations meet with internal or external pressure to advance a mission, to expand and evolve, but many need assistance at critical growth points. Fund development, something else I'd worked on for various nonprofits, is often part of the challenge to sustain meaningful growth. Luckily, the process was also creative and motivating: Somehow, we had to keep the doors open.

Fundamentally about relationship building, development offered rewarding work on many levels. But as a serious writer, I was also eager to keep exploring the intricacies of the human condition via spirituality and sociology. My intuition was strong; curiosity dependably fueled my desire to delve more deeply into my insights.

After falling in love with books as a girl—the mustiness of our Carnegie Library, its endless treasures—I'd shared the organic wisdom of the prairie culture and landscape in a book of my own, and wanted to dip into poetry, maybe fiction, someday. But when 2007 rolled around, I was researching the power and purpose of memories. Fascinated by their artful complexity, how they weave our days on Earth into stories that feel sharply real, as things turned out, this was a book I would never write.

June changed everything, even though life, before then, was the usual whir of activity. Stuck on a juiced-up merry-go-round, I, like most, wondered how to manage a plethora of priorities. Could I decipher the demands of time—break the code of life, so to speak?

Using calendar time wisely wasn't so much about career development, however. I'd never craved (or trusted) the common trappings of material success, but I did believe in following through on promises, commitments. Figuring out the best use of my energy was often the difference between living in a haze of frustration and having enough time for what really mattered: investing in those I loved and cared about while honoring quiet longings I hadn't quite figured out—the deeper side of life, you might say.

But news that rattles the soul, triggers a frigid, surreal reality, and no one, *no one*, lest a Gandhi or his counterpart, is prepared. So when the call all parents fear came, my entire being reverberated with a sickening sensation.

Its stark message—its timeless, deafening echo—permeated every cell, yet none at all, as it crushed the very goodness from a gentle day in late spring. But neither disbelief, nor a stumbling, searing pain was enough to alter reality. Grass pushed higher, daylilies bloomed, the sun stood bright, steadfast. And *still*, death had come.

At 27 years of age, Matthew had committed suicide sometime after midnight. Parked in a remote meadow on a slight hill west of a family hunting cabin in northern Missouri, on a Sunday, only nine days before a trip home to Indianapolis for the Fourth of July, a life I loved ended. And even though precise timeframes lack importance when death and its ability to shock and stun us arrive, three days prior I'd talked to Matt, and that brief conversation began to play back in my mind ever so slowly—over and over, commonplace words generating a suffocating wave of nausea.

In the aftermath, it reminded me of a sad, beautiful song you can't stop listening to: Matt's measured words reduced to ash against infinity, against what he chose not to say.

Had I missed the deeper message; had it even been there?

Eagerly, he'd confirmed his travel plans, but simultaneously, Matt sounded distracted, as though struggling to hold it together. Catching the discrepancy, his patchwork efforts that did nothing to reassure me, I retreated to familiar centers of worry.

Is he staying clean; does he need medical care?

Can anything be done to prevent another insidious relapse?

Matt, are you there? Matt?

Bottle-feeding two spindly looking calves named Thelma and Louise, he said: "Calves are hungry; gotta keep moving."

Rushed, reluctant to talk, his tone of voice fluctuated, varied in intensity, in quality, like a radio station with poor reception. With the voice I loved imperceptibly fading, I stood frozen, cell phone in hand.

"Well, Mom, I better get going," Matt finally muttered, his reluctance noticeable. "Love you."

"Love you, son."

And with that our five-minute conversation faded to silence.

I tried to shake that fuzzy sense of dread, told myself to remain calm. I would see him soon, could search those greenish-brown eyes for whatever he hadn't shared. Matt was an adult; somehow I could wait. Besides, phone calls had obvious limitations. Maybe I was overly concerned, needlessly anxious—even over-reacting.

Yet my son's challenging history led me to believe otherwise.

When pressed for information, Matt usually grew silent or distant, or would abruptly end a conversation. And whenever we discussed communication issues during fleeting periods of recovery, he explained that he couldn't talk to family members when using drugs.

"It makes me feel bad, because you'll know right away."

So, unfortunately, his reluctance to engage in conversation that morning spoke loudly of Matt's state of mind. Conversely, words are tools of manipulation for addicts, so well before our last phone conversation, I'd learned not to trust everything he said, especially during, or right before, a relapse. I would have to be patient. Clinging to a thin thread of hope, I knew I wouldn't be able to gauge his location on that eerie, teetering continuum between relapse and recovery, until he drove east, walked through our door. When Matt looked gaunt, too tired to smile, as if hiding behind faded eyes, he was in relapse mode, just hanging on.

I *knew* that tentative tone: the wobble in Matt's voice that signaled another downdraft.

Mothers, via their intuition, are tuned in to the vibrations of their offspring, even when they are adults, so I had little choice but to trust my frightened instincts, even as I yearned to quiet my fears. Panic was of no value—that much I'd learned. Besides, Matt seemingly had been taking greater responsibility for the details of life, getting along better, overall. We felt hopeful.

But what is hope when dealing with addiction—what is realistic versus fantasy versus wishful thinking? Sometimes I had no idea how to answer that question with any degree of certainty or clarity, because no matter how good Matt *seemed* to be doing, I was never easily convinced, even as I had to settle for whatever he was willing to offer.

Addicts lead sketchy, secretive lives. And most are caught up in day-to-day mind-sets laden with high risk, uncertainty, disapproval of self, and sustained, purposeful distance from those they love. Hiding behind a cloaked world of deceit and despair, they seem to defy anyone to penetrate a makeshift veil of secrecy.

It's easy to get caught up in the innumerable highs and lows, in a journey of shifting shadows that defies all understanding. Had I possessed supernatural power, I may have seen the ending that lurked in the silence, the worrisome pauses in our conversation that warned of *something*. But summer stood tall, gallant, like life itself. Tragedy couldn't be hiding nearby. To say we were numb to Matt's ups and downs—a perpetual reality of imminent calamity—isn't really the case.

But after living through a host of close calls, we avoided prediction. The weather or the universe might be more predictable, after all.

Perhaps he dreamt of lasting recovery, but Matt envisioned the next thrill with equal fervor. The tension—the grating inner conflict—must have generated tremendous pain.

Smoke and Mirrors

As Matt ushered in perilous periods of carefully veiled experimentation with controlled substances that morphed into a serious, uncontrollable problem, the steamy underworld of drugs was known to me only on an abstract level. Their dangerous appeal impossible to fathom. I'd studied related societal issues—i.e., deviancy, social control, criminology, and so on—while a graduate student, but seeing my own son drawn into such a turbulent, deadly world was like watching a terrifying movie clip.

If you haven't navigated this brutal tightrope firsthand, it may be difficult to imagine the helplessness and pain that such harrowing circumstances engender. And even though addicts of any age must ultimately help and heal themselves, this seemingly obvious fact rarely springs into view like perky yellow tulips.

That would be wishful thinking at its very finest.

Life in this frightening lane goes something like this: phase versus problem; serious use versus experimentation; relapse versus recovery; life versus death. How, you might wisely wonder, are such elusive lines drawn, especially in the midst of something so fierce, so intrusive, that we could scarcely grasp the unfolding of one shocking development before another crisis materialized around us? But this was my only son—I would not give up without a fight.

To counter my naïveté, I read George McGovern's book about his daughter, Terry, and her lifelong struggle with alcoholism. Learning that his middle child lost her life when she froze to death in a parking lot during a final relapse was jarring. The brutal reality of addiction—a gut-wrenching scenario my heart wanted to reject as unique or unlikely—also left me wanting to learn how to prevent a similar tragedy in our family.

But as the devastating power of drugs and alcohol came into sharp focus, I also began to understand that full recovery is always an impermanent, iffy state. A fitful, gray zone. McGovern explained how Terry's final relapse came after an extended period of sobriety—when everyone believed (after years of treatment and hopeful struggle) she'd made it. What a dreadful surprise. But "doing good" can delude those fighting drugs or alcohol, because they believe *now* they can use again—*now* they can "safely" manage their habit.

Addiction, the proverbial land of smoke and mirrors.

As a cautionary sidebar, if you know or love an addict and feel somewhat optimistic, even confident about apparent progress, there is also good reason to be watchful, if not alarmed. Such is the bizarre terrain of mind-altering drugs, along with other substances that belong in this category. And despite the extremely limited odds of someone "making it" once addicted to meth or its close variants—recovery runs as low as 3 percent—most of us desperately want to believe in the people we love. I did.

I prayed for a miracle, for deep-seated, long-lasting change. *Surely* statistics should be interpreted with a mature perspective, relevant contextual details, since societal issues are often cast in their most distasteful light—while precisely definable truth, as we know, is mostly an abstract, shifting concept dependent on perspective, timing, and so on.

David Sheff, sharing his son's journey as a meth addict in *Beautiful Boy*, describes the treacherous terrain of drugs with eerie precision, stressing how an abundance of shocking milestones, life-threatening setbacks, broken promises, and failed attempts to reverse a situation that seriously impacts brain chemistry made it difficult to believe in anything. He's absolutely right, I'm afraid.

Believing in anything, good or bad, often felt like a ridiculous form of self-delusion.

Advice, generic treatment options, and dire predictions are mere words in comparison to the urgent concerns of aggressive, unrelenting addiction. Plans disintegrate, schedules disappear, trust vanishes. Predictability fades like the sunset, or a silly, childhood dream. Yet, my optimistic spirit rallied time and time again, until firmly crushed by a blinding act of violence. Until fingers, as though gasping for air—*a perpetual solution*—connected with a cold, metal trigger, instantly extinguishing all signs of life.

And, yes, Matthew, like Nic Sheff, was also a most "beautiful boy."

The Cloak of Night

I couldn't help but wonder how Matt, drugs raging in his veins, had been able to choose, then find, his final destination—engine running, headlights on—until discovered around three in the morning. On a purely practical level, exactly how had he managed to sustain a muddled thought process long enough to contemplate and commit suicide? Was there no way for him, for someone, to stop this deadly sequence—nothing to come between him and eternity? And then to find him. My heart raced at the thought.

I'm pretty sure life never prepares us for the gravity of something like this, but I was told an unidentified noise, in the black of night, woke up one of Matt's uncles. Spending the weekend in the nearby hunting cabin, he stepped outside to scan the darkness for the source of the noise, and glancing up the hill, spotted streams of light, firm against the cloak of night, from a vehicle in a most unlikely place.

I cannot imagine my son leaving the world like this.

The piercing sound of gunshot against a peaceful country silence when life and death equally shared that split second—the precise moment when Matthew's life came crashing down. A fallen soldier, tired, utterly defeated by the battle. Everything in me resisted this shattering image; yet somewhere in the far reaches of my awareness, I sensed I would have no choice but to fully embrace it. *Someday.*

Cosmic Connection

Strangely, the night Matthew died, we slept, miles away in another state, but also awoke suddenly. Noah (our schnauzer) was scratching on an upstairs screen and barking loudly, so I got up, rushed to check on him. He liked to sleep on a futon in a spare bedroom that also served as my husband's home office, but rarely, if ever, barked during the night.

Fear hit my brain like a powerful shock wave.

Something was wrong.

Noah was extremely agitated when I found him staring intently out a window onto our lower roof. If the air conditioner had been on, the window would have been closed tightly, but night temperatures were mild, so we'd left it open a few inches. Following Noah's gaze, I spotted the raccoon. The night raider stared back, his black mask startling me. Flinching, I closed the window, lowered the blinds, so Noah couldn't see the intruder should it return. Within minutes, the quiet of night resumed: incident over.

But sleep eluded me. I couldn't shake the heavy sense of dread trying to take root in my soul. Spiritual leaders often discuss the possibility of signs, but, in this case, a sign of what? Where was the connection; what might it point to?

Adding to the mystery, my husband and I woke up again with a start, an hour or so later, after hearing another odd noise—a loud bang—we were unable to identify.

"What was that?" I ventured.

"Don't know," John said, in a sleepy voice. "Probably nothing."

But I could almost hear our thoughts racing around in the dark, somewhat frantically, as we tried to pinpoint the disturbing noise—or convince ourselves we'd imagined it. As the minutes ticked by, we slowly dozed off again. We lived in a safe suburb; there was no reason for alarm. But I will never *ever* forget that harsh sound at about the same time we lost our beloved Matthew to this world.

A cosmic connection, an unusual coincidence—absolutely nothing?

I was clueless, but apprehensive.

In retrospect, the intriguing theory of quantum entanglement comes to mind. Maybe a phenomenon called clairvoyance.

For many months thereafter, I woke up, almost precisely, at three a.m.

When a silvery dawn crept over the horizon that morning, the aggressive raccoon, the jarring noise, zoomed back into focus. Of course none of it made a shred of sense. Not until the news of tragedy lit up my mind like lightning bolts racing across an endless sky. It was a disabling truth. And in that sinking moment, I wondered if my own heart would grow still. I couldn't imagine what would possibly provide the impetus for its continued beating: its lifesaving rhythm. It felt like it had skipped a few beats already—grown pale and faint, as if overcome by severe and sudden exhaustion.

Sensing the ultimate sacredness of the moment, I searched for a candle. Finding a white taper in the dining room, I lit a match, held it to the wick, stared blankly. I suspect this had something to do with not having any idea *what* to do, as my faded eyes turned to thick salty burning pools. A candle's flickering flame, hardly anything when set against the starkness of the unknown: a limitless power slamming into my life with a vengeance.

Still, I watched the warm light dance higher, as if it knew no bounds. As though nothing had changed.

But within minutes, the candle was dripping; I bent close, blew it out. The familiar scent of something burning lingered. Memories of "Candle in the Wind," Elton John's haunting song, popular during my college years, filtered into my awareness. Something about the rain setting in and do we ever really know what to do. The album cover from *Goodbye Yellow Brick Road* was also unforgettable.

The general ease of college life in the mid-1970s—its luxurious sense of time ahead—placed beside the stripped canvas of death was an overwhelming comparison. The grip of absence tightened, making it difficult to breathe. I walked in a new world now—one I'd never seen or envisioned, one I couldn't distance myself from, or hardly ignore.

I could hate it, though; that much I could do.

But things are merely beginning to unfold. The formal days of loss, a prayer service, a morning funeral, a country burial, loom somewhere ahead. *Somewhere ahead.*

Inviting the Bell

"The Way of Heaven is to
benefit others and not to injure.
The Way of the sage is to act
but not to compete."

—LAO TZU

Consciousness Itself

What remains to be said after a sudden death, when everyone has left the cemetery, gone home and mailed you a lovely sympathy card, and you are alone as never before? This deceptively simple-sounding question haunted me for a long time, followed me around, drug me all over in search of an answer. Lacking insight, I was determined to find out, so I kept writing—all the while confronting the surreal nature of loss—but more than once, I failed to trust my intuition. Missed the answer time and time again, even though I sort of thought that life, at its most meaningful, must be about the basics. How could it be otherwise?

Tea and poetry. Nature. The foggy notion of time. Beginnings merging into endings and vice versa; life and loss swirling side by side in a frothing universal stew. A sunrise, a sunset, that startles us with its intensity as if delivering an unspoken message. Anything and everything can point us back to simplicity: to the roots of our existence, to Zen-like principles like emptiness, silence, meditation, breathing, and peace. But it seems we resist the inescapable return trip: oppose living with genuine regard for this fundamental truth.

Do we really believe we can leave our spiritual origins behind, pretend they are no longer needed, as unimportant as that old winter coat in the far reaches of our closet?

For some reason, we run too hard, too fast, in all the wrong directions.

This dynamic may be unconscious but, nonetheless, it's there. Of course I had to walk many challenging miles to unearth and embrace what now seems relatively obvious. Like most, my life evolved in fits and spurts, in largely unexpected ways, generating a personal map I never could have envisioned as a youthful dreamer. Then, life was a poetic palette: bright, endless days simply waiting for my imagination and energy.

This curious feeling of "how did I get here" isn't uncommon, especially when you've stretched, willingly or otherwise, beyond the safe, predictable confines of home, routine, and tradition—venturing into the unknown, head held high, or otherwise. But, for me, the real game changer was becoming a parent. With no idea how two spirited children would steer my average life and dreams in unforeseen directions—how abiding love, fearsome challenges and, finally, a sudden death, could look and feel more like a spiritual mission when viewed from a long-term, higher perspective—when considered more deeply, this is precisely what the journey suggests, and reveals.

I didn't see it in the moment. The great unraveling of experience hadn't happened, nor had the thread of time revealed its purpose.

Like most, I thought of parenting in terms of biology, the family tree: an extension of marriage. I also believed that spiritual missions were *special* undertakings reserved for the holiest among us. Priests, monks, rabbis, pastors, spiritual teachers, nuns, preachers, theologians. It never occurred to me that my plain-clothed life would demand and deliver a spiritual voyage—a cosmic trip into the unknown depths of my very human soul.

Haven't you also presumed that spiritual missions, or ordained paths, originated with overt clarity: a purposeful, identifiable launch; a fully conscious commitment to a well-defined religious path; a formal dedication to serve God, a higher power, a humanitarian cause; major goals written in strictly spiritual terms? Assuming such an orientation was well beyond the scope of my ordinary life, I believed this path was something to admire from afar: to read or hear about, to imagine. In coping with Matthew's death, however, I was compelled to reach beyond *thought*.

The moment had come to insistently question and, perhaps, transcend everything I'd been taught to accept as truth. Dogma, traditional belief systems, religious frameworks, even some definitions of spirituality and spiritual practice. Nothing could be spared. Already, I'd left too much of it behind. Not so much by choice, but because I wanted to understand life and loss from a more enlightened perspective—wanted to jump into the deep end of the pool, see if I could keep my head above water. And now, I'm convinced that spiritual missions enter our lives in various guises—that we are *all* called, or invited, to live from a higher purpose. Often in surprisingly common ways.

Or in ways that, on the surface, appear simplistic and routine, even irrational, to those who are curiously eager to judge from distinctly different vantage points that are distant, invariably incomplete. And perhaps we accept (or reject) this gentle call to service, this nudge to confront the vast unknown, unwittingly, yet, certainly, as we secretly wonder if this is a daunting life test, a strange and potent challenge, or a profound spiritual gift in disguise. While we must look to our beliefs, values, and history for answers to ethereal questions, having known Matt's arduous journey—painful addiction, hopeful rehabs, countless recovery-relapse cycles, incarceration, and finally, a violent death—it's quite clear that these overwhelming, hypnagogic experiences have been my mentor: my greatest teacher. Not academic pursuits, professional ambition or accomplishments, nor anything I've encountered or experienced during the block of time we refer to as a "lifetime."

The painful, tangled process—Matt's infrequent, yet, hard-won victories; his crushing, often life-threatening defeats, persistent mistakes and misgivings; wrestling with life and death issues for many hard years—tested me in a multitude of ways. Just the need to love my son unconditionally in the face of agonizing setbacks, intense worry, mind-numbing fear, and digging deeper for a particle of well-being when clouds of despair engulfed me, taught me a great deal about my son, myself, family, friends, society, and ultimately, the world beyond—in spiritual terms.

Reaching for an inner strength I rarely expected to encounter, I had little choice but to persevere against the turmoil of my son's addiction. And with his sudden absence, again, I had little choice but to evolve—seeking solace in a garden of stones that looked barren, unwilling to surrender its wealth of secrets.

Dark Complexity

An unexpected window to my soul, Matthew's death was the catalyst that exposed life anew. But even before his loss, during the excruciating years of hope, prayer, setbacks, and silent sacrifice, I repeatedly asked the God I knew one simple but daring question: *why?* Why did I have to watch my son suffer endlessly; why were there no answers; why couldn't anyone seem to help him; why couldn't he help himself; why didn't people try to understand drug addiction from a health perspective (mental, physical, spiritual); why was this tragedy happening—to him, to me, to us—in the first place?

In the wake of loss, I also asked God why my son's life ended when least expected—almost like a horrible joke. Finally, we were growing accustomed to extended periods of normalcy and recovery, witnessing hopeful signs, relishing the hard-earned, unmitigated pleasure of seeing Matt enjoy the simple, safe, and sustainable things in life.

Painful questions, like these, however, are never answered with finality; instead they beg for answers that are only generated by a deeper spiritual awareness, by searching within for as long as needed. Likewise, there are few universal answers to such personal questions. Still, with Matt's life and death, a sterling invitation to explore the peaks and valleys arrived, and as I navigated this formidable path, I grew even more convinced that this journey with my son was an incredible spiritual invitation.

Through his struggles, Matthew grew, I grew, and family members grew. Beyond our family circle, I am also confident that people I will never know, those who met him along the way, grew from having known him. *Think about it.* If no one generated problems for the world—if there were *no problems* to solve at all—how would anyone grow, evolve?

Keep in mind though that, for us, personal growth wasn't optional.

Family systems are forever interconnected, inherently flawed and dysfunctional, yet, this is a *normal* aspect of the human experience. Imperfect individuals create imperfect systems. Still, despite (and because of) an abundance of so-called flaws, we can discover and embrace endless opportunities for insight and growth—if we are receptive.

A contradiction in terms, perhaps, or a painfully ironic twist, that Matt, easily labeled in one-dimensional, harsh, or negative terms, gave of himself anyway, even if indirectly and unknowingly, in surprising and spiritual ways I am understanding better each day.

Matthew's struggle to conquer dangerous temptations, life-threatening problems, and serious human shortcomings ended abruptly, without the joyful resolution some of us had envisioned but, nonetheless, he touched the lives of many, inspiring some in subtle ways, and reminding others, in eloquent, unspoken terms, to remain forever humble in the face of adversity or agonizing realities that can manifest at any time … *in any life.*

Even though these dynamics usually went unspoken, in searching for the underlying story—the imperceptible, often revealing truth—I noticed such moments. Witnessed the gift of growth my son's problems offered others, even virtual strangers, in a sad, strange, complicated kind of way. Matt's utter humanness speaking quietly to others, reminding them that perfection is another great illusion. Yet, societies, cultures, and individuals of all ages and persuasions insist on chasing this tempting mirage.

But, still, why *my* son? Was this a cumbersome blessing, a curse, the luck of the draw ... or merely a random experience? Questions like this burned in my soul, a summer storm gathering momentum, and naïvely, I believed others would perceive the dark complexity of sudden death. Most didn't, however. This, almost more than anything, spoke loudly to me of the need to share this deeply personal life chapter with others. Creating awareness around issues that defy full, or even logical, understanding is important; helping to stem destructive tides of ignorance and apathy that paralyze and encumber us, may encourage greater compassion, as well. It's not an easy world, after all.

Sacred Quality

Losing Matt to a lethal combination of methamphetamine and self-inflicted violence, obscured reality, and even though I'd been through difficult experiences with him along the way, I possessed limited emotional context for something as riveting, as devastating, as suicide. His abrupt loss confounded me—shredded life into the tiniest of bits, pieces. Giving voice to the dimensions of grief that are easily minimized, obscured, or forgotten by a frenzied, frantic world, is what I have left to offer.

Like hard-earned emotional ashes, I sense a sacred quality to what remains. Initially, though, it was a far different story. (Weaving the personal days of loss with some of the more far-reaching issues helps to shed light on the universal aspects of grief and spiritual exploration; thus, experiential story layers unfold gradually.) Tentative, early steps, for instance, didn't feel remotely sacred.

Customary expectations, like fine sand washed out to sea, vanished. I caught myself writing poetry about the "relics of routine." Faced with unimaginable sorrow, I learned how individuals and society struggle with the intricacies of grief, desperately rushing to sweep sadness away, lest it contaminate that glorified well of life. Getting in the way of what many frantically *want* to believe is so much more important. But grief, too, is life, and loss steps into everyone's world, sneaking with deliberation and precision from the barest of shadows: a potent force robbing us of those we love.

The twining of life and loss, like quicksand under my feet, felt unbearable. Subconsciously, I yearned for one without the other.

So how did I move beyond simplified frameworks to honor a clumsy process that was neither linear nor logical but, without question, gut-wrenching?

Initially, runaway swells of hopelessness arrived in the form of panic. The next breath, the next moment—it all felt impossible. And I soon learned that pain of this magnitude doesn't lend itself to ridiculous recipes for successful grieving: simplified steps or phases, one-size-fits-all thinking.

Death, assuredly the greatest unknown we must face, is something our "enlightened contemporary society" fails to embrace as though belonging to all of us. And sadly, we learn to fear it—hiding death, running from loss, as if possible. John Donne (1572–1631), preacher, lawyer, Jacobean poet and author wrote in *Devotions upon Emergent Occasions, Meditation XVII*, "Any man's death diminishes me, because I am involved in Mankind … never send to know for whom the bell tolls; it tolls for thee."

Death is a collective experience, and once grief arrives, it's not unusual to feel trapped in a fitful state somewhere between life and death: dazed, bewildered, and perpetually exhausted. Of course these unwieldy circumstances wind their way into family systems, entire generations, work and educational settings, communities and organizations and, invariably, impact relationships of all kinds. Somehow we must learn to give ourselves permission to cope with loss in ways that acknowledge and serve our most human needs. Catering to a demanding, highly dysfunctional society as though *grief conformity* were a legitimate, rational expectation serves no one.

Given these grim realities, I could barely envisage how I might one day transcend deep suffering. It was clear I would have to summon the courage to ignore senseless cultural norms. So about a year after Matt's death, I began work on this book. I knew of no better way to plumb the depths of such an intense experience. Putting other projects on hold, the urgency of this story was clear—too many people drowning in a restless, churning sea of discontent that leads to many forms of addiction. Yet, our focus is stuck on "individuals"—on "fixing" him or her, when people and societies are inextricably linked.

The world always has been about *connection*.

If nothing else, I wanted the book I would write to stimulate, maybe even elevate, the national conversation. Isn't it mostly reactionary, mostly dull, lifeless? And while some voices—loud or pensive, young or old, powerful or otherwise—seem hopelessly fixated on arguing about drugs (what to do, or not do), others die. Go to prison. Give up. Drop out of jobs, schools, families, and society. But I also sensed the root causes of addiction were largely unexposed, unexplored. That "cause" was buried somewhere within every human being, manifesting as a futile search for whatever society insists is important, necessary, good, fulfilling, or fun. Pointing us in a multitude of unfruitful directions, it's common to believe that happiness and contentment reside *somewhere else.*

Somewhere external to us.

St. Francis of Assisi exquisitely states the problem and the solution: "What we are looking for is what is looking."

Another troubling tendency is treating symptoms, period. Does it seem practical or expedient to settle for so-called solutions that are mostly knee-jerk reactions taking us far afield from what might actually help? History, repeating itself *ad infinitum*, reminds us of this pattern.

Shared Vulnerability

Because we sense only those closest to us truly care to hear about our troubles or worries, it's not unusual to walk a difficult path (knowingly or otherwise) without saying much—especially if there isn't ready access to societal cushions of fame and fortune (ill-fated, trick cushions that rarely make a positive difference). Fearing people will turn against us if our lives don't resemble the fantasy land of television and movie screens, sitcoms of old with cookie-cutter parents and sweetly charming children, we are reluctant to share the struggles that threaten to overwhelm us. During the years of *not talking* about Matt's life or ours, I realized that suffering, directly and indirectly, from life-threatening issues is merely one aspect of living with extended trauma. Keeping things under wrap because of insidious cultural expectations is another kind of suffering: more unfair, more draining.

Long before I studied sociology, I knew we needed to look closely at social systems from forgotten or enlightened perspectives, because we seldom do. We are bogged down in the status quo. Captivated by popular stereotypes that rarely shed light on *anything*, we haven't noticed how mindless conformity can be useless, mostly dysfunctional.

So whether or not others are willing to listen, speak up. Don't suffer in silence because you fear negative repercussions. We live in a judgmental world—opinions derived from limited information, the shadowy influence of ego—thus, some are noticeably eager and willing to look down on anyone, especially those struggling, searching, or simply trying to get it right. But from a spiritual perspective, everyone struggles, even though some are unable to openly acknowledge this. Some are happy to distance themselves behind self-righteous, religious walls by clinging to doctrines that appear to offer a safe set of rules.

But when I confronted my safe set of beliefs, they disintegrated. This was liberating too, because simultaneously, I also discovered a hidden door. One urging me beyond time and self, suggesting I peer through the tricky veil of custom and convention more closely. There, of all places, I detected a strong desire to ignore the many constraints of a fitful world seeking enlightenment only sporadically, if at all. I also sensed, ironically so, the discernible fragility of humanity—everyone covering up, attempting to compensate for perceived imperfections in countless, ineffective ways.

Matt chose the slippery promise of controlled substances.

Just one approach of many, albeit an extremely common one.

Forced to confront a vast unknown without warning, preparation, or noticeable grace, I definitely felt newly fragile, and easily languished in a murky well of uncertainty. Only when owning the vulnerability we all share, did I sense a deeper connection to a spiritual dimension that felt incredibly alive: like consciousness itself.

My journey, however, was unpredictable. A shape-shifter in every way. My expectations were diverse, irregular.

One thing, thankfully, was clear: I craved understanding of the swampy relationship between life and loss. Something *real*, something useful, was lurking there because the pairing made me so uncomfortable.

Could an innate discomfort with death—its brutal force, its inevitability, and how it shapes brief mortal sojourns—lead the unwary to some form of addiction? Not consciously. From a fuzzy, indistinct, and trembling place within that is disconnected from the wonder and luminous simplicity of spiritual awareness.

Isn't the question itself, the observation, rife with potential for deeper consideration?

Inviting the Bell

"The Way of Heaven is to
benefit others and not to injure.
The Way of the sage is to act
but not to compete."
—LAO TZU

Silence is the universal refuge....
—HENRY DAVID THOREAU

The Face of Hardship

*B*arely functioning in a consuming gray haze, I agonized over a troubling scene lodged in my mind's eye. Matthew, scared, alone, hunched and shaking in the driver's seat of an idling vehicle in the stark hush of night with the primal intention to end his life reverberating through his psyche. Was he cold with fear, hopelessly confused, while still trying to *think* about the pros and cons, or merely reacting to a false impulse in white hot haste, determined to get the dreaded, final moment behind him, as if inevitable—tucked in the cards of destiny all along? Then again, was he remotely capable of rational thought while viewing his life from a riddled landscape of unbridled, drug-laden emotion?

Such useless questions flooded my senses, as we sat crumpled on our old blue couch. A relic of the corduroy era, it was still comfortable, even comforting. John, Matt's step-parent of 12 years, looked faded and stunned—tears erupting, subsiding, erupting. I was locked in an enervating silence, devoured by feelings so visceral I felt stripped of my ability to function. Noah's soulful, deep brown schnauzer eyes, studied me with a worried look.

But even with a mind disabled by shock, I grasped for a thought, an emotion, maybe a memory, to somehow *explain* this blinding moment.

Did the location, like our worn couch, soothe Matt? Did the lonely, remote spot harbor something special he wanted to be near: memories he loved, abandoned dreams, peace? A verdant meadow scattered with wildflowers, cattle grazing nearby, a small stock pond he'd fished in probably only days before, a place where he listened for the unmistakable call of a bobwhite—but then, the final push of time. Matt responding with a deadly plan, methamphetamine pulsing through his veins—as the lab report confirmed.

Relentless questions, logical to absurd, stormed my foggy awareness. Exactly how had the dominoes fallen, I wondered. A lack of viable information didn't squelch my internal pacing. Had Matt's befuddled mind generated an artificial reality that led to an accidental suicide, or had he harbored suicidal thoughts for years—was he *aware* of his choice? In vain, I tried to imagine him sitting here, talking with us. There had been plenty of conversations on this couch. Some more difficult—more memorable—than others.

I could see him tossing aside the cushions, pulling out the mattress. "Mom, where are the sheets?"

Maybe the house was crowded with holiday guests; maybe friends were spending the night. But the poignant image was too much— too full of family, safety, and routine—and the crucifying weight of mind-numbing questions returned.

Experts on addiction have linked suicide to methamphetamine. The withdrawal state is agonizing and the addict's sense of remorse can easily overwhelm. Some addicts tuck away the idea of suicide as a last resort. During the long course of his addiction, we worried about an overdose, a fatal car accident, a lethal brawl in an ugly drug deal—rarely suicide. In hindsight, there is no sacred territory in this devilish context: no place of safety, nothing out-of-bounds. But ... Matt always appeared to have the will to live. Perhaps he was simply a decent actor, because one could easily argue that addiction itself represents a strong desire *not* to live. At a minimum it suggests a deep reluctance, an ongoing inability, to embrace and sustain the expectations of others or to adopt a healthy lifestyle.

We all harbor secrets of the heart, and since Matt suffered from bouts of depression, ADHD, and related issues—such connections aren't unrealistic. Never eager to address his ongoing struggles—human imperfections so many face—was that just camouflage? When scared or worried, pretending not to care is a common defense mechanism. Matt didn't have much faith in medication, nor was he convinced of the need for therapy ... it's possible he was self-medicating (intentionally or otherwise) with drugs or alcohol—with whatever fell into his hands—which is how some wind up addicts in the first place.

Andrew Solomon, professor of clinical psychology at Columbia University, wrote in *The Noonday Demon: An Atlas of Depression*, a book that won 11 national awards, that "depression and substance abuse form a cycle." That "self-medication with illicit drugs is frequently counterproductive...."

Of course prescription drugs are another insidious issue—also readily abused and, as statistics reveal, even more so than street drugs (heroin, however, is making a comeback.) Enter Philip Seymour Hoffman, a gifted actor, now deceased. And not long ago another life lost to these insidious issues.

Deeply moved by his son's tragic death, Edward Hirsch (poet, author, president of the John Simon Guggenheim Memorial Foundation) wrote a book-length poem, *Gabriel: A Poem* (Knopf, 2014), about the inescapable emotions of overwhelming loss. In a subsequent interview, *Poets & Writers Magazine*, Hirsch compared the experience to a tsunami: "… when you're in the total grip of grief, you're inarticulate." How very true, and our sons sounded so much alike—both impetuous, even "unstoppable."

Touching Truth

Somehow, like lethargic ghosts, we rose from the blue couch, made some tea. I worked to convince myself the steaming liquid was soothing but, honestly, it was merely something to do: an attempt to survive an overwhelming moment. In many ways, *the exact moment* I'd been trying to survive, or prevent, for years. Reeling from the fresh news of tragedy, I didn't see this connection then. Not consciously. Nor could I sense the unbroken spirit of the trusting but inquisitive girl within, the one sipping tea with her grandmother, not a care in the world. Such days of simplicity and joy seemed lost forever.

Unraveling the complexities and contradictions of addiction can feel absolutely futile. A bizarre, barren landscape, and it doesn't help that so few seem to grasp that addiction is truly addiction—not a bad habit masquerading as a troubling pattern of behavior, not only a dysfunctional repetitive choice. Addiction, as I've come to understand it, flows from a powerful, all-consuming set of thoughts and actions motivated and sustained by chemical modifications in the brain: overwhelming cravings for the next high, frightening impulses that trick and cajole the addicted, along with those who love them.

Addiction, as witnessed in Matt, was a persistent inability to alter thoughts or actions, even when the very harshest of consequences stared him in the face: even when wanting desperately to change. Sadly, I'm unable to do this foreign, mixed-up reality justice via mere words. Encountering addiction as a progressive disease, largely without a known cure, is, in many respects, beyond our limited human language. A place where customary expectations are turned upside down, inside out, and sunlit days take on the dark, difficult hues of danger, uncertainty, fruitless wishing, and interminable waiting.

Ultimately, it is a life and death issue, one that individuals and many societies tend to shove under the table while pretending it only happens to "bad people" or "bad families" or defective individuals who don't care about their lives. Very little could be further from the truth. But, sadly, a widespread societal *and* individual disease invites a stereotypical response, finger-pointing, and vast suffering.

The menacing dynamics of addiction only complicate matters. What appears fixed, inevitably isn't; what should be routine, winds up being involved, difficult. Running a few errands; locking a door; planning ahead; basic communication; honesty, trust, dependability. Even a conversation about following up on a commitment can quickly become strained. Things mysteriously go missing.

"What happened to Matt's golf clubs?"

"He probably pawned them."

"Probably. I wonder when."

"Or where."

With Grief at My Side

One night when making yet another cup of tea—the only thing I could manage that offered a moment's respite from an indeterminate surge of powerful emotions—I noticed it had become a ritual that bleak summer of 2007. While the relentless march of calendar time persisted, I faced its passage with a solid sense of denial. Some days I felt like a contrary child who couldn't, or wouldn't, get it straight: Matt was gone. Not temporarily, either. Other times, I felt like a failed, imperfect mother: the one person in the world who should have gone one step further, done one more thing, to save her son's life.

I'd tried to do what was in Matt's best interests, even when sorely tempted to give up, and especially when all reasonable efforts to support his journey felt futile—like a fuzzy, girlish daydream I couldn't shake. But this must be a common reaction, an agonizing sense of failure after a child's (regardless of age) loss.

Looking over boxes of tea in our pantry—green, spice, peppermint, Earl Grey—my thoughts swirled like a curious combination of all four. I remembered another mother, what she'd written about her son, Johnny. In a classic about the loss of a brilliant 17-year-old son from a brain tumor, Frances Gunther shared this truth in *Death Be Not Proud*, a book I'd read and loved well before my own tragedy: "I think every parent must have a sense of failure, even of sin, merely in remaining alive after the death of a child. One feels that it is not right to live when one's child has died, that one should somehow have found the way to give one's life to save his life."

No matter how or why a child leaves this temporary world, most parents would swap places without hesitation. Something in us urgently and persistently wants our children to prosper. To contribute to our extended human family—enjoying long, happy, purposeful lives. Yet, our sons, our daughters, have destinies of unique design; an indisputable fact providing only minimal consolation. Even when our egos convince us our willingness to help makes a lasting, remarkable difference in the lives of others, a touch of humility conveys a more subtle truth: What we do to impact another life may not be earthshaking.

Conversely, we know that the right kind of help, at the right time, can tip the scales of survival and success. You've heard the claims. Without my mother, father, grandparent, or sibling, I couldn't have made it. Or maybe tremendous credit is given to a close friend, an inspiring teacher, counselor, coach, minister, aunt, uncle, step-parent. Touching another life in meaningful, life-saving ways does happen. Obviously, there is no single right answer, no definitive concept to be accepted or rejected, and most of us will go on helping others, hoping our efforts—amazing, sacrificial, or largely ordinary—make a positive difference: in the moment or later on.

Some parents, in particular, hold especially high standards when it comes to helping their offspring; and if, by chance or circumstance, they must say good-bye to a child of any age, a swamp of wishful thinking, a quicksand of regret, pours from their vulnerable souls. Likewise, it is easy to get lost in punishing conjecture. Either way, we are largely alone with our internal barometers when we navigate this trying terrain.

But ... back to my tea. Earl Grey, a favorite. I also enjoyed green tea, and with all the hype around it, decided to make a cup to take upstairs. John's career required travel, a schedule that gave me ample time to ponder whatever was on my mind. Sometimes, in such moments, I evaluated myself on how well I was doing. It's something we all do, but I considered it much more frequently now. I'd heard about those who collapse under the strain of grief, those who don't make it after a death in the family.

I had no idea where I fell on such a frightening continuum, but felt evaluative eyes on me, people watching to see if I would crumble under the strain of Matt's death, so I tried to worry about my "progress," my state of mind, privately. Quiet and reflective by nature, I'd noticed a strong, insistent pull from within. An inner voice that seemed to understand loss differently—better than anyone I knew, especially myself.

I was willing to listen.

I'd grown up hearing that lemon and honey could cure almost anything, so I stirred honey into my cup, added a light squeeze of lemon. Curiously, as I left the kitchen, my grandmother's sweet smile came into focus, along with her peaceful gaze, her lined face perfectly framed by gray-white waves. A welcome, comforting memory. Turning off the lights, I called for Noah. He raced ahead of me, taking the long flight of stairs in his usual effortless fashion. I marveled at his energy. In contrast to mine, breathtaking.

Flipping on a bedroom lamp with subdued lighting, I changed, sat on the edge of the bed in my robe with my tea. I dreaded going to sleep: dreams too often darkly laced in sorrow. I stalled. Decided to light the white candle from June 24. I could at least mark the endless hours since that day, honor *whatever* kind of journey I was on.

Watching the flame—its warmth, steadiness—I again sought my grandmother's face. Taking a plain white cup to withered lips, there she sat, as I watched her every move from across the table. A girl captivated by her kind, gentle ways.

If I could just talk to her, ask her what to do now that Matt was gone.

On my own, I hadn't figured out too much. Only that there was a great deal more to this (and any) story of loss than superficial, simplistic explanations lead us to believe.

There was something so wrong about it, yet how could it be wrong and natural at the same time, so critical to the ongoing evolution of the planet? Feeling chilled, I pulled my favorite blue robe closer, wondered if I possessed the courage to dig deeper. When I tried, I wound up back at the beginning, caught in an endless circle of disbelief.

Studying the dancing flame, I reviewed what little I knew, that grief was initiated by a deeply shocking event that forced an intense confrontation with the vast unknown. A dark angry sea had risen up in me, pushed me up and over and down. A turbulent energy that was exhausting and demanding, but if Stephen Hawking, the famous theoretical physicist, could probe the distant, disturbing world of black holes, couldn't I somehow muster the strength to confront *all* the dimensions of death—to *look at it* without flinching, without reservation or hesitation or fear?

Closing my eyes I tried to chart an imaginary death sequence on an abstract level. Maybe if I took a dreamlike experience like suicide, and placed it in a broader, boundless context, it would reveal something more. After a deep breath, I envisioned a spring day ripe with contentment. Maybe you can visualize the same kind of day.

Birds, clear sky, warm breeze—a peaceful setting that draws you in, comforts you as never before, and you feel strangely trusting, calm, and joyful. Life is good.

Then an enormous black hole appears from an invisible and unimaginable dimension; arising, in fact, from your relaxed state of mind. And unwittingly, you step through, free-falling to the other side, but only when time itself makes it so, and in that instant, you are swept away, as a horrifying helplessness overwhelms you. Until your life—the one you understood, experienced, expected—ceases to exist.

Grief has come to stay.

Like fine dust snaking its way under your back door, it moves in, takes control, even as you seek, in vain, to steady yourself, hoping you will feel like your *old self* someday.

I opened my eyes. The candle's flame persisted against my thoughts: dark, somber, choppy.

Does loss transform those left behind by pushing us to the very brink of extinction?

No sign of life, no need to go on. Definitely no reason to push beyond yesterday, to laugh or strive, to reach out to friends, family, or colleagues. What was the point, after all?

My grief was raw and intricate, uniquely intertwined with the mountain of moments that comprise a mother-son relationship of some 27 years.

I glanced at the candle, now dripping. After admitting how much I was struggling within that frightening black hole, I dared to wonder where I would find the energy to counter the cold assumptions, the predictable misconceptions, the unfriendly judgments on Matt's life—its dark, violent ending.

How would I explain his sudden loss, when I didn't understand it myself?

Extinguishing the flame, I felt a deep weariness settling in like a heavy sky before a storm. Would I defend my son, rage against the facts, or simply deny my pain?

Reaching for my cold tea, I winced at the prospect of conversation. For one thing how many can even resist a tempting piece of chocolate cake, let alone something as physically addicting as meth, cocaine, heroin? Yet I sensed some would be eager to judge—to compare, to shore up personal images, to minimize Matt's loss—when I needed compassion, empathy, and understanding. After all, time had come completely undone: a monumental sensation.

Living in a nation, a turbulent global society, addicted to almost everything—video games, credit, shopping, prescription drugs, alcohol, controversy, drama, sex, conflict, gambling, sugar, and even thinking, according to some—why would anyone assume that harsh or difficult circumstances would never penetrate his or her protected world?

On any given day, any time, for any reason.

Addiction knows no boundaries, takes on many external and internal forms, and will claim anyone in its path regardless of socio-economic status, race, gender, religion, age, education, political pref-erence, family heritage, birthplace, or residence. But, still, we are too often an abrasive, rush-to-judgment society comprised of individuals who behave like ruthless children, acting oddly convinced, via false bravado and obvious fear, that *certain problems* will never grace their *perfect lives*. Most are dead wrong. No one is immune.

Dr. Hawking has now begun to question the impact, the existence, of black holes. As a social scientist, I find his research fascinating—his life story, hugely inspiring. How very tempting it must have been for him to have given up, simply succumbing to a diagnosis of amyotrophic lateral sclerosis (also known as ALS or Lou Gehrig's disease).

At only 21, his original prognosis was dire: three years to live.

Veil of Disbelief

Iris Bolton, therapist, author, and mother to Mitch, a son who committed suicide at their home, offers a prayer: "And help me to be aware always that it is through suffering that we humans meet one another, knowing no strangers, and that life can regain its meaning through that precious kinship." All we have to give our children is our "humanness," the imperfect gift of ourselves, Bolton points out. "I saw that my son's death was his choice," she wrote.

On an intellectual level, she was right.

But sometimes "knowledge" isn't enough; we need the deeper story.

Yet, I was hopelessly stuck that summer, always prodding my soul for *real* answers. Time stood still. Firmly so. The sweltering summer day when even a zephyr would help.

Tonight I'd stared at bad television for a couple of hours before thinking about sleep. Then I noticed Noah patiently standing by the patio door, so wandered outside with him. The evening air was pleasant. I grabbed a deck chair to sit for a while and, intermittently, a slight breeze would whistle through an oversized lilac bush—the same kind I'd planted so long ago in our country yard.

I heard the soothing sound of wind chimes, glanced out at bird feeders, a bird bath, hollyhocks of pink and white, Noah roaming about without a care. Our backyard, teeming with life.

But I saw it all through that funny veil of disbelief, as I fought the stiff marriage of life *and* death. Interwoven, running hand in hand like twins, an inevitable pairing that was so very troubling. As I spotted a striking male cardinal, Iris's penetrating message surfaced again; I considered it more deliberately. How the decision to live, or not, resides within each individual: life invariably, a most personal responsibility. I wanted to remember this on notably bad days, but also when subtle signs of life caught me by surprise: bare, brief moments when I felt almost safe, like a skeptical, uncertain child learning to trust again.

Yet it was *entirely* too soon. The perils of grief waited in the wings, descending on me like thick black fog. No warning, no noticeable trigger. Even the old Alan Jackson song, "Remember When," could push me to the edge of despair within seconds. Its melody and lyrics leading me down a treacherous emotional path: the jaunty curls in Matt's blonde hair before getting a real haircut; small hands reaching for chocolate frosting on his first birthday cake; his affection for cats; his unassuming style—his voice, the way he talked, walked, moved. Simple things he loved: Saint Louis Cardinals, chocolate-covered cherries, challenging ski slopes, collecting arrowheads, visits home, and country music artists like Waylon Jennings, Johnny Cash, George Strait, Merle Haggard, Hank Williams Jr.

Matt admitted to his sister that hearing "Travelin' Soldier" by the Dixie Chicks always made him cry. *Why*, I wondered? When younger, he liked music that was loud, animated, popular, and intense, but as he matured, soulful country music seemed more to his liking.

Noah chased a squirrel; it was almost dark. Our neighborhood was growing very quiet. Could I sit outside all night, stare at the stars? Why did everything, even sleep, feel pointless?

Unacceptable Diagnosis

Once in bed, I stared at the vaulted ceiling, wished I'd stayed outside longer, as Matt's voice drifted through my awareness with eerie precision—his eyes, his face, illuminated. If someone asked me about his personality, his demeanor, I considered my response. I had to plow this rock hard ground, had to think deeply about Matt in the past tense, but describing him, even to imaginary listeners, only brought more useless tears.

Condensing his life into descriptive paragraphs didn't feel right. I wanted to capture Matt's spirit, the part of him that transcended everything harsh and unthinkable. Images drifted through my mind like pictures without frames. I found his face, how it changed, how it stayed the same, at all ages. And that keen sense of humor: his contagious laugh. Matt had a kind nature, was a fan of programs and comedians that mocked life. Monty Python, Homer Simpson, Jim Carrey, Steve Martin, Adam Sandler, and Jack Black, for instance. Matt also had an enviable smile that conveyed a calm, caring warmth.

But as a boy, even as a young man, Matt was shy with strangers, with those he didn't know well. A counselor once told me he was just a shy, sweet kid—someone especially vulnerable to the lure of drugs. Her keen observation made perfect sense to me. Yet, as worried global citizens, most are reluctant to think of drug users in the context of naïve innocence, and realistically, as a progressive disease, the many motivations for drug use are forever shifting and swaying while, more often than not, advancing steadily.

Mere curiosity must lead to dependence in a heartbeat.

Matt's attributes revealed many things, including a well-meaning person. Someone who, by and large, wanted to do what was "right." But hopeful periods of promise and understanding seemed to inevitably circle back to something much heavier: pronounced frustration, impatience, and an ongoing search for *something* he couldn't identify or find. In the end, it was a lethal internal mix that Matt couldn't master or survive. One wonders how many times we should be able to get back up after falling. Is there a limit to mortal endurance, to our tolerance for pain, torment?

We are all only human, so naturally such limits exist.

Most of what went on within Matt was a private matter—him sharing tiny pieces of whatever he deemed acceptable to others—until that closely held world disintegrated. If you've ever been in a similar situation, you know that pushing someone to share what they don't wish to reveal, or can't begin to effectively articulate, is a no-win situation.

Still staring at the distant ceiling, a car door slammed. Noah, sleeping near my feet, instantly went into high alert mode. When silence followed, he lowered his head to the bed, sighed. Is it okay to admit how much comfort a dog, a beloved pet, can be in the lonely black of night? Poet Mary Oliver gets it. Her poetry collection, *Dog Songs*, is all about moments of canine connection, and affection, not easily dismissed.

Tossing and turning, wishing for sleep, I closed my eyes, but Matt's life—all it had entailed—swirled on in living color despite emotional exhaustion. I imagined someone asking me to share what it was like coping with the hurdles and issues of my son's fatal addiction.

How would I begin to reply?

Again my eyes snapped open, the question instantly overwhelming me.

One thing was true—not every moment was about staggering doubt, grappling with yet another painful decision, or the expectation of a call from an emergency room, the police station, or maybe a concerned friend. There were *good moments*, no matter what, and we loved Matt, no matter what.

Plenty of drug addicts, I'm pretty sure, are just like you and me and those we love, but they are also people who chose, consciously or otherwise, a dreadfully difficult path: one most would love to leave behind. Despite serious mistakes, unmanageable problems that threaten to negate their best efforts, some, if not all, have numerous redeeming qualities. Quiet fears, humble hearts. But as a stubborn, simplistic society, we don't get it.

Pervasive stereotypes, plus expedient labels that define and limit our thinking, help to explain why we rarely approach reality with open minds: choosing caring, constructive, watchful attitudes; developing and enforcing an intelligent, humane policy of inclusion by striving to understand why so many people around the globe easily become addicted to everything and anything. What is it about the human species—cultures and societies—that drives so many to try and escape life one way or another?

Isn't that the real, the deeper, more urgent and universal, question?

Yet, unbridled fear, confusion, and reactive postures dominate popular attitudes.

We see the river shrinking, but just keep fishing—trying different bait, new techniques, better equipment from a bigger boat or sunnier location along the shoreline.

I also could compare this unfortunate dynamic to watching someone you love suffer from an illegitimate disease—an unacceptable diagnosis—as Matt finally would make his way into remission (or hopeful recovery) just as deadly symptoms surfaced again with a vengeance. In the face of harsh, accessible drugs like heroin, cocaine, methamphetamine, don't we desperately need inquiring, enlightened minds to focus on these issues from a comprehensive, and creative, vantage point?

Interpreting addiction as a character flaw takes us nowhere fast. *Mom, you know it doesn't help to worry.*

So what exactly would have helped? Not worrying—what an unrealistic luxury.

The room felt heavy with uncertainty, and suddenly too warm, even with the ceiling fan whirring overhead. Tossing back covers, sighing at my frustration, I again framed the question: What would have helped? *What?* Numerous mental and physical issues create a predisposition to addiction. That could be a viable place to begin.

Since human beings seem largely susceptible to addictive patterns of all varieties, why not dig in—discover what is actually driving this unyielding, often terminal, reality?

Perhaps our national and global search for answers will lead us to an unexpected path that points to intangible qualities like humility, compassion, and healthier, more inclusive cultural values. *Maybe* even to a significant shift in universal consciousness.

Seriously, addiction can't be wished away, enforced away, or prevented, once and for all, so it's imperative we begin to see this vast and destructive issue with new eyes. Even if you are in the "not-a-disease" camp, addiction and addictive behavior, in all its guises, are telling us *something* critically important about ourselves as a struggling, seemingly locked in fight-or-flight mode, species. But *what* is it, and do we really want to know?

Are these deadly, troubling patterns an insightful and revealing window into the soul of contemporary cultures—a dark terrain that suggests deeper exploration, or something more benign, but still offering critical clues to our long-term survival?

Viktor Frankl, Viennese psychiatrist and survivor of Nazi death camps, in his famous work, *Man's Search for Meaning*, wrote this: "In fact, the drug scene is one aspect of a more general mass phenomenon, namely the feeling of meaninglessness resulting from a frustration of our existential needs, which in turn has become a universal phenomenon in our industrial societies."

My breathing slowed; I inched toward sleep.

But what about Frankl's compelling insight?

Wasn't there some way for our vast global society to assimilate and apply such crucial knowledge—to finally graduate? To move beyond politicians and police, therapists and prisons, overdoses and suicide?

The addiction conversation: stale, ineffective, shallow.

Bozos on the Bus

Waking up several times that night, like every night in recent weeks, I vowed to stay up later in the days ahead. A new day was unavoidable, yet my weary mind rumbled about in a restless, unsettled mode. *What about suicide, another pressing issue that nearly always mystifies us?*

Kay Redfield Jamison, renowned professor of psychiatry at Johns Hopkins University School of Medicine, wrote in *Night Falls Fast: Understanding Suicide* of her attempted suicide, explaining she learned as best she could, as much as she could, about the "moods of death." Only 28 at the time, Jamison's word choice was gripping.

Moods. Moods of death.

It captured the mysterious gray zone in the shifting space between life and death; the finality and peace of death in contrast to the mesmerizing twists and turns of daily life. Because, yes, the lovely reality of life ushers in the disturbing reality of death; and that, per se, is the treacherous gray zone that provokes us, taunts us, with its stern ambiguity.

I considered Matt's final days as I adjusted my pillow, glanced at Noah. Had powerful forces, beyond my awareness or comprehension, been at work?

The end had come when least expected. An inglorious end, according to social mores. But why are we so overtly judgmental; what are we so afraid of learning or feeling?

What was the *real message* of loss? I had no idea.

I hoped, however, that someday I would be able to look beyond a shocking, untimely ending to thank Matt for his life and for giving us the rare opportunity to experience and practice unconditional love under daunting circumstances. Love transcends like nothing else. And even though Matt wasn't a shining star in the conventional sense—the limited, sacrosanct ways society promotes and values—he fought a valiant struggle with life and death (one that many will never face firsthand). He experienced love; knew pain, joy, and fear; grew, learned, made mistakes, and shared of himself; cared, set goals (missed some, made others), and believed in a sacred, eternal life force—a divine force many call God.

Sometimes, despite obstacles that must have felt painfully insurmountable, Matt even believed in himself. Days when optimism, even conviction, radiated from his words, his eyes. It was impossible to miss how much he craved the willpower, the desire—perhaps the "vitality" that Dr. Andrew Solomon refers to in relation to depression—to sustain his dreams. Ordinary, uncomplicated dreams, at that.

Elizabeth Lesser wrote in *Broken Open: How Difficult Times Can Help Us Grow*, that we are all "bozos on the bus," part of the "standard human operating system" that negates an imagined need for pretense, false superiority. Isn't that the truth? Matt's shortcomings, visible, undeniable, were also gifts of imperfection that provided ample space for the rest of us to mine (expose, confront, understand) our weaknesses. So I never saw him as "less than."

Rather, steep challenges served as poignant reminders to tread lightly: care deeply in the face of hardship, struggle. Our bozo status shared equally on life's crowded bus—this *short short* life with its hard edges, abrupt endings.

Inviting the Bell

"The Way of Heaven is to
benefit others and not to injure.
The Way of the sage is to act
but not to compete."

—LAO TZU

Don't follow in the footsteps of the old masters.
Seek what they sought.
—MATSUO BASHŌ

A Wicker Chair

*E*xperiencing an odd sensation of pinpricks against my skin when I learned of Matthew's suicide, a dull mental numbness followed. Suddenly thrown, like a naïve child, into the furious fires of grief, I'd wondered, as you know, more than once how to survive my own terror. But was this truly possible?

Lately, it seemed implausible—too much to ask—when before, I'd been the calm, quiet person in the room thinking, of course, we *can* do this. Whatever "this" was.

Seemingly etched into my character, I'd long believed one more courageous step—energy, time, creativity, love—could make a positive difference in nearly every context. The strange notion of "can't" rarely landed on my internal radar, and facing it head-on, even if slightly untrue, scared me. *What if I can't do this, really ... can't do this?*

Barbara Rosof, psychotherapist for 30 years, notes in *The Worst Loss: How Families Heal from the Death of a Child*, that loss and helplessness are two of the most painful experiences human beings have to bear.

"Losing a child," Rosof notes, "is a different kind of loss. Its dimensions are more profound, and the swath it cuts across families' lives is much broader than that of any other loss." Realistically, had I read this sentence before Matthew's death, I would have gleaned her message primarily on an intellectual level, not on an experiential level. The difference is significant. Unfortunately, with firsthand awareness, I knew she had it right. A child's loss—of any age, under any circumstance—strikes our vulnerable human core: instigating a primal, overwhelming sorrow.

For me, loss marked an unwanted initiation into a realm of pain I didn't know existed. A realm beyond the moon, over the stars, and definitely nowhere near a rainbow. Trying to sleep or just rest, the haunting lyrics from "The Dance" (written and composed by Tony Arata, recorded in 1990 by country artist Garth Brooks) would creep into my awareness. Yet, I *did know* the way it would end, the way things would go, and there was no retreat: no way to avoid this crash landing. Increasingly, I understood why most of us have no idea what to say or do when death occurs—even when earnestly wanting to comfort friends, family.

Plainspoken words fall flat, come out all wrong, and tend to sound twisted, insincere, or hopelessly cliché. Hearing them aloud: we wince, we run. Well-meaning expressions of sympathy (flowers, books, cards) are met with blank stares, silent tears—the disturbing rustle of someone trying to breathe.

Rosof draws on people who have experienced this kind of loss, noting she has not lost a child herself: "I have not walked in the dark country of their grief. The voices of those who have experienced this loss should speak the clearest; they are truly experts in living through the worst loss."

A painful distinction, one that fell in my lap without 10 seconds' notice, so I turned to books like hers because the void in my brain, heart, and soul lacked all boundaries, and I felt wildly disoriented. Even when I couldn't read more than a single page, a paragraph or a phrase, every morsel of encouragement and understanding was of value. Books, since I could listen to the words or delight in the colorful illustrations, were central to my world. A comforting, dependable treasure and, in times of crisis, we turn to what feels familiar. When lost in the dense jungle of a foreign city, we need a knowledgeable guide.

Drawn to insightful authors like Elisabeth Kübler-Ross, who died in 2004, I hoped her ideas would resonate and console. And the towering book by Harold Kushner, *When Bad Things Happen to Good People*, was a sympathy gift, but when I opened it, I could only stare blankly. *I can't read this. Not now, not yet. Someday, maybe.*

But, gingerly, I picked at his words and tried to comprehend the advice that had been consumed by millions, while fervently working to convince myself that if so many others had survived this mind-numbing reality, so could I. Yet, it was a feeble thought in many ways, one I could barely consider at all, and was Matt's death a "bad thing happening to a good person" or, more aptly, was it the very nature of the human condition?

The yin, the yang, of our brief earthly stay.

I wanted to stumble across books with the right tone, finding compassionate authors to help me navigate the long days ahead that stretched before me like shattered glass I could feel but not see. That meant searching them out. That meant deciding to seek out helpful voices on my own instead of rushing off to counselors. I've never been drawn to endless talk therapy sessions, but always have believed in self-discovery and deep reflection via books and the inherent wisdom of my surroundings: nature, place, people, lifestyle, landscape, and history.

The Look of Loss

Venturing into a large bookstore to look for books on grief and loss on a warm, trusting summer day, a young woman with a kind expression guided me to some lower shelves on the opposite side of the store. She offered a stool for browsing. I'd never realized, until then, how uncomfortable it was to spend time browsing books that lived on the bottom shelves, and I didn't have a physical disability, nor was I elderly with bad knees or hips. But the wooden stool looked like something a child would love to perch on, and by the time I was finished, my back was sore, my head ached.

A minor detail at the time, yet it occurred to me that bookstores could greatly benefit from eye-level shelves tucked within an innovative, compelling design to maximize customer experience. Don't book lovers love to browse? Even my grief-laden mind could conjure up unique layouts, comforting visuals designed to emphasize the subject matter of various sections. A visually engaging bookstore (to compete effectively with online sites) should be a creative, thought-provoking space, so why do straight lines, long rows stacked high, and short wooden stools prevail? Such orderly boredom is nothing like the worlds of wonder, despair, and enlightenment so richly conveyed in books themselves.

Scanning various titles I noticed several themes running through the literature: losing a parent, losing a spouse, losing a child. Books on suicide or on losing someone after an extended illness. Some were focused on religion per se: biblical passages and so on. One was about coping with death when it also brings relief. Unsure what I wanted in these turbulent, uncharted waters, I merely wished to spend time with an author who could touch my relentless pain, minister to my private despair in ways that were honest, yet, insightful. Flipping through books, scanning contents, I settled on *The Undertaking* by Thomas Lynch and *Beyond Tears: Living After Losing a Child.*

The Lynch title looked like a book John might want to read; I would give that one to him. But I wanted to read a thin yellow paperback that shared the stories of nine mothers whose children had died as young adults. Edited by Ellen Mitchell, I felt an immediate bond with these women.

Not trusting my emotions in public, I wasted little time choosing. Whatever I carried to the register would have to suffice until the protective walls of home felt less necessary. Grief robbed me of my composure. I wanted to rush home: wanted to be invisible.

Seeking privacy was my new calling, as I vacillated between dueling desires: wishing others would mention Matt, and hoping, praying, he wouldn't come up until I felt ready to talk more openly. Even in a public setting, like our church, didn't I have a strained, absent expression—that look of loss? Wouldn't even complete strangers detect the intense sorrow buried in my soul: the dark country that was mine?

Night Thoughts

When I learned of Matt's death, as if on remote, I picked up the phone and made calls to immediate family members. Several advised calling a physician for medication to get me through the sequence of events thrust upon us: unexpected travel, stopping by the funeral home (I wanted a rosary placed in his hands), ordering flowers, publishing an obituary, attending a prayer service, a funeral—a burial. What horrifying nightmare had taken flight in my life, anyway? In a mindless moment, I recall asking God if there was nothing anyone could do to forestall the despair I would be forced to endure in the days ahead—nothing anyone could do to alter this suffocating truth.

Surely, there had been a dreadful mistake.

Might it have been another young man perhaps; had the wrong body been innocently identified? Of course, that's not something I actually wished for, but the alluring thought crossed my mind like a slight breeze in the far reaches of my awareness.

Matt had made it this far, why not at least for another day?

I pleaded to the gods, any of them who might listen: it cannot be over—*not like this.*

Trying to talk myself free of sudden death created nothing but a trail of tears, the cold finality of loss devouring my energy, dragging me under.

I am not ready, not able to do this. Not ever.

But I didn't call for a useless prescription to help me sleep. How could I sleep—why, in the name of all things holy, would I want to? What difference could it possibly make?

The unthinkable had happened. An unimaginable scenario had been explained to me in fateful black and white words I could scarcely comprehend. Surely, the world, in sum, had stopped spinning. Could I even breathe, or did it matter?

I'd never been a fan of taking *something*, had never gone there.

I preferred to work through things quietly, resolutely, by following my intuition like a laser. By slugging it out one day at a time, seeking personal growth and insights along the way. Shortcuts didn't appeal to me when it came to difficult, unexplored waters. Even if things were extremely painful, I wanted to stay awake and aware, not letting my own life slip by me in a sleepy blur—in a haze of makeshift solutions from the local pharmacy.

Making no attempt to sleep that first night, I collapsed in a wicker chair instead. Slumping, I stared through a bedroom window at the empty night: disbelieving, shaking, stunned, and wondering if the sun would rise again. Surely, if it did, its light, too, would be tarnished, diminished in concert with the radical truth of death. Though it may sound sophomoric, fitfully trying to grasp the severity of sudden loss—its barren, unthinkable force—produced nearly infantile thoughts.

Glancing at numbers on an illuminated clock across the room from my straw-colored chair, I knew this must be my worst hour. Alive, yet dead, wanting to see Matt for a last good-bye, but knowing only my flickering imagination could produce such a scenario. I loved Matthew unconditionally—and mine was a determined love, a love tested in many ways—so how could this have happened: Wasn't love enough? And how could he decide to leave it all behind, giving up on himself, on us, on life, on *his* God?

Absurd, ridiculous, wrong.

Or was Matt merely riding a chemically induced wave that carried him far beyond the shore, leaving him to drown in his own confusion?

Had an impulsive decision rooted in fear—paranoia, the kind meth produces—been made? Had Matt found himself unable to endure the excruciating pain of withdrawal, or simply grown exhausted fighting his own addiction? Possibly frightened for his future—the bleak resignation that things would never get better—or driven mad by the starkness of mortal limitations—ones we all face—an ending, *an immediate ending*, may have seemed extremely desirable.

Sometimes I wondered who this person was, the one who had taken his life. Was it the same young man I'd golfed with, laughed with, patiently listened to as he talked over his life, its urgent challenges? The gentle soul who loved to imitate quail, easily nailing their famous whistle: *bob-white, bob-white*; the boy with the easy good looks and kind heart who once asked me, while we were driving somewhere, him, about five, in the passenger seat, leaning forward to peer over the dash: "Do all roads go to the same place, Mom?"

Well, yes, Matt, as a matter of fact, they do.

And was this the same young man who gladly planted the three apple trees we gave him for Easter in 2006—a symbol of our faith in his future?

Frequently, I'd encouraged Matt to believe in himself no matter what, to return to the love and faith of family when questionable choices disappointed. I also encouraged him to pray, to take the principles of recovery seriously, while accepting the need for humility and continual learning. Our conversations were meaningful, real, relevant; I'd hoped they were also honest. Matt talked of wanting a stronger relationship with God, of wanting to find a lasting peace and contentment in the ordinary moments that consume most days. He talked about temptation, as well, and when he felt the most vulnerable to the shiny allure of drugs: stress, boredom, feeling unhappy with himself or others, or discouraged about the array of demands that flowed into his day.

He talked about relationships that were important to him, and those that troubled him. Friends of old were to be avoided, he knew that, but Matt hesitated to connect with those who didn't share an interest in drugs—in the escape and excitement seemingly promised. At times, I sensed Matt was stuck on a mighty bridge, about half-way across and unable to decide which way to go, because he wasn't convinced he could make it across to the side offering a drug-free life, a different group of friends, a more fruitful, peaceful way of life.

Totally pulling away from the past—from habitual drug use—even if possible, must be terribly difficult, but for Matt, it was a life-threatening struggle: an arduous, grinding endeavor that sapped his youthful soul of energy, vitality, and joy. Most thrash around with the big questions, ultimately settling for a large chunk of uncertainty, but he hadn't found that kind of resolution: wanted to *know* exactly what it would be like on the other side of that daunting bridge before he committed to finishing a painful trip that seemed slightly out of reach, forever in its nascent stages.

In other words, he wasn't entirely convinced the other side was that much better.

The wicker chair grew increasingly uncomfortable, but being stiff and creaky, it was probably appropriate for eerie night thoughts that flew around the room like swooping, diving bats emerging from their cave.

Sharp Edges

Only months before his death, Matt adopted a pair of black labs, Boots and Coal, to join his gray cat, Mickey. A cat that had shown up one day and moved in. I'd embraced the high-energy puppies as a good sign, inferring that Matt was growing more content and comfortable with what life could realistically offer. I was also relieved that he still cared about animals, was able to love something that would give back to him in safe, healthy ways (companionship, loyalty, fun) without all the dangerous, life-threatening complications.

Mostly a mother's hope, I'm afraid.

The kind that *wants* to believe in happy endings, that mostly sees what is bearable, not unbearable; that sees her son, his soul, with subjective clarity, while patiently waiting for change, redemption, and a new day.

I suppose a father's hope might fall along similar lines.

As the pinkish hues of dawn edged into our bedroom, I asked myself why I'd believed my son was incapable of suicide. Naïve, foolish. Had my maternal instincts led me astray, distracted me with a flower-filled valley in spring and the persistent optimism to believe I could keep my son from an early grave?

Getting to my feet, reluctantly, as though my body suddenly weighed much more than its usual 140 pounds, I walked to the window, stared at the pale flicker of light to the east. The persistence of the universe seemed unfair, inappropriate, and I noticed how the mind reels at harsh discrepancies, at uncomfortable inconsistencies. And there was the chaotic churning of the universe, the unpredictable manner in which things occur: for better, for worse, for obvious and obscure reasons that intermingle freely.

Later, making travel plans for a morning funeral—a bleak word I couldn't say aloud—my brain must have resembled a barren sketch pad. Void of energy, I looked for a travel bag, pulled one from the back of my closet, unzipped it. Packing decisions loomed.

Must I wear black? Why?

The press of time swirled around me.

Functioning in a sea of dread, we made hotel reservations, rushed arrangements for pets. Blinding sorrow followed me, as I went through the motions, making me keenly aware of how much life had changed in a matter of hours. It was a staggering sensation, the kind you might feel when viewing the wreckage of a terrible accident.

Months later, in contrast, I caught myself wondering about the evolution of emotional pain. Would the sharp edges soften, or not really? How would I feel as the years elapsed? Would I forget the sound of my son's voice, his smile, or feel his physical and emotional absence differently? These were a few of the sinister questions the grief-stricken voice in my head insisted on producing in a stream of steady gray. Frequently, I asked, in vain but pointedly: How can life have true meaning without the ones who matter the most?

I was prepared to reject the days on my calendar that continued to show up: unbidden. Despite a quickly morphing culture that emphasizes impermanence—from pictures on a cell phone that are deleted moments later (are we intent on *not* remembering?), to texting, instant messaging, and blizzards of email—once my son was gone, I wanted to remember.

Only wanted to remember.

Insistently, I drug my feet against the sands of time, focused intently on the mother-son relationship stolen from me in the most alarming way conceivable.

Understandably, the immediate moment felt invisible, and the comfort of knowing those I loved the most were still part of this world, was gone. In its place, only a piercing silence that seemed to offer nothing.

Inviting the Bell

"The Way of Heaven is to benefit others and not to injure. The Way of the sage is to act but not to compete."

—LAO TZU

Early on you will have to fortify yourself against insensitive comments from blundering friends, relatives and acquaintances, some of whom should know better and others who have no idea that you are bereaved.

—ELLEN MITCHELL (AND OTHERS), *BEYOND TEARS: LIVING AFTER LOSING A CHILD*

Humble Belongings

*I*nteracting with others loomed. I railed at the prospect. What could be more undesirable, more trying? Lacking an easy explanation for inquiring minds, I knew of no public way to discuss the magnitude, the shock, of this situation.

My eyes, my face, would have to communicate for me.

With no memory of getting ready for an evening prayer service, I recall, with laser precision, my heavy sense of dread as we neared our destination—as I tried, in vain, to brace myself for my son's casket and a sea of people, many unknown.

Conversely, the weather, as if wishing to deny the absolute gravity of death, served up a carefree summer evening. Inviting, warm, gentle. Knowing Matt would no longer enjoy such welcoming days, drained all possible pleasure from my veins. The lightness of such evenings now out of reach for him, and what about the many lost days overall—the time and beauty my son had surrendered?

Had Matt simply left the light of day behind or had he discovered a new, stronger light in death? A radiant, spiritual light, perhaps. Must we relinquish one to find the other—had Matt felt compelled to look in a contrasting realm?

Driving straight north in light traffic, we neared the funeral home. *This really was happening.*

How had death arrived, us unwittingly going about our days? A stream of questions that I couldn't shake escorted me inside the small, plain building. Had Matt sifted through the dark details of suicide well before this, on an ordinary day when he was of clear mind, or on a gut-wrenchingly, gloomy one—no sun, no light, anywhere?

Of this and more, I wondered.

Part of me assumed an impulsive, in-the-moment reaction to the agony of extended turmoil—unbearable stress, feelings of hopelessness, uselessness, or overwhelming confusion.

Nic Sheff, wrote about the dynamics of rehab and relapse in his book, *Tweak—Growing up on Methamphetamines.* "Honestly, I was as surprised by my own actions as anyone else. The morning of my relapse, I had no idea I was actually going to do it. Not that there weren't ominous signs."

Blurry, wandering thoughts sailed on, as people I hadn't seen in a long time, hugged me, greeted me, offered condolences.

The movie had begun, one featuring my son's funeral, burial, and shocking absence. If ever there were an out-of-body experience, for me, this was it. But what I discovered that night, as friends, family, and strangers formed a slow-moving line to reach out, say a few words, was that everyone was gracious and caring.

I felt terribly ungrateful, though, because every ounce of me wanted to be left alone. I wanted to walk to the front of the room and politely ask everyone to leave.

No one does such a thing, of course.

Instead I made myself stand there—size 6.5 feet in black shoes standing on a carpeted floor—in a disconnected state.

So lost and protective of my private sorrow, I was nearly lightheaded.

Surprisingly, I heard myself utter a polite thank you in response to "We are so sorry."

A senseless charade, an acceptable and meaningful tradition, a painful obligation. All of the above. Much (most?) was left unsaid, and I sensed that this massive gap—emanating from deep within— was the real story.

Only a Monet, Renoir, Van Gogh, or Cezanne could capture such a discrepancy.

Matt's girlfriend made a 30-second appearance.

Gently, I told her I was Matt's mother, but in a river of tears herself, she disappeared. Matt's other friends offered a long sigh, a nod, a look of deep shock. Apparently he was alone that night, and even though some had gone looking for him when it got late, they eventually, and understandably, had given up.

Another Shock

I couldn't make myself dress in black. I had no energy to focus on my attire for one thing, but I also knew a black dress, a dark suit, accomplished nothing. Besides, a prayer service meant another chance to deny reality—to tell myself this was *not happening.*

I merely had to look the other way, until an improved reality appeared.

Not one to court pity or sympathy, I also wanted to avoid a color that said death had arrived and everything around me was falling apart. Privately, I had no idea what to expect of myself and wondered if I might collapse in tears or sit and stare, unable to talk or look at anyone. Perhaps I would lose my mind entirely, trying to avert my eyes from my son's coffin. Grief served up such bizarre worries, conjuring up devastating images of helplessness, panic, and public humiliation.

With no warning or preparation, there had been no moment of surrender—no dress rehearsal. I remember someone leaning over, whispering: "Whenever you need to leave, just leave." This should be obvious, but hearing it was extremely helpful. When forced to function under duress, we need to be reminded (frequently) that we're not superhuman. That it's okay to feel frail, weak and unsteady; perfectly fine to limit exposure to painful, public circumstances. So when pools of exhaustion welled up, I escaped to the far end of a sofa at the front of the room near Matthew's closed casket.

Sitting next to a table lamp, that light—that light alone—was a tiny comfort.

A moth to the flame, right?

When it was time to go, I hated to leave my son in that impersonal place. Why do we immediately separate the living from the dead with iron walls of societal convention?

Even with people standing around, beautiful flowers, and lovely landscapes on the wall, the room felt cold, dark, lifeless.

Before we made it out the door, however, I was blindsided by a painful conversation.

The owner of the funeral home, a petite, elderly woman (kind, soft-spoken), didn't want me (or family members) to view Matt's body. Wrongly, I'd assumed this was a standard practice, something we would do before the funeral, in private. Or something we should have done before the prayer service. I was his mother, after all.

Listening to her rattle on, I sat speechless and numb to cold-sounding words I could barely comprehend. While viewing Matt's body wasn't something I looked forward to, I would bear it. Worrying about his physical appearance seemed grossly superficial, and though I remained reserved and polite during our hushed conversation in the back of the room, my heart rattled in nonbelief. I didn't tell her this was one good-bye that was *not* happening through the walls of a casket, but I knew I could never distance myself from my son like this, as if unable (or unwilling) to honor his last moments on Earth.

We would find a way beyond her resistance. Old-fashioned, generic. She'd spent a lifetime attending to dead bodies, but seeing my one and only son would be too much for me? No logic there.

An Imagined Refuge

Heading south to the hotel, maybe a 20-minute drive, I sat silent and staring out my window, noticing nothing and hopelessly lost on poignant memories of the young man with eyes that held such life and joy and pain only days before. A choir of voices behind me had recited the rosary during the prayer service. I'd only heard their subdued tone as through a tunnel, as though far away, as if I were an invalid, a stroke victim perhaps—someone suffering from emotional paralysis brought on by a sudden, debilitating trauma. The closed casket, like a protective shell, refused additional clues about the lifeless body inside, and blocked from Matt's new reality, we were all held at bay—undeserving, uninvited.

Still, I wondered: was he aware of us somehow?

Could Matt sense our presence on a spiritual, afterlife level? If able to communicate, what might he have said? What final words would have been shared given the magnitude of an earthly departure that he, most likely, didn't foresee? Questions without answers—futile, mind-based attempts to grapple with the vast and intimidating unknown.

It didn't occur to me then, but I'd *needed* to distract myself, so had occupied myself with a useless mental noise that resembled an emotional cushion: fleeting, abstract notions, and rhetorical questions offering an escape, an imagined refuge from the abruptness of saying good-bye to the beloved son who grappled with seriously difficult issues. The kind unimaginable when he was a child, a boy. Poignant images of beginnings and endings, like bookends, were daringly incompatible.

A Struggling Servant

I woke up early the next morning. The urgent need to see my son immediately in focus. Advice and resistance had been offered, and while well-intended, after consulting with a family friend, also the owner of a funeral home, we knew we were within our rights. The decision was personal, best left to the wishes of the family.

John called, identified himself, told the woman we were on our way.

After another feeble warning about how this experience might negatively impact us, now or sometime in the future, *okay*, we could have a few minutes with him before the funeral. *Only a few, though.* Legally, our request couldn't be denied, but it strikes me as odd that it was even an issue. I'd given birth to the son I'd loved through a maze of ups and downs, so seeing him at rest was the absolute least I could do—for Matt, for myself. I'd always believed in his soul, knew that external conditions were largely irrelevant in the face of death—the timeless spiritual journey our lives represent.

We drove in silence, and when she met us at the door of the funeral home (along with the undertaker: eyes of icy indifference), I hugged her, said thank you. Wanting to quietly reassure her—*I'll be fine, this is something I must do*—she looked largely unconvinced, reluctant: at a loss for words. A spontaneous expression on my part, the hug, but for some reason, I felt sorrier for her than for myself.

Folded, lifeless hands, black beads of a rosary intertwined, spoke of an ending—trials and tribulations endured—that I never could have captured in my imagination. Seeing Matt clothed in his favorite shirt and jeans, I closed my eyes, took a deep, excruciating breath. The miserable merger of life and death in plain view.

But closure? Another author—a father also coping with a son's death—once wrote that closure is for real estate deals, not the loss of children. So this stark moment didn't offer anything resembling closure. At least Matthew's final moments were visible to me, though; I began to *see* that his physical journey had ended. A circle of mortality: closed. No more suffering or struggling to conquer (or understand) a disease—*a need*—that had plagued him like a magnetic shadow from a former lifetime. A treacherous, unrelenting battle that so many are intimately familiar with.

I remember telling Matt, in the privacy of my mind, that it was okay: if I had to let go, had to accept this tragic ending, I would find a way. Wanting to offer his spirit something for the afterlife (whatever that was), I reminded him of eternal love, continuing prayers, and promised my memories would never fade. What stands out for me now though aren't my words, but the deep, wordless moments—enormous and spacious, like something I knew, but quietly resisted.

Finally, after silently wishing Matt a peaceful journey, I also made a request. I asked God—the assumed God, any God, his God—to remember Matthew as a dear, struggling servant: to have mercy on his soul. I've never felt quite so inept, though. The room, eerily quiet, dreamlike, and I had no idea how to get this right. Strangely, my maternal instincts kicked in. Even in death, I wanted to shield Matt from my most despairing thoughts.

But silly, mortal problems were no longer relevant: he was free.

Clinging to this bittersweet facet of death, I reached out to touch and kiss motionless hands—symbolic of everything he'd known, feared, and loved. Then, much too quickly, the time came to pry myself away. Once again, time and convention dictated the agenda, and I resented it deeply. *What, really, was the rush?*

A Country Cemetery
After a brief burial service, people lingered, talking or standing silently on the cemetery grounds—a serene country setting tucked off a narrow, country road—and I stood by the casket gazing blankly

at pinks, yellows, blues, whites. An abundance of flowers shielded by a dark canopy. Heavy waves of incredulity swept through me; I felt almost airborne, propelled into deep space, no other place to go. Did I even remember the funeral, sitting in the front row, trying to listen to the priest—his generous words of comfort?

What was that he'd said, exactly?

I had no idea.

Lightheaded, I sat amidst the rows of empty metal folding chairs and wondered, more intently, about that night: the anguish in my son's heart, or not at all. Which was worse, knowing you were about to die, or being so unaware of your reality you had no idea what was coming: what you were about to do. A horrible choice to contemplate. I sat quietly with the question, and somehow noticed the day's continuing warmth, as a faint breeze rustled the June leaves of towering oaks only a few feet away.

White banners that said "Son, Brother, Cousin" waved in the warm air, as though trying to get my attention. What was their purpose? To honor Matt's past, to label the reality of fading relationships, to soothe the bereaved? Maybe all were valid reasons, but they felt useless. Labels and roles suddenly irrelevant, wistful sounding.

My eyes could barely touch on them, especially the one with son. I'd called him son, frequently; it seemed to mean so much to Matt. And I knew it meant a lot to me.

"Hello, son."

"How are you, son?"

Reminding him of our connection, our shared spiritual roots, I hoped to convey a quiet strength, a deep confidence in the resilience of the human spirit. Maybe he would sense the joy I felt in talking with him; maybe it would be enough. Surely, love and acceptance would fuel his journey. But like the sun setting at midday, instead of when expected, our relationship was only relevant in the past tense now: so it seemed. Staring aimlessly, I felt distant, jumbled thoughts taking flight: the seeds of a windblown dandelion.

I'd acquiesced, worn black to the funeral—slacks, a jacket with thin gold stripes.

In hindsight, why hadn't I worn blue? Matt loved blue.

I doubt I'll ever wear that jacket again.

Draped in plastic from the cleaners, the July 5, 2007, ticket still stapled to it, when I happen across it in the far reaches of a closet, instinctively, I turn away. Its memory, its purpose—too bold. Sometimes, though, I pause to study the petite six wool jacket with a skeptical eye, hushed emotions; the dark cloth, its orderly stripes, almost startling me: an unexpected reminder of a day etched in my soul as one without compromise, comparison. One featuring a brand new threshold of human pain.

Now, though, standing graveside, the future already hovered like an expectant parent, a demanding boss, an insistent sunrise, and I sensed the requirements of daily life would resume with a startling vengeance. As people wandered over to stand with me, to utter a few kind, rambling words, I wondered how I would keep going. With pressing questions of life and death at the forefront, where would I find the desire, the energy, to water the garden, run errands, cook dinner, do laundry, or resume a professional position begun only weeks earlier? Curious rituals that suddenly lacked meaningful context.

Small Treasures

Before leaving for home that afternoon, I ventured again into an east-facing bedroom—in the comfortable, well-worn brick ranch Matt's grandparents had built, raised five sons in, back in the '50s, '60s—to see if I'd missed anything, and to feel Matt's lingering presence one last time. Clothes hung neatly in his closet—summer shirts, warm jackets, navy robe (a birthday present months earlier)—and tossed on the floor, laundry, boots, slippers, and white tennis shoes that still looked new, never worn. I picked them up to take with us; unworn shoes that now hold a place in our hall closet.

I also spotted a beaded leather belt, a Christmas gift from the year before. Scattered pictures, prints and posters, with no discernible theme, lined the walls. Books rested on a bookshelf. One I'd given him about health and recovery looked untouched, but he had been reading *Marley and Me*, a hardcover in Christmas red, and *Giants in the Earth*, a favorite classic of mine about pioneer days in Dakota by O. E. Rölvaag—Matt's bookmark on page 293. I recalled selecting it for him because of its inspiring message from Ralph Waldo Emerson: "Every step is an advance into new land."

Maybe I needed the bookmark now.

I brought both home—can still see the book, the tip of the bookmark, from my desk. He hadn't finished Rölvaag's lengthy story—531 pages in all—but was more than halfway there. An impressive arrowhead collection from a family hobby that began on the farm with his grandfather and father, was displayed on a dresser. Staring at the historic stone pieces of various colors, shapes, and sizes, I sensed Matt's pride in his collection.

Strangely, his room and humble belongings looked useful, organized, ready: a snapshot of things he would need—the owner, a young man who would be back any minute, just out to feed cattle, fix some fence, pick some berries, run with his dogs, or tackle a few errands. Surely, my mind insisted, even pleaded, Matt would walk through the door any minute to grab a clean shirt.

"Hey," he'd say, a slight smile on his face, "what's everyone doing in my room, think I wasn't coming back or something?"

Everything *looked* like Matt. With an endearing sentimental streak, he never missed birthdays, holidays, or special days of any kind, always mailing cards with a short note scrawled inside, always calling. Could I hear his voice, my eyes frantically raking every inch of his bedroom to somehow detect his vanished presence?

As clearly as church bells on a calm day.

Whenever there was a noticeable sadness in Matt's voice, as if longing for something he couldn't explain or begin to understand, I offered words of reassurance: reminded him he was never alone. We all cared, always would be there for him. Sometimes I asked him if he prayed—if he thought it helped. But it's increasingly clear to me that we all must find our own path to the divine ... in our own time. Wisdom can't be taught; insights must come from within, not just consumed intellectually.

After gathering up a few more small treasures—things to keep—I walked to the large, country kitchen; glancing out the west window that framed a sprawling green pasture, I recalled time spent there when Matt was a baby. His grandmother, an extremely energetic woman, loved the company of another woman in her kitchen.

Kathleen, a professional with the county school system for many years, also raised a family of boys that she and Matt's grandfather kept busy on the family farm; the same one in northern Missouri where Matt was living, working. A devout Catholic of Irish heritage, Kathleen had red hair, freckled face and arms, facial lines from the sun and age, and a spirited temperament. So, yes, her family gave her a most fitting nickname: the red raisin.

Loved, respected by those who knew her, Kathleen also had a warm sense of humor, an unpretentious manner, and a tolerant disposition. But how she earned her master's degree (educational administration) with five young boys at home is still a puzzle to me.

Stepping closer to the kitchen counter, I noticed a Crock-Pot. Seldom interested in preparing time-consuming meals, and after working outside, sometimes in inhospitable weather, he preferred easy dinner options. As things had quietly spiraled out of control, I doubt that Matt had done much cooking at all. Other things, illegal drugs, a girlfriend, probably took priority. We didn't meet until the prayer service, but I recognized her voice because she'd been answering Matt's cell phone in the weeks immediately preceding his death.

Another red flag.

I'd wanted to talk to him about it, but Matt was sensitive about the subject—felt his family would disapprove of their relationship because, apparently, she'd struggled with drugs, too. Attempts to discuss things like this with him were met with a strained silence. Addicts want to believe they can help each other—and sometimes they can when both are actively committed to recovery—but it's more likely they will only enable each other.

Gazing at the peaceful countryside, it wasn't difficult to imagine how they may have rationalized their choices and behavior in the pursuit of some kind of love.

Chameleons

In early June, about three weeks before tragedy struck, John drove to the farm to spend the weekend. Concerned about Matt's heightened veil of secrecy, we hoped a visit might reveal something helpful, pry open a few doors. But as he left Indianapolis for northern Missouri, we wondered, realistically, what to expect.

Matt had sounded pleased, not suspicious, when John called to talk about a weekend visit. Still, we didn't know if there would be troubling signs—glaring, alarming—or if John would detect indications of growth and stability offering a welcome sense of relief. Most likely, the signals, as usual, would be mixed. A terrifying awareness of what could go wrong at any instant couldn't be denied; we'd lived along this rocky shore for years.

"Matt seems okay, pretty happy," John observed. "No evidence of drugs unless he's hiding them extremely well."

Naturally, he wanted to reassure me, but we knew Matt could find *happiness* walking down a dangerous, ill-founded path. So even though he denied using or planning to use, we couldn't rule it out. I studied the pictures John took: searched for clues in Matthew's eyes, and expression. Also my first glimpse of his girlfriend (off and on for a few months prior), I didn't notice anything odd or shocking, but there was a noticeable weariness, the same weariness I detected in my son's face.

Still, both wore a smile, seemed at ease.

After dinner, they'd gone outside to enjoy a pleasant summer evening. Sitting around a table on the deck I remembered so well from Matt's childhood, pictures revealed two young adults talking, laughing, mostly oblivious to the sun dipping below the horizon.

I wasn't surprised to see them sharing a glass of wine, even though, alcohol, for most addicts, will trigger a relapse. Matt *knew* the risks all too well; and, to no avail, we'd had that particular conversation innumerable times. But he had to want change more than we did; had to make healthy choices on his own if he ever hoped for a sustainable recovery. Besides, whenever I mentioned it, gently reminding him that he'd told me he could *never* drink again, Matt insisted that *now* he could handle it. Surely, but not necessarily—given how brain chemistry is modified by substance abuse—he knew he was kidding himself.

We could have refused to spend time with him if any amount of alcohol was involved, but addicts tend to "go under" when pressure or limits come their way. Chameleons. We also knew, from experience, that Matt would have quipped, "Fine, don't spend time with me. Up to you."

The extent to which anyone can significantly impact another person's behavior, at 27, is seriously limited. An adult by anyone's measure. And even with all the well-meaning advice that came our way, we'd arrived at the discouraging conclusion that, in the end, hardly anything works. No one *really knows* how to help addicts, because *they* must be their strongest advocate; they must want help. And even if it appears otherwise, the ball (pardon the cliché) is always in their court.

Plenty of programs sound good. New and old ideas swirl in the air, inching their way through social networks, relevant organizations, various disciplines. Yet, it's common knowledge that durable change is extremely complicated, and under deeply challenging circumstances, rare. I've set out to change; so have you. Anyone reading this book has heard its alluring call. And often we respond with a "plan," but even shiny resolutions made to greet a new year seldom become something that we can point to months later.

I believe that significant change originates from deep within; so when someone hasn't found that place yet, everything else is superficial, destined to fail. Profound change—lasting, encompassing, transformational—seems to occur in our souls, in other words.

It's encouraging, though, to see new research pointing to plausible explanations for adolescent behavior. A *New York Times* article by psychiatrist Richard Friedman is one I wish I'd read many years ago; the title says it all: "Why Teenagers Act Crazy" (June 28, 2014).

Specifically, he notes that "adolescence is practically synonymous in our culture with risk taking, emotional drama and all forms of outlandish behavior."

Most of this, until recently, was largely explained away by psychology, but Friedman points to an improved framework: "But there is a darker side to adolescence that, until now, was poorly understood: a surge during teenage years in anxiety and fearfulness. Largely because of a quirk of brain development, adolescents, on average, experience more anxiety and fear and have a harder time learning how not to be afraid than either children or adults."

Apparently, "adolescents have a brain that is wired with an enhanced capacity for fear and anxiety, but is relatively underdeveloped when it comes to calm reasoning." He also writes, "As a psychiatrist, I've treated many adults with various anxiety disorders, nearly all of whom trace the origin of the problem to their teenage years. They typically report an uneventful childhood rudely interrupted by adolescent anxiety. For many, the anxiety was inexplicable and came out of nowhere."

Obviously his research holds far-reaching implications for drug treatment, including the considerable drawbacks of current practices. Friedman notes that "the prevalence of anxiety disorders and risky behavior (both of which reflect the developmental disjunction in the brain)" suggest a "biological contribution."

Falling Forward

When the farm visit hadn't revealed anything overtly alarming, we questioned our deepest fears, our customary concerns.

Were we imagining things?

Was Matt in love, real or otherwise, and simply needed time alone—privacy? Were we clinging to habitual worries, fears—afraid to let go or give him space to manage his adult life? Had we grown to expect the worst?

All reasonable concerns, yet, once an addict, always an addict, so legitimate doubts gnawed at my soul. During the long, dark days of winter, a relapse had loomed like ominous storm clouds. When Matt was home for Easter weekend (two short months before John's farm trip), we'd had a candid conversation about it. What caused his relapse—winter's predictable hush, depression triggered by cold dark days, loneliness, stress, or wanting to believe that *this time*, because of an inflated (false) sense of confidence, he could manage recreational use—and how was he supporting, sustaining a shaky recovery?

"I can handle it, Mom."

While wanting to fully share Matt's optimism that day, I knew too much to be blindly supportive, which is what he appeared to want. If history repeated itself, and with addicts that is too often the case, there were valid reasons to seriously question his ability to stay clean. Acknowledging my doubts about his lifestyle and priorities, I feared another giant step backward. Still, did *anyone*—myself, John, Matt's sister (she'd spent a week on the farm in May), his father, stepmother, friends, or the uncles he worked with—sense that a family tragedy was imminent?

The predictable setbacks had been painful, discouraging for everyone who loved Matt, but no one saw an untimely death in the cards. Such is the land of meth—the destruction it invariably leaves in its wake—and though we *knew* the innumerable ups and downs of his journey, the final twist descended like a malicious fire. An unyielding weapon and an uncompromising shot shredding time, and all variations of hope, as it penetrated and absorbed the utter fragility of a precious human life in a secluded meadow on a faded summer night. An unbearable image. An anguished landing during the seductive month of June—nature in full bloom—made death even more startling, incongruent.

I wanted to hate the sixth month of the year.

⚮

Leaving Matt's house after the funeral, I wondered how to handle questions from people I hadn't seen, talked to, in years, those I didn't normally confide in. Would I just explain Matt's death as a terribly unfortunate accident?

If not unduly influenced by a chemical substance, he wouldn't have taken his life.

I believed, still do, that Matt wanted to live ... without the torment of drugs. Without agonizing cycles of recovery and relapse bearing down on him like torture treatments from the Middle Ages. He frequently mentioned how much he wanted to be like those who didn't have to fight addiction. Those with *average lives*, unafflicted by intense challenges—content with the basics.

The ongoing emotional and physical struggle must have been exhausting, but what Matt couldn't understand, or accept, was no matter how rosy things looked, *everyone* struggled with something. A fact of life: inherent to the human condition. Like the need to evolve—spiritually, emotionally, intellectually—hardship of some kind impacts even picture-perfect lives that, of course, are *never* picture-perfect.

What I wouldn't have predicted, was how, as time elapsed and people mentioned him, I often wanted to avoid their bleak words of curiosity. It may be difficult to understand if you've not yet walked with grief in a deeply personal way, but much of this felt hollow— like feigned concern that failed to dignify a human life. After all, it was *my son* they were talking about, not a TV personality or some fascinating character in a best-selling novel.

Matt's loss, for me, was as real as drawn blood, and the utter casualness of someone's tone could depress me, instantly. When that happened I would simply withdraw from a world that felt upside-down, because there was nothing casual or generic about the depth of my sorrow. Nothing words could touch. The gap between my inner world and that of others, wide—a turbulent river without safe crossing.

Yet there really was no polite way to let people know that unless they wanted to share empathy, compassion, and love from a place of genuine understanding, the less said, the better. Sadly enough, it was easy to detect pity, obligation, judgment, or twisted curiosity when I craved the warmth of sincere, heartfelt communication.

Soul to soul, an orientation of "we are in this together," resonated.

Don't most parents treasure their relationships, no matter the challenges, with their children? Ask anyone who has lost a young child, then written about it—someone like Sukey Forbes (*The Angel in My Pocket*), or Ann Hood (*Comfort: A Journey Through Grief*). Sukey lost her six-year-old daughter, Charlotte, to a rare genetic disorder; Ann, her five-year-old daughter, Grace, to an antibiotics-resistant strep infection.

Ann's memoir shares how, at times, she felt as though she'd swallowed stones—that grief made her feel heavy, and slow. I knew that feeling. The instant grief arrived in my life ... I felt unable, unwilling to rush anywhere. And when I shared my book title with Sukey, she said, "I understand the *silence of morning*—a gutting reminder with nowhere to hide, but also a space to keep sacred and process." Of course the loss of a child *at any age* is a parental nightmare. While editing this book, I watched a presidential debate just to hear Carly Fiorina say she had buried a 35-year-old stepdaughter from drug addiction. Another challenging, painful situation, I'm sure.

Relationships with our children possess a quality, a depth, that is unique, powerful, and primal, and when that deeply significant connection is severed without warning, emotional wounds are profound, abiding. So when someone acted like it was perfectly okay to plop all sources of grief into one giant emotional basket, I felt more alone. Maybe even invisible. More at a loss for words.

And early on, lacking the gift of perspective that comes from living beyond the loss of someone you love for a period of time, it seemed presumptuous, if not slightly arrogant, when someone I barely knew claimed to know the unspeakable agony of *my* heart.

Though unpleasant, it was another good reminder that I was on my own: would need to turn inward for strength and solace.

A book on my shelf mentioned that parents who suffer the loss of a child often considered ending their own lives. I believed this without reservation. Even though I hadn't felt suicidal—not per se—my will to go on was shaky, feigned at times. I was falling forward, if at all.

Inviting the Bell

"The Way of Heaven is to
benefit others and not to injure.
The Way of the sage is to act
but not to compete."

—LAO TZU

Shakespeare Remembered

*T*wisted time and logic pursued me like a pack of hungry wolves. On a stormy Saturday afternoon, tucked away in my writing study and looking for a broader perspective, I diligently searched the headlines: to see what else had happened on the 24th of June.

Rather quickly, I unearthed another tragic story.

Drawing close to my computer screen, I began to read.

Natasja Saad, 33-year-old Danish rapper, reggae singer—career on the rise—had died in a car accident in Jamaica on the same day and was buried in Coppenhagen's cemetery for artistic, pioneering personalities. Pausing, I offered a moment of silence.

Next, I ran across a hopeful story. The World Children's Festival, a quadrennial event sponsored by the International Child Art Foundation (ICAF) in Washington, D.C., was the world's largest celebration of children's creativity and imagination.

From their website: "Let young artists and performers inspire you, spark your creativity and imagination." Sounded good to me.

Website visitors were encouraged to help children build a more just, prosperous, and nonviolent world with a contribution. I'd been a fundraiser and development professional for nonprofits, so of course I read on: "Once we recognize the power in a child's art, we can foster their creative development and harness their imagination for positive social change." I loved the exquisite sense of possibility. "The ICAF serves as the national arts and creativity organization for American children and the international arts and creativity organization for the world's children."

I also considered their stated vision: to inspire children to make the difference and change the world. And since 1997, their mission: to employ the power of the arts for nurturing creativity and developing empathy, key attributes of successful learners and leaders. *Inspiring*. Also convincing proof that June 24, 2007, existed in a positive, uplifting way despite my immediate reality.

Otherwise, the national news had raged on that day with topics like the Iraq war, the sputtering economy, sporting events, and such. The Roman Catholic Church celebrated the feast of the birth of Saint John the Baptist, and the Stern Grove Festival—after some 70 years in San Francisco—featured the Idan Raichel Project, an "entrancing blend of Ethiopian and Middle Eastern flavors."

June 24 is also the 175th day of the year in the Gregorian calendar, leaving 190 days until year's end. And, June, the sixth month, has 30 days; again, per the Gregorian calendar. The month is named for the Roman goddess Juno, wife of Jupiter and equivalent to the Greek goddess Hera.

June, the month with the longest daylight hours in the Northern Hemisphere, is in spring until the 21st. The birthstone is the pearl, its birth flower, the rose or the honeysuckle, so June is sometimes coined the Rose month. It's also the month of Gemini and Cancer per the zodiac.

In Europe, Latin America, and Scandinavian communities in the United States, June 24 marks the summer solstice, the holiday called Midsummer Day. In some places the main event is a bonfire or fireworks, and fairs are commonly held in Romanian villages and cities. On the Irish calendar, Midsummer is one of the four Irish Quarter days that divide the official calendar. In Quebec, June 24 became a legal holiday in 1925. Many celebrations around the globe, besides those of Catholic tradition, are also linked to prophet and preacher Saint John the Baptist.

I read on, feeling somehow comforted. These events weren't about me, my pain, and while it wasn't much relief, I was open to any reasonable diversion.

In Estonia, Midsummer marks the end of spring sowing, notes the smooth transition to summer haymaking. According to some, the traditional celebration of Midsummer's Eve, from ancient times, was based on a belief that midsummer plants had miraculous healing powers when picked at night. Bonfires were built to protect against evil spirits thought to roam freely when the sun was turning southward again.

Then there was the Shakespearian play, *A Midsummer Night's Dream*—written circa 1595, and likely performed for the first time in 1604—that featured a mischievous fairy in a moonlit forest. The romantic comedy set in Athens, Greece, never grows old. And I learned about Midsummer traditions that focused on its midpoint: beginnings, endings, merging as part of the cycle of life and death, a turning point—a luminal period.

Did I believe Matthew picked June 24 for a specific reason? Not at all. An array of troubling, ultimately, fatal, circumstances fused into one uncontrollable spark that day.

So, even though my son's death occurred on Midsummer, it was mere coincidence. Not evil forces or dark-spirited fairies lurking in the meadow, not even Matt's conscious mind could be blamed for a death caused by a serious relapse: his powers of rational thought seriously compromised by harsh chemicals. He'd apparently understood the risks on an intellectual level, but like we all have done, Matt probably decided to dismiss them as "unlikely."

During periods of recovery and treatment, he learned a great deal about the physical, mental, and emotional ramifications of meth (or whatever chemical was on hand). Yet it was Matt's nature to see how far he could push his luck. In one conversation we had, he said he hadn't gotten to the point where he could reach out, ask for help, before or after a relapse, but wanted to believe that ability—that day—would come.

So did we. We knew that relapse was part of recovery: addicts must fall time and time again before something (time, treatment, luck, maturity, belief in a higher power, suffering, strong desire, or sheer determination) alters a deadly pattern more permanently.

We hadn't stopped believing in an eventual transformation: durable, authentic.

But, now, the summer storm intensified.

When a powerful flash of lightning moved across the darkened August sky, I turned off my computer. Further research would have to wait.

Yielding to Tomorrow

I slept for a while that afternoon, waking to find sunlight, everything in the backyard still soaked, dripping. John had gone out on errands, so I grabbed a towel and headed outside. Drying off a lawn chair, I planned to sit with nature for a while.

If there was any comfort to be found, it was right here: amidst squirrels and birds—cardinals, goldfinch, blue jays, wrens—flowers and sky. Once I'd even spotted a blue heron in landing mode just beyond our fence near dusk. Such glorious creatures.

I depended on nature for many things.

For organic beauty, a sense of life continuing without interruption, and most of all, to console the part of me that was forever connected to Matt's spirit.

The air was steamy in the storm's aftermath, but wanting to soak up everything around me, I didn't mind. Counting on nature to work its magic—the green grass of summer, a towering old oak tree in the back corner of our yard, a pair of white pines, a stunning row of tiger lilies—I inhaled deeply, looked for other signs of life: birds came and went, squirrels scurried up and down tree trunks, the sun dropped lower in the sky. And for some reason, my heart raced.

As the realities of Matt's suicide consumed me once more, I asked for the millionth time, *why him?* While several theories are advanced by professionals from various disciplines to explain why people turn to drugs, we, including Matt, were unable to pinpoint any one issue, dynamic, or belief in particular. If serious mental issues are behind many suicides, maybe he had undiagnosed problems that compromised his ability to pursue a safer path. And some, genetically predisposed, are apparently at higher risk for addictive patterns.

It also seemed, however, that 99 percent of us could find *something* in our lives to blame on some kind of addiction. By way of observation, we are a restless, uncertain, ever-shifting country and world: *people with issues*. Yet, curiously, we dedicate ourselves to a toxic, competitive mind set—which addiction, problem, or issue is the worst; which solution is the best—instead of aiming for a better reality for everyone. We *never* seem to see the forest for the trees (yes, a cliché, but a good one). Have you noticed?

Likewise, we must move beyond mind-dulling myths surrounding addiction, realizing that addictive behavior is often linked to the most ordinary of problems—human beings, one just like the other, searching for life's meaning, purpose, and peace. Many manage to gaze in all the wrong directions, but don't *most of us* stumble around, working our way through this mortal maze step by tentative step? That illusive magic wand: only an enticing dream.

Drug wars, drug lords, or those with absolutely no interest in living without addiction are an entirely different matter. I'm not referring to the ramifications of destructive drug rings and related violence, but plenty of people out there are simply caught up in something larger than life, turning to drugs or alcohol on a purely personal level out of pain or frustration or loneliness. Motivations may be as mixed, as mysterious, as the universe itself.

Ice in my glass of tea was melting rapidly. A blue jay hollered from the oak tree. Wind chimes, like a familiar voice from the past, offered a melodious whisper.

Like many (don't most of us dislike excessive routine, schedules and tasks that repeat themselves without pause?), Matt lacked a serious interest in the mundane: the unavoidable banality of the mortal path. Surely this generated a nagging inner tension.

Why? Because most of life happens on this very level.

Maybe he turned to drugs to combat a nameless anxiety, to keep secret worries at bay, to serve as a buffer between him and the world. Sometimes, as if wishing for *something* more intriguing than a traditional framework, Matt also lacked interest in social pretense and familiar middle-class trappings. At least he was honest about it.

As a creative person, I relish the opportunity to develop new ideas, explore innovative thought, professionally and personally, but understand the need to channel creativity in constructive directions. But my son hadn't identified a satisfying outlet: a motivating path that resonated. Short attention span, sometimes, but there was also a cynical streak—the kind a comedian might love to tap into (but the addiction battles and reported suicide of actor Robin Williams come to mind). Matt also seemed troubled by perceived unfairness.

Of course many are puzzled, even seriously harmed, by life's inequities, complexities; and finding safe outlets for frustration mandates a degree of maturity, understanding, and perhaps a great deal of spiritual awareness. Seemingly, it's built into the journey.

Still, tolerance levels—*because we are all different*—vary significantly.

Clinical depression and related mental health issues are real, even as possible causes are countless. I can also conceive of a spiritual (or existential) depression.

When Philip Seymour Hoffman died of an apparent overdose in 2014, fellow actor Jim Carrey described him as a beautiful soul, reportedly tweeting along these lines: for the most sensitive among us the noise can be too much. Tuning out the extraneous—life is extremely noisy, literally and figuratively—can challenge and annoy us as we try to sift through *everything*, rapidly depleting our precious energy in the process.

Jim Carrey is also a fan of Eckhart Tolle, perhaps for good reason.

Tolle, like many spiritual masters and teachers of Zen, teaches how to quiet the mind. A great number of our thoughts—repetitive, drama-generating, evaluating, planning, and projecting—are merely another kind of useless noise. The worst kind, perhaps, because it is lodged in our very own heads, and we aren't sure how, if ever, to escape it.

The "voice in the head," as Tolle often describes it, pretty much rattles on, with us, the captive audience, unaware that we are actually generating much of our own suffering.

Russell Brand, comedian, actor, author, and addict in recovery, also wrote about Philip Hoffman. In a most insightful article from February 6, 2014, Brand explains: "In spite of his life seeming superficially great, in spite of all the praise and accolades, in spite of all the loving friends and family, there is a predominant voice in the mind of an addict that supersedes all reason and that voice wants you dead. This voice is the unrelenting echo of an unfulfillable void" (*Guardian News & Media, Ltd.*).

A Creative Torch

Still outside, I leaned back in my chair to consider an early evening sky dappled with thin clouds, and a common question came to mind: *Where do dreams come from?* It seemed that I'd been born with many of mine, including a deep appreciation for the promise, the potential, of each amazing life. I believed, for instance, that schools could be transformed into fountains of creativity, encouraging children of all ages and situations to discover, to nurture, their unique talents: not to merely memorize a well-worn path.

Conformity is an understandable concept, and given human nature and burgeoning populations, necessary to stabilize societies and their dynamic components, but when children display creative tendencies—most do when self-discovery is encouraged—we need educational systems and global environments (cultural milieus) that respond in empowering, supportive ways. Otherwise, we risk losing more children and youth as they opt out, rejecting a world order that feels narrow, inflexible, and stagnant—a "mad world," as the song goes—and therefore difficult to navigate or thrive in. I have no way to know if more positive or engaging educational environments could have significantly helped Matt, but the multifaceted problems of addiction beg for innovative thinking.

Are we willing to let go of outdated methods and models that fail to engage students fully? Children are as unique as snowflakes; average is a solitary peg, and not everyone fits such an expedient description. Many great minds in history have experimented with controlled substances. What were they seeking, what did they find? Did a desire to tap into creative energies more intently fuel their interest in mind-altering drugs; were they nonconformists seeking alternative—brighter, kinder, more humane—realities?

Can we benefit by asking if we lean toward excessive conformity out of convenience, insecurity, or habit—perhaps to ensure the traditional power structures that maintain and serve select segments of society?

The founders of modern-day sociology, giants like Max Weber and Emile Durkheim, explored such concepts and, as a perpetual student of society myself, I wonder what it may take to actually "change us" … in the collective sense.

Was Durkheim, a French sociologist, correct when he claimed that society itself can cause suicide, that only a life of utter conformity ensures a long life?

The light was shifting, growing pale. I glanced at sparrows gathered under the feeders.

Sadly, none of these intriguing thoughts, nor the most outstanding academic discourse, would bring Matt back to life, nor ease the pressing concerns of millions struggling to unearth a more meaningful, less painful path through life. But *maybe* there will come a day when we look with greater understanding on those who don't fit the arbitrary mold of convention—those with something unique and special to give, those wishing to explore or challenge the status quo in constructive, creative ways.

A mother's hope, perhaps, but in the grand scheme of things, a popularized culture with an abundance of dicey issues should be eager to look in new directions: at what hasn't been considered, discovered, or imagined. What could we possibly lose?

Tossing melted ice into a barrel of pink geraniums, I darted inside.

Hungry mosquitoes had arrived.

Greatest Teacher

The next morning I jotted down these thoughts: Despite my desire to put hope aside, as senseless and naïve and childish, without it, I'm unable to go on, and while the things I actually hope for have changed, it is hope, per se, that illuminates the dark road ahead. Without its abiding fire in the face of death, my spirituality—*my belief in life*—would vanish like crisp autumn leaves blowing aimlessly down an abandoned street.

I wanted to remind myself of these truths frequently, because obvious was no longer obvious. Even my strongest beliefs were under scrutiny. The grinding days of grief had yet to generate a predictable path. There were no runway lights. Life seemed chaotic: random, disorganized, unmanageable. Many days felt poorly constructed, an emotional labyrinth. I sensed, however, that only by weaving the past, present, and future into an organic, newly revised reality could I transcend loss.

And since grief wasn't a neat, tidy, package dropped at my front door, but a dynamic, comprehensive process that seemed determined to defeat me, I needed to remember that there was no right, good, or better way to explore this disturbing foreign terrain.

Our success and accomplishment culture made it challenging, though.

When I caught myself thinking there was a right, a better, a faster way to maneuver this volatile passage—these highly personal days—I turned within. By confronting my thoughts, I hoped to release superficial, useless, or inappropriate standards. Suffering is the greatest teacher. I wrote that down, too, as if grasping this unwelcome truth for the first time. Suspecting there was hidden value in my realization, with deeper ramifications to come, I wanted to accept the perils of this path—wanted to hear grief's quintessential voice speaking to me of legitimate human needs.

Hope faded extremely fast when I asked the wrong things of myself, so I vowed not to be pushed or pulled by anyone: not to pretend to resume a life that no longer existed. Nor would I succumb to subtle messages that whispered *it's time to move on*. Not abundantly clear then, but when I listened very deeply to my inner voice, stayed on a quiet path that honored my intuitive wisdom, time began to lose its wretched grip.

And I could see that unlike fads and trends, we don't leave those we've loved behind—they, too, are part of the mystery that never dies. Though we bloom briefly, then fade, the universe always returning to itself, when we allow life to touch us deeply, even in sorrow, somehow, it extends our mortal view, and our glory.

Inviting the Bell

"The Way of Heaven is to
benefit others and not to injure.
The Way of the sage is to act
but not to compete."

—LAO TZU

We all want expanded consciousness and bliss.
It's a natural, human desire. And a lot of people look for it
in drugs. But the problem is that the body, the physiology,
takes a hard hit on drugs. Drugs injure the nervous system,
so they just make it harder to get those experiences on your own.
—DAVID LYNCH, *CATCHING THE BIG FISH:*
MEDITATION, CONSCIOUSNESS, AND CREATIVITY

Today's Canvas

Setting down words in a straight line like an orderly stone path is an interesting process. It creates the illusion that things like death happen in isolation, not tucked into the layers of life occurring simultaneously. If I studied a bird nest closely, for instance, could I tell precisely where the twigs, leaves, grasses, plant fibers, string, and scraps of whatever begin or end? Not really.

Likewise, it is slightly easier to grasp the intricate twining of life and loss when I don't fixate on Matt's death as an isolated event in a time-based world.

Death, it seems, can only be carved out, singled out, in an artificial context. But more realistically, it continually dwells within each breathing life form: a mysterious presence; a persistent knocking against the formidable walls of time, the dark echo of memories. So, in stark contrast to the unfathomable silence that a manifested death leaves behind, *what happened when*, the more chronological aspects of any story, is minor.

Only by probing moments, ideas, and feelings that are newly relevant can I explore, perhaps illuminate, the amorphous nature of existence. This vantage point gives me a canvas to consider what is tragically personal, yet universally significant.

Nellie White

One day I realized how much music—I like New Age, classical, or contemporary artists like Adele or Alisha Keys—reminded me of Matt. Especially country music. While I'm not what you would call a big fan, I'll admit that even when lyrics are overly dramatic or annoyingly simplistic, some songs express a familiar sentiment, one we all recognize.

Country artist Gary Allan reminds us that life ain't always beautiful—for instance.

Conversely, we love beauty when it steps into our lives—in its myriad forms, with or without warning. Natural, manmade, hard-earned, fleeting, long-lived, unique, daring, powerful, spontaneous, intricate, even poetic. Flowing from an endless array of sources, inspired by the seen, the unseen, or just a vivid imagination, beauty knows no boundaries. Even unique personal qualities showcase an inner beauty, along with special experiences, which are sometimes labeled beautiful moments.

This beauty, life's incredible bounty, had been a source of dependable joy for me, but now, even as it defiantly wormed its way into my surroundings, I was mostly oblivious to its influence.

It seemed, in fact, impossible to experience genuine pleasure in the things I'd once enjoyed, and while I *remembered* joy, it was as a flimsy ghost: a relic of a former life.

In some ways, I actually felt resistant to joy and beauty.

While wildly confusing to myself and others, *this* was today's canvas. Today meaning post-tragedy; today meaning not yesterday, when Matt was my living son.

In bleak contrast, I used to notice (and gravitate to) beauty everywhere. *Everywhere.* A lifelong knack for finding contentment in the commonplace—a spectacular sunrise or sunset, brave tulips on a cool spring morning, poetry that stayed with me for weeks, an author who daringly danced beyond the predictable and safe, strong coffee with cream—was part of my wiring.

The list once seemed endless: cheesecake, brownies, or cherry pie, a cozy quilt, hot soup on a subzero day, the perfectly comfortable pillow, a road trip with notable scenery, a leisurely walk on a sunny autumn afternoon, a movie with Steve Martin, Jack Nicholson, or Dianne Keaton, a long nap on a rainy afternoon, talking to someone I loved, to Matt or Erin, in particular, taking Noah to a field where he could run free, jotting down insights in my journal, listening to music, or visiting art museums.

What I'm trying to explain is that I "got life" on a purely fundamental level.

Somehow I'd sensed, even as a girl, that life is a pretty serious endeavor, replete with opportunity and formidable challenges, so why not notice, relish, and do those things that aren't complicated, expensive, or far away?

Take flowers.

Walking around our backyard, I appreciated how they bloomed on, regardless. Lilies, stargazers, and cherry chimes (daylily tubers mailed from a thoughtful friend in memory of Matt's love of chocolate-covered cherries) standing tall, colorful, convincing. I'd also planted miniature lavender roses—dainty blossoms, like summer snowflakes—proud moss roses, and sturdy zinnias in a rainbow of color. And midsummer, why not notice rows of towering hollyhocks? Deep pinks amidst placid white blooms that seemed to be racing to catch up—both rising up through thick, overgrown mint leaves for summer tea, mojitos.

Even a brief trip to cyberspace to peruse online nurseries could be intriguing. There, I'd discovered a plethora of red lilies: Scarlet Orbit, Signal Sunup, Seductor, Sir Wilford, Street Urchin, Stop Sign, Superlative, Apple Tart, Jewel, Cardinal's Crest, Papal Guard, Chicago Brave, Timeless Fire, and even Happy Memory.

I also liked to grow traditional white lilies. Easter lilies—often potted in green plastic, wrapped in foil with a colorful bow—when done blooming and planted outside, return in the spring, blooming late June, early July. Such a wonderful study in contrast. Brilliant white against the soft green of spring; a spiritual symbol of renewal, redemption; a sign of peace and hope amidst the angst of our average daily lives.

The essence of the Easter lily—inspiration for *Easter Morn*, a moving poem by Louise Matthews—yields images like: "sweetest offerings" and the "heavenly towers of God." Research also led me to the origins of the Nellie White: a traditional lily cultivated for commercial production by James White, the popular store variety named for his wife.

Curiously, I found myself drawn to such details, noting coincidences that felt like symbolic markers of Matthew's abbreviated life. Our outdoor Easter lilies bloomed during Matt's 4th of July visit in 2006, then again in late June of 2007, the week of his loss. The timing, noticeably ironic, reminded me of the words of a different Matthew (6:28-29): "See how the lilies of the field grow; they neither toil nor spin, yet I tell you, even Solomon in all his glory was not arrayed like one of these."

Nonetheless, a dark shadow stubbornly surrounded these thoughts and poetic images, no matter how inspiring or beautiful. But this is the true nature of grief: it tarnishes our predictable joys, steals our innocence, and rains on our parade for an indeterminate time.

It trails us; seemingly stays too long. The party guest who remains after everyone else has gone. Even as our Easter lilies bloomed again, summer of 2008, most of their natural beauty was lost on me. The bigger story was that I didn't trust life anymore. Instead, I felt like a pathetic sucker when I allowed myself to be taken in by beauty or joy.

Both seemed like remnants of a silly, girlhood innocence.

Lure of the Prairie

When I published *Where the Heart Resides: Timeless Wisdom of the American Prairie*, I wrote passionately about the prairie's striking beauty: its subtle powers of transformation, its dependable comfort. In reflecting deeply on a spacious landscape—place, people, history—I was able to share an organic wisdom based on unpretentious lifestyles. Growing up in the capital of South Dakota, a beautiful river town planted in the midst of open prairie, I felt compelled to articulate special, yet easily trivialized, qualities.

Years later, in a local newspaper, I ran across an article that shared this tidbit: "South Dakotans are among the nation's most extroverted and agreeable people in the country, according to a personality map designed by a British university."

The University of Cambridge research findings had concluded that South Dakota is "more sociable" than most states. So there you have it. Apparently, I had grown up in a place deserving of a closer look. I'd also written in the book that the prairie, known for its magnetic pull, its harmonic overtones, was good food for the soul. It had long been part of my world, as mentioned already, to notice, to value, the simple, attainable joys in life—and the wonderful guises of nature, for instance. Rather basic aspects of existence, easily (and sadly) downplayed in the crazy shuffle of hectic routines.

Still, like most authors, I had to live with one sarcastic-sounding review. The only negative one encountered, I knew the anonymous reviewer missed the book's point, in sum, or perhaps had come up with something in haste to meet a forgotten deadline. But, luckily, it was irrelevant, because the people I wrote the book for "got it" immediately; they valued its spiritual perspective, its inspirational, and hopeful, viewpoint.

Mining the deeper story of an ordinary yet beautiful place with a lifestyle that some seem eager to disparage because it doesn't conform to the dark culture of consumerism that fuels our national economy (especially noticeable when we face down recessions, depressions, high unemployment, and stalled growth forecasts), was very meaningful. In light of a troubled global society—its turbulent, violent nature, its superficial emphasis—it's also good to know that authentic lifestyles are still possible. In looking at what was, instead of what wasn't, a reasonable degree of wisdom emerged.

Overly analytical minds gravitate to negative, critical thinking, but framing the area's shortcomings wasn't my intent. That's been done, often under the guise of objectivity or academic discourse. I wanted to go beyond that to uncover something old, yet new, and the spiritual tenor of the book opened those doors.

What is readily apparent to some is foreign to others, however.

Author (*The Promised Land*, 1912 autobiography) and activist, Mary Antin, offers this: "We are not born all at once, but by bits. The body first, and the spirit later; and the birth and growth of the spirit, in those who are attentive to their own inner life, are slow and exceedingly painful. Our mothers are racked with the pains of our physical birth; we ourselves suffer the longer pains of our spiritual growth."

So, yes, understanding and appreciation vary widely. A premise, also noted eloquently by Gustave Flaubert: "There is no truth. There is only perception."

I loved Fred Egloff's (*Booklist*) take on the book, however: full of historical tidbits, personal anecdotes, and interviews, Hickman's book provides a virtual trove of thought and wisdom. Thanks, Fred, for "getting it." Supportive voices like his convinced me to publish a second edition in late 2014: *Always Returning: The Wisdom of Place*. Due to timing, I'd missed a chance to connect with Oprah during the release of the first edition, plus my publisher's priorities and staff changed swiftly when William Morrow was purchased by HarperCollins in 1999.

Needless to say, as I experienced the ever-changing, complex world of publishing, I quickly learned that having arrived in Oz ... there really was no wizard.

But, as part of today's canvas, when studying the first edition's cover (and there's yet another very interesting story behind that) with its bronzed prairie grass, I'm reminded that writing, like the prairie itself, has seen me through some difficult days. Growing up there, in the '50s and '60s, its unspoken heritage was always near—quietly comforting. Innumerable hardships and soul-testing were thickly weaved into the area's historic lore, but this was also part of its enduring charm: its compelling depth.

At key junctures—times of intense spiritual inquiry, significant personal growth—not surprisingly, I've drawn considerable strength from my unpretentious prairie roots.

Matthew's loss was no exception.

After his death, on road trips to South Dakota, when I caught sight of home—prairie grass waving its silent greeting, breathtaking sunsets, powerful skyscapes—I knew how much I needed these familiar landmarks. An avenue back to myself that I trusted: a place I'd known intimately before becoming Matt's mother; a place I'd loved as a girl; a place I'd written an entire book about. But, mostly, an area where people had known me since birth—where I'd known an uncomplicated joy amidst the innocence of childhood.

Still holding the book, I flipped through, studied the black and white photographs by artist Bob H. Miller that introduced each chapter. They all spoke to me about a place I missed. I yearned to throw my belongings in a bag, run for cover. A subconscious pull to safety or the illusion of escape, maybe, but also understandable. Grief made me doubt myself in fundamental ways—pushed me to question everything—so what I'd known and loved, in my earlier days, felt like quiet reassurance.

Besides, this sense of starting over from scratch could feel most alarming. Like straining to see critical markers through a thick fog when hardly able to detect the faint outline of a tree laid bare in winter or a rusty mailbox perched on the edge of a dusty gravel road, I was drawn to anything deeply familiar. Our desire to escape pain must be written in the stars. I *knew* it wasn't possible, though. Pain must be confronted, endured, turned upside down, approached from a multitude of vantage points, to explore its unsettling presence, its hidden purpose, and terribly draining contours.

Neither graceful lilies, nor my prairie roots—influential memories, an enduring love for wide-open spaces—offered a *real* escape route.

But did this stop me from pining for an alternative reality?

Not that I recall.

The human heart isn't good at accepting the unacceptable.

We fight back, consciously, or otherwise; and we stare at days on a calendar as though they should have a certain meaning but, in the end, they don't. The illusion of time traps us, leaving us to muddle through, and sadly focused on questionable priorities.

Wrong Wish List

What exactly was the point, I asked myself one morning, sitting with a book in my lap but staring out at the world beyond. *Why should I bother writing anything after a life I loved was extinguished without warning—when there were positive, hopeful signs?*

Admittedly, though, I'd already "bothered" via books, reflection, and spiritual inquiry. I'd turned, for instance, to the movie *Conversations with God;* bought Neale Walsch's books (the foundation for the movie), and read about his uncommon dialogue with God.

I was fascinated, deeply moved, by his message, and even though critics have spoken, who among us avoids all criticism?

No one; it's the way of the world.

"To avoid criticism, do nothing, say nothing, be nothing" (Elbert Hubbard). "The dread of criticism is the death of genius" (William Gilmore Simms). "Criticism is an indirect form of self-boasting" (Dr. Emmit Fox).

Offer most anything, *anything at all*, and someone will rush to object or vehemently disagree or quietly ridicule. Human nature, mind polarities, ego, immature personalities, fear of being wrong, competitive desires, conflicting philosophies. Still, I craved a more peaceful, encouraging world, one in which more of us saw beyond the tedious back and forth.

I loved this powerful point from Walsch: "There is only one reason to do anything: as a statement to the universe of Who You Are."

Sounded good—straightforward, focused—but *who* was I these days? I had a decent idea before June 2007.

Among other things, I was Matt's mother and reasonably hopeful while cautiously looking forward to better days not dominated by problems, worry, or fear. In 2003 he'd lived through a nearly fatal car accident. Driving back to the family farm after a night out with friends, Matt missed a sharp curve (fell asleep or otherwise) and landed in the emergency room with serious internal injuries and broken ribs.

He had the apparent will to go on then, and vowed, once more, to stop using drugs and drinking and, after the accident, made it through another arduous relapse, recovery cycle: a convoluted process, supposedly necessary for growth, awareness, and lasting change.

But Matt's near-death accident scared me deeply, and helping him up from a hospital bed to slowly walk the corridors for exercise, I wondered if this was another ugly version of hitting bottom, or merely one more tough bump along the way.

A harsh, or final warning, perhaps?

This passage from *Conversations with God* aroused my curiosity. "Accidents happen because they do. Certain elements of the life process have come together in a particular way at a particular time, with particular results—results which you choose to call unfortunate, for your own particular reasons. Yet they may not be unfortunate at all, given the agenda of your soul."

I mulled this around to see if it might buoy my spirits or convince me major life events had an inevitable meaning, a divine purpose. But what was the agenda of my son's soul? Had he completed his earthly mission, albeit prematurely by most standards? This was a tough one, but I wanted to consider it, even as I fought the unwieldy notion.

Unfortunate, fortunate, unfortunate—how could this matter be up for debate?

Surely, Matt's passing at such a young age was a tragedy, a profound, nonsensical loss for him—those left behind. We all must go sometime, yes, but it seemed that 85, 90, even 100, would be better ages to leave this incredible planet: *after a full life*. After a lifetime of experiences had refined and polished his spirit as intended.

Was it better to focus on quantity or quality when measuring his life? Or any life?

I had no objective idea, because I wanted both for him, and my wish hadn't seemed all that unreasonable until denied. Until I began to chastise myself for holding even average expectations that nurtured a time-based reality. Spiritually speaking, a mere handful of pivotal life moments might complete the soul's journey.

After all, long-life guarantees don't accompany birth certificates and maybe less was more but, no, I wanted more time with Matt; had hoped he would build his dreams on the solid ground of a drug-free life. Maybe even get married one day. But I'd also prayed he would build a spiritual life—one with a stronger connection to an inner wisdom, one that would sustain him during days of temptation and mind-numbing challenge—to help him live with greater peace. And contentment.

You might say I wanted the customary things parents want for their children, but now I can see that it was the wrong wish list.

I'd again relied on a mother's hope, and even though I believed his spiritual growth was linked to everything in his life, it was impossible to know how, or if, it would ever come to pass. Searching Walsch's writing—seeking passages for meditation—this was comforting: "Love is the ultimate reality. It is the only. The all. The feeling of love is your experience of God. In highest Truth, love is all there is, all there was, and all there ever will be. When you move into the absolute, you move into love."

Reaching for my coffee, grown cold, I considered how Matt had unknowingly taught us how to love unconditionally. His greatest gift, perhaps. It's easy to love someone who does the *right thing* most of the time, but a young man drawn to dangerous extremes can cause others to question their affection.

Had I come to know God, my spiritual dimension more deeply, because of Matt, and everything he brought into our stress-filled lives?

Without a doubt.

Easy come, easy go never adds up to much of anything.

We remember the steep mountains in life, the times we fell off the cliff, stumbled over our own two feet, much more than routine days filled with the predictable: the cushion of innocence, good times, easy laughter, minor victories. But despite comforting insights, I was still trapped in a painful void between light and dark, life and death, wanting to dwell on memories and wishing to repel them at the same time—only permitting them to surface when I felt up to the emotional content, holding most at bay until another time. A time when I might feel stronger, able to withstand the sharp rush of yesterday.

For now I sat quietly with my doubts and resistance, letting an internal war rage on, and maybe (probably) that was the very best I could do. The canvas called today had its rough edges, its soaring limitations.

Inviting the Bell

"The Way of Heaven is to
benefit others and not to injure.
The Way of the sage is to act
but not to compete."

—LAO TZU

❧

So we are grasped by what we cannot grasp.
—RAINER MARIA RILKE,
RILKE'S BOOK OF HOURS: LOVE POEMS TO GOD

French Lyrics

Driving home from the funeral, I was overcome by images of the son just buried. In an uncanny sequence, pictures came into my awareness as if purposefully selected from a tattered photo album. Sometimes, in winter, Matt grew a beard: dark brown laced with red (a color inherited from his Irish grandmother). With hazel eyes and perfect teeth, no braces needed, his smile seemed to communicate many things. Don't worry, I'm fine, or more often, joy and love, and maybe a slight mischievousness—a shy playfulness.

Matt had a spirited, generous laugh. A forgiving nature. About five foot ten in stocking feet, a shade taller in cowboy boots, he was of average build, weighed about 175 pounds when drugs weren't involved. Serious meth users don't bother much with food or sleep because it produces a euphoria most of us can't imagine. How, I'd wondered, does one return to a plain life of ordinary colors, one with unpretentious goals demanding steady focus, hard work, and determination, after the intensity—the addictive rush—of drugs?

On a common sense level, it seemed unlikely, perhaps rare.

David Sheff wrote this about his son: "Nic had been a sensitive, sagacious, exceptionally smart and joyful child, but on meth he became unrecognizable."

Nic, he added, felt he'd been searching for meth for a lifetime.

Routine and sameness, even though the average life depends on both, must seem like cruel enemies after this kind of high.

Heading east into an overcast afternoon sky, the unpretentious country cemetery we'd left behind less than an hour before zoomed back into sharp focus. Tears poured out of me for most of those highway miles, despair pounding me like pitiless sea waves. I hated how the uncompromising nature of time had yanked me through the experience without the slightest shred of mercy. And it occurred to me, even as we drove *away* from the cemetery, that Matt's final unbelievable moments—his entire 27 years—was coming along with us. *Everything was coming with us.*

How many, I wondered, constantly crave an intoxicating feeling of well-being—some way to suddenly feel all bright and shiny? The number, most likely, staggering. But how can artificial highs be taken seriously, and shouldn't this reasonable question be a deterrent? Given the vast number of youth and adults using street drugs and/or prescription drugs—seemingly eager to embrace an artificial experience—most must not worry about differentiating between real and artificial in this context.

In fact, the persistent desire to escape a time-based reality—its myriad forms of pain, its humdrum nature, its challenges, setbacks, and mysteries—in exchange for "amazing peak experiences" (euphoria, harmony, bliss, deep connection, or creative rapture) must be highly motivating. Conceivably, unless the human condition changes significantly, the use of drugs may never decline. Even a pronounced desire for excitement, or a headlong collision of opportunity and circumstance, can seemingly lead the unwary down this dark, desolate path.

Author Dirk Johnson in *Meth—The Home-Cooked Menace* (2005), noted that the drug was "hitting hard in the heartland" (and Matt died in 2007). As still may be true, many confiscated meth labs were in the Midwest. "Missouri," he wrote, "had more labs confiscated than any other state." Demographics and statistics fluctuate, but the dynamics of habitual use are predictable: "Addiction to stimulants happens rapidly, and withdrawal can be hellish. During use, the brain learns to stop producing dopamine and serotonin on its own."

Meth addicts, Johnson explains, may see people who aren't there, and "life without the drug seems pointless." They may believe that no one cares, nor should. Meth, he tells readers, is "far more powerful than plant-derived cocaine. Smoking meth produces a high that lasts eight to twelve hours, compared to a cocaine high ... twenty to thirty minutes." An award-winning journalist, known for his work with *Newsweek*, the *New York Times*, Johnson's book was published by the Hazelden Foundation.

Hazelden, a nonprofit organization, has promoted the dignity and treatment of people afflicted with the disease of chemical dependency since 1949. Based in Center City, Minnesota (Hazelden merged with the Betty Ford Center in 2014), these facts about meth, are likely still available on their website: made from dangerous chemicals in makeshift laboratories; increases the heart rate, blood pressure, and risk of stroke; overdoses can cause heart failure; affects brain, body, and self-control. A powerful stimulant, in other words, meth produces addicts from all walks of life.

The World Health Organization, and various other sources, documented that meth is one of the most widely abused illicit drugs. At one time, an article I read suggested that there were 1.4 million meth users in America with an expanding demographic.

Called crank, Tina, tweak, ice, or glass, meth's impact is deadly.

During withdrawal or when tweaking, users can experience acute psychosis. Meth can also cause depression so debilitating, so severe, that individuals want to commit suicide.

We stopped for gas; my thoughts refusing respite.

∾

The road home seemed endless. But *now*, what did that mean? My perception of home was much more than a physical definition—a house, an address, a comfortable tree-lined street with familiar landmarks—and, in Matt's absence, strangely and suddenly altered.

Did it feel grossly unfair that my adult son had fallen prey to the death grip of meth? Of course. Was it tempting to look for someone, something to blame? Of course. Did I want to change the course of history, exchange a summer burial with tempting fantasies of intrepid survival: a movie-like ending where miraculously Matt was able to beat the odds and win a valiant struggle to live in peace, freedom? Absolutely.

If there is a universal takeaway, it might be this: judging others is an enormous waste of time and energy. Anyone can develop a drug dependency when potent circumstances collide. Addicts, of one kind or another, are everywhere. Everyone on our spinning planet has a weakness to conquer; some are just more life threatening than others. And if we live in the midst of an addictive culture, what are the possible root causes? For one thing it's conceivable that, inadvertently, we've generated an artificial civilization or society—one failing to address basic human needs in healthy, positive ways. Thus, drug use, like other forms of addiction, may be revealing mirrors that reflect insidious cultural values. After all, an artificial environment will likely generate "more of the same," right?

Clearly, empathy, humility, and enlightened perspectives will be needed to conquer deeply embedded social issues. While answers are elusive, a compassionate stance may reveal better, more constructive definitions all the way around. How a *problem* is framed (conceptualized) is significant, because this is what indirectly prescribes the quality (and quantity) of solutions considered. So it's fairly easy to see how an artificial culture could engender equally artificial solutions.

Glancing at a road sign, I realized we were finally nearing our destination. Drained and exhausted, I dreaded *whatever* came next.

Howard Kaplan, sociologist and director of the Laboratory for Social Deviance at Texas A & M University, suggests that punishment (for drug users) "lowers self-esteem, thus increasing the likelihood of continued deviant behavior." Likewise, many are strongly suggesting we drop the "war on drugs" because of its ineffective posture.

Johann Hari, author of *Chasing the Scream: The First and Last Days of the War on Drugs,* in a 2015 article in the *Huffington Post,* suggests we are actually increasing the "larger drivers of addiction" via this so-called war. Hari also considers the pressing need for meaningful connection in a society that tends to shun people with problems.

No man is an island, yet we insist on living like this fact is pure fallacy, don't we? Hari suggests that we "change our hearts."

Of course. Because that is where our personal (and collective) power resides.

"Loving an addict is really hard," he admits. "When I looked at the addicts I love, it was tempting to follow the tough love advice ... shape up, or cut them off." Pointing to erroneous logic, Hari suggests that this may actually "deepen their addiction—and you may lose them altogether." Tough love, I'd agree, is largely ineffective in the long run. Addiction in its many forms, as a physical, mental, spiritual issue (disability, disease, or brain disorder), asks individuals and society to dig deeper: to find the true keys to transformation.

For the living, the still-struggling, I hope we find new ways to respond to drug-related issues if we are serious about impacting this treacherous terrain—this deadly symptom of an addictive, artificial culture—instead of trying, in vain, to contain it, minimize it, or condone it. Giving up doesn't strike me as a viable option, and "not caring" flows much too readily from a narcissistic society, easily and strangely distracted by things and stuff and irrelevancies of all kinds.

Slow Dance

Arriving back in our Indiana driveway, I had no idea what to do next. Fortunately, some things, like caring for pets, weren't optional. The only self-advice I could muster was to take it slow: a laudable idea adopted like a mantra of survival, until I figured out it was mostly impossible to put into practice. "Take it slow" sounded reasonable, sensible, but life has a funny way of pushing, pulling us—insisting we maintain the established pace by staying in sync with a fast-paced, immediate gratification, overnight delivery world.

After a few days I couldn't decide which approach consumed more energy: swimming against an invisible tide, or a feigned attempt to keep pace with a frothy stew of spoken, unspoken expectations. But I didn't have to think about this for long; apathy, profound weariness made the choice for me.

I felt drastically changed, but if pressed, couldn't have articulated a useful reference point. The utter vagueness of the days ahead frightened me. Was I meeting myself for the first time on a deeply spiritual, eternal level, or merely crawling toward some destination offering no clues or reassurance? Never great at living without a strong sense of purpose, that is precisely what the gods seemed to ask of me. But could I trust this uncertain new world—did I have a choice?

Future Memories

Staying busy had the potential to distract me and, professionally, I wanted to maintain my customary standards. When I agreed to do something, it was important to me to make a consistently strong contribution. Never fond of coffee breaks, chit-chat, flimsy excuses, mediocre or half-hearted efforts, when taking on a job, project, or heartfelt goal, I asked a lot of myself—expecting the moon, perhaps.

Even in the face of stiff emotional demands, when at work, I wanted to be there fully. At the time of Matt's death, I was an interim executive director (a strategic, transitional role that often helps organizations to evaluate their direction, change course, or consider long-term issues), and fortunate to be in professional position that was motivating. Most nonprofits are committed to their missions, but funding and, therefore, planning, can be difficult; likewise, staying competitive with salaries (retaining key personnel) can also be a major challenge. When I could help an organization improve its financial position by adopting refined growth (or fund-raising) strategies, it was rewarding. Work that weaves core values, professional training, and creative skills together is an invigorating gift.

When I wasn't at the office, I thought about writing. I liked to work on projects pre-dawn or late into the night—when I couldn't sleep. Tonight was one of those restless nights, but I couldn't write, either. Not during the summer of 2007. Not for a long while, actually. So I found a quilt, went downstairs to read and reflect—I liked to linger with certain passages. Landing on our blue couch, I perused a short stack of books perched on an end table, and reached for one that a kind colleague had given me: *Saving Graces: Finding Solace and Strength from Friends and Strangers.*

Written by Elizabeth Edwards about life's hurdles, including the loss of her son Wade, I wanted to glean her survival strategies. Opening the hardcover to no page in particular, I read: "There's a trick to being strong, and the trick is that no one does it alone." As this advice sunk in, slowly, like a gentle spring rain, I considered it in terms of my work with nonprofits, a context where collective efforts weren't optional. Whether fundraising, or helping an organization to evolve and transition, key ingredients had to come together.

Of course, I had to bring persistence, creativity, and courage to the table, along with an ability to inspire staff, board members, volunteers, and donors; it also took an arsenal of good ideas. Wisdom, timing, and intuition came into play before this unwieldy mix of luck and skill could be knitted into a compelling vision.

Blessed with a somewhat uncanny ability to visualize the sequence of steps needed to spur growth and development, numerous individuals still had to commit to the process—willingly endure the growing pains of change. Guiding organizational change usually requires a systems approach (in sociological terms, systems theory comes to mind), and includes a willingness to take the heat for emotional reactions that are all too human in the face of painful, or controversial, transitions. Luckily, my work, lodged in an inspiring and meaningful context, forced me to step beyond myself, my free-floating angst, for at least several hours each day.

But while work was manageable—a worthwhile, necessary respite from the things my mind so doggedly wanted to dwell on—unstructured time was predictably treacherous. A twisting mountain road speckled with signs that warned of falling rock. That's when I felt the most alone and adrift. Without my solid professional instincts to steady me, propel me forward, free time was when a deeper reality zoomed back into focus.

The paradox was that I also experienced an enormous amount of relief when I didn't have to meet the needs of others. Perched here under a blanket with only a reading lamp to illuminate a dark room in the middle of the night was safer ground. During the day, when I walked Noah, for instance, I was relieved when our neighbors didn't try to strike up a conversation. I couldn't talk about Matt, myself, or much of anything then—words, if unspoken, kept his loss at bay. And I was positive his death would come up if I paused, even briefly, to engage. So on and on I'd walked, gazing straight ahead or staring at my feet, the sidewalk, while hoping to lose myself in the moment. I had no way to know if our neighbors understood my reluctance, my inability, to chat with them, but something about this experience had moved me well beyond the need to please others.

Somehow, this was liberating. Maybe because my emotional reserves were depleted, I was deeply reluctant to take unnecessary risks and was convinced that something private or negative—sorrow, avoidance, distance, displeasure—would spill from my face when I lacked all energy to explain or fake the thinnest of smiles.

Self-protection is a necessary, normal aspect of grief.

That's another thing I was learning.

Glancing at Noah, now asleep next to me, I remembered that day I stopped at a coffee shop, impulsively buying an unknown CD with French lyrics: *Rendezvous à Paris*.

Foreign lyrics sounded safe; I couldn't trust my car radio.

Too many songs resurrected memories of life and Matt when they were intact as one, and this easily led to a surge of tears at the next stop sign. So the foreign tunes had played on, stacking invisible bricks around my car, while I pretended they could shield me from a world I planned to ignore.

Sometimes, though, even a few words on a Starbucks paper cup would draw me in—quietly reassure. I saved two during the summer of Matt's loss. From "The Way I See It" series (discontinued amidst some unfortunate controversy, according to Internet articles), one of them, #187, shared this gem: "Life is a school for angels. Love is the Teacher, so do your homework without fear. Death is merely graduation."

What a hopeful thought.

Another one, #282, by Lyall Bush, executive director of the Richard Hugo House, a center for writers and readers, seemed to wistfully capture childhood memories. "Childhood is a strange country. It's a place you come from or go to—at least in your mind. For me it has an endless, spellbound something in it that feels remote. It's like a little sealed-vault country of cake breath and grass stains where what you do instead of work is spin until you're dizzy."

Spinning until I felt dizzy sounded blissful; escaping into childhood memories could work. Cake breath reminded me of pink-iced birthday cakes, dancing candles, and friends toting presents wrapped in bright paper, bows, curly ribbon. Pointed party hats and those annoying whistles that roll out flat like colorful rulers when blown, magically curling up to deflate, were safe, gentle memories confirming the whisper of innocence.

Putting Elizabeth's book aside (what a courageous woman), I thought about sleep, but lingered with those innocent, intoxicating images instead. My reverie was brief, though, as a string of lost birthdays paraded into my tired awareness. Shadowy, future memories strangely, and suddenly, canceled—my suffering inevitably linked to my belief in time. But grief makes time feel oddly salient, almost all-powerful. Would we even know who we are without time as a primary defining condition? Would we recognize ourselves without dates, deadlines—a bodily form that changes constantly, an unpredictable outline in the mirror somehow and, mostly, beyond our grasp?

Only an illusion could sustain this anomalous dynamic: this phenomenon. But I hadn't figured all of this out yet.

Still locked in a narrow, time-based reality, I believed the past and the future were at least as important as the present, and now, since the dreadful past had already stolen the future, a happy merger of all three was impossible.

Like a prairie windmill silenced by time, life felt heavy and still.

Inviting the Bell

"The Way of Heaven is to
benefit others and not to injure.
The Way of the sage is to act
but not to compete."

—LAO TZU

Sorrow makes us all children again—destroys all differences of intellect. The wisest know nothing.
—RALPH WALDO EMERSON

Spiritual Roots

The summer of 2007 leaned leisurely into fall—the season of harvest and fulfillment—and ten butternut squash produced from random seeds in our small compost hill were ready to pick. But the fervent vines were puzzling. Sweeping across our yard with abandon, they produced massive, cheerful, orange blossoms that opened each morning with an ineffable brilliance.

Were they blazing a trail of insistent green?

Difficult enough to get garden vegetables to grow when carefully planted, fertilized, and watered in a fenced garden, the seeds from a delicious butternut we had for dinner one night took off effortlessly when simply tossed in a decomposing pile of leaves, organic matter. Igniting like fire, their fortuitous growth pointed, metaphysically, to transformation—and the enviable bounty of nature. Prickly vines were hollow like drinking straws, yet rich in color.

But when I reflected more deeply on their symbolism (as writers do), I struggled to unearth something tenable. Obvious ideas sprang to mind: circle of life, death begets life, spurious growth. None seemed quite right, however.

I considered how conditions, things, and people can grow or develop spontaneously, unplanned, unintended, when the right conditions merge—a fertile mix yielding a variety of positives, negatives, or neutral results. In this case, thriving squash plants that required virtually no work or planning were an unexpected bonus, as they romped across a carpet of summer grass making it difficult to mow.

But in looking for the symbolism in relation to Matthew's life—its untimely ending—I found it difficult to imagine a positive from the net result except on a purely spiritual plane. Had unlikely things transpired that fair weekend in June, a fateful blending of circumstances that set the stage for unplanned, horrific results?

Perhaps the stars were aligned just so, allowing a lethal mingling of racing emotions, powerful drugs, impulsive decision-making.

Whatever maze of events led to a tragic ending, I tirelessly wished this scenario could have been prevented. If just one minuscule moment in the series of steps leading to death had been different, right? The inevitable *Where was God?* rose to the surface frequently. Realizing it wasn't necessarily helpful to query a higher power along these lines didn't make my questions any less painful or pressing. After supporting my son's challenging journey, I had to ask, *had to know*, where God was that night and early morning.

Fair enough, right?

Surveying the daring squash vines, I looked for God—*any kind of God*—right in my own yard. Surely nature held the key to all understanding. I had grown up in the Catholic faith—spent my elementary years at Saint Joseph School, was baptized and confirmed and received my first communion, went to confession, and so on. As you know, I believed in a divine cosmic force that some call the-one-and-only God, even though others call "it" something else. I prayed as part of everyday life. Not in the formal sense, but in a more organic, spontaneous, and relevant way.

Spirituality was intrinsic to my way of life, embedded in a predictable, unglamorous lifestyle: days of quiet contentment, a deep respect for nature, an abiding appreciation for depth and substance, an avoidance of superficial distinctions and stereotypical thinking, cultivating a peaceful existence that avoided dwelling on the "dark side" of things.

I desired, like many, an inspiring life path that consistently challenged me to make a creative, meaningful contribution, and because a strong spiritual dimension had fueled my values and priorities, I was drawn to authentic people with open minds, good hearts. Interestingly, after starting law school in my late twenties, I decided within weeks that it wasn't for me. An emphasis on conflict and controversy, when held under a classroom microscope, didn't inspire, or motivate, me. Yearning to dig deeper, explore life on a more philosophical, qualitative level, I opted for a master's degree in sociology. A perfect fit, if there is such a thing.

Raised to believe I should become a trial lawyer, I'd bought into that ever-so-logical, middle-class dream for some time; I had even completed an undergraduate degree in legal studies. But listening to the first law school lecture (an experience recalled with clarity), I was seriously disappointed. The tone was pompous, shallow, and antagonistic.

I'd matured between degrees: was the mother of two by then, felt increasingly drawn to the dictates of my soul, and social conscience. Difficult to admit at the time (how had my dreams been misdirected for so long?), but I was no longer interested in learning how to navigate an antiquated system that (mostly) revolved around combative clients, hyper-competitive colleagues, and fee generation. There are *many* smart, hard-working, and ethical lawyers out there, but something in me had shifted.

I craved a lifestyle with purposeful work that I believed in.

Boxing up massive textbooks (who could lift them?), I sold all but one, never looked back. I've wondered, though, how I had the strength to walk away. How many aspire to go to law school, and can't? Undergraduate grades, LSAT scores, finances, family concerns, health limitations, or geographic restrictions. The lure of high income and community status would have been enough to keep many enrolled, but neither captured my passion or priorities, so in the end, I had to pass.

"Gutsy decision," a friend said with a smile.

❧

Our wild squash vines were now a memory, and I'd gone outside to soak up sunlight for winter. Enclosed by a wooden fence of mixed heights, our backyard was unusually calm. Birds, squirrels, friendly neighbors—eerily quiet. No dogs barking, car engines, slamming doors, or jets overhead (and we weren't that far from the Indianapolis airport), no distant voices. Our trees stood tall, motionless, as if a strong breeze had never graced their branches.

A beautiful Saturday afternoon, a comforting silence.

A day when our Carmel, Indiana, suburb typically buzzed with leaf blowers, lawn mowers, kids on bikes, cars and motorcycles coming and going. Our lawn looked tired, the insistent green of summer fading to allow a new season, and the hearty squash vines that seemed to be rushing toward something nameless ... felt dreamlike.

Nature, such a wise and noble teacher.

Just ask Thoreau, Whitman, John Muir, or Rachel Carson, to name a few.

Staying with the ambitious vines—an autumn harvest of pure chance—I pried into this once more, hoping nature would divulge its secrets, its timeless wisdom.

Supercharged growth had occurred, when?

When stringy, slippery white seeds were tossed aside to decompose. That's when they came to life, putting down roots quickly and easily. *Is that where God also comes into sharp focus: below or above the surface of things, in fertile places that somehow transform us?*

I'd finally begun reading *When Bad Things Happen to Good People*.

Harold Kushner, a rabbi, who lost his son Aaron to a rare disease in his teens, had also suffered a crushing loss. Sensing readers would want to know why God hadn't intervened to prevent his death, he wrote "God, who neither causes nor prevents tragedies, helps by inspiring people to help." So, Kushner sees God as working through us in critical, albeit indirect, ways, explaining that while He may not prevent calamity, God is still the source of our strength, the perseverance, to overcome it.

The author and father also suggested in his book that maybe (when tragedy strikes) we need to forgive the world for being imperfect, and to likewise forgive God for not making it better in our eyes. Kushner challenges us to love this world anyway. Clearly, it's all we have, and despite unbearable experiences and considerable strife, there is "great beauty and goodness." Reasonable thoughts from an obviously reasonable man suggesting that God needs our maturity and understanding.

Accepting that we may expect too much from God, I was willing to consider his point. I had, in fact, expected God (mostly subconsciously) to be there for Matt—for those who loved him— in concrete ways that fulfilled *our* mortal, time-drenched dreams, when ... surely, God's (whatever your definition) standards and goals were vastly different.

Letting my thoughts idle for a while, I scanned the yard.

Our massive oak was sporting sharp new colors—threads of yellow, orange, brown—and the first stab of winter hit me.

Instantly, I dreaded it.

That "first" winter—an unavoidable holiday season.

But not wanting a surge of sadness to overwhelm me, I turned again to my memory of the lush vines, Kushner's thought-provoking message, and the reassuring sun, its warmth on my face, neck, hands.

Kushner's preface to the twentieth-anniversary edition of his book offers this: "people going through a tough time need consolation more than explanation." Since Matt's death I'd needed, more than anything, to feel heard, understood: I agreed with him on this. But there were some who seemed intent on talking me out of my feelings, curiously trying to point me in another direction, as though it were wise (or possible) to distract me from Matt's absence. Some acted like grief was a broken casserole that needed a quick repair. Absurd? I'm afraid so.

I didn't need *fixing*—I needed sincere concern: people strong (empathetic) enough to care and to listen, to appreciate (without judgment) the well of trauma and consternation that defined my existence. It didn't seem like that much to ask, but not everyone is strong in that way. Many shy from deep and powerful emotions, from the reality of life and death. But this interesting suggestion from Kushner surprised me.

"I now tell bereaved parents: you have inherited from your child all the years he or she never got to live." My logical mind rushed to question this grandiose idea, but he insisted their years were a "precious legacy." And he instructed: "Live their years along with your own, and feel their presence as you do so."

A very tall order that felt unattainable … in the moment.

Shifting my gaze to a bird bath littered with leaves, as if on cue, the consoling silence began to slip away. Children's voices, synonymous with a trust in life, an unspoken promise of a future that would be safe, long-lived, drifted in the air. Neither, factually true, of course, but the conditioned mind is oblivious to such distinctions. We can only hear what the world has taught us to hear, and to expect.

Soon another voice rang out.

"Time to come in, bike in the garage, please."

Sighing, I closed my eyes in retreat.

Kushner also advised readers to focus on *where* to find helpful resources. I suspected that searching for illusive inner resources was also part of the process. But this can be a bit of a scavenger hunt, with grief insisting, like a pushy friend, that it might be necessary to dig even deeper this time—to see tragedy as an unsolicited reason to push beyond traditional beliefs or a limited vision.

Maybe, I thought, my head feeling pinched, my heart resisting.

Such an enlightened perspective required a generous frame of mind, plus an ability to feel grateful for spiritual growth regardless of the catalyst. But a stifling darkness seemed to prevail, and life as I knew it seemed to be shrinking—vanishing right before my green, sometimes blue, even gray, eyes—so I wasn't at all sure how to endure the sharp sting of this kind of gratitude. Gratitude for *anything and everything* was another very tall order.

Neighborhood voices grew quiet again. A small relief.

The space of silence led to an inner stillness: to insights edging into my awareness, to old ideas imbued with new meaning. We live in a confusing world with a dark, turbulent side, but I could still invite the light. Like a brilliant harvest moon against the black sheet of night, light is magnificent in many contexts, but most vivid, in total darkness. There is universal wisdom—pointed to by ancient and contemporary sages—in this complicated, see-saw relationship between good and evil, light and dark, as each allow and inform the other. But this isn't a new revelation.

Our minds rush to interpret events as good or bad, positive or negative, as we eagerly watch for the "good" and, more cautiously, for the "bad." But when darkness descended into my world with absolute force and determination, abstract concepts became fiercely personal, and I was drawn to profound life questions as never before.

Was I encountering, deeply so, my spiritual roots?

Like the hardy vines, might something "good" grow from apparent tragedy?

I didn't know, but the question alone held promise: was even enough to finally get me out of my chair and back inside.

The Human Condition

A few weeks later, autumn penetrating in deepening layers of rusty gold, I encountered the idea of spiritual roots again. I'd hoped to spend time outside—with nature, my wise and worldly friend—but the morning was dark, blustery, so I opted for a chair near the fireplace. Neither John, Noah, nor Lola (our white cat with calico markings) had stirred, and the exquisite play of night and day, dark and light, marched boldly into my thoughts. Had I greatly feared the darkness before Matt's loss, naïvely believing I could wind my way through an entire lifetime without *knowing* its full weight?

But it wasn't like my life had been a fairy tale lark.

Of course there was no such thing—only silly expectations for a "good life" without undue difficulty or long-term suffering.

Turning on a reading lamp, I squinted against its brightness, and picked up a book I'd already started. Eckhart Tolle's compelling perspective had found a lasting place in my heart. In his second book, *A New Earth*, I'd read "suffering has a noble purpose" because it helps us to evolve. Specifically, "the fire of suffering becomes the light of consciousness." Or some awaken to a new consciousness through loss and suffering, thereby becoming the light of consciousness.

I winced—the process sounded daunting. Winter was nearing, and I couldn't imagine being the light of anything.

The idea sounded blissful enough (allow something good to emerge from the ashes), but I struggled to grasp the full depth of his message, even though I wanted to stay open to what might unfold.

What did I possibly have to lose?

Tolle also described some individuals as "frequency-holders"—those who "anchor the frequency of the new consciousness on this planet." Their lives may appear ordinary, but Eckhart believes they may serve a greater purpose in the evolution of the universe, noting that some have a difficult time fitting in and may "turn to drugs because they find living in this world too painful." *That*, I could see.

Could Matt have found this mortal framework, as a whole, too painful?

Most would agree we live in an imperfect world comprised of people, organizations, systems, and groups that are noticeably dysfunctional; so, indeed, life can be painful, even under circumstances of promise. Doesn't life, for instance, fail to live up to most of our lofty ideals about what is desirable—assuming such vague notions could be defined and understood in terms relevant to each living being in both practical and spiritual terms? And what if someone wants to transcend the cultural demands of an ego-based existence, knowingly or otherwise? A lonely, even impossible, endeavor, perhaps.

Leaving the needs of ego behind, as some suggest must happen if we are to evolve as a civilization, might feel like crawling out on a flimsy limb.

I glanced outside. The wind had picked up. Watching brittle leaves being tossed about like a winter salad, I thought, *It's true, we are all works in progress.* A landscape that *looks* the same morning after morning is in perpetual motion, always changing, just beyond our perception. And nothing remains the same for long, unless we reside in an artificial land of quiet denial and stunted growth. Even then, there is movement: subtleties occurring just below the surface.

But it was still early—my thoughts were tentative, sketchy.

Should I make tea, coffee?

Instead, I sat quietly, feeling starkly aware I would never know the precise mission of my son's soul, nor would I ever know if Matt even believed in such things. The universe, far more complicated, purposeful, and interconnected than I could begin to comprehend, rarely makes us privy to such things. But since surface events tend to have a deeper relevance, a cosmic purpose, a divine principle, again, I wanted to leave the door open.

Glancing outside I hoped to see a vibrant sun peeking through heavy clouds. Maybe a few birds jetting around. But nothing. Tolle's words tugged at my soul. An international spiritual teacher with a humble background, he writes: "Even if both of your parents were enlightened, you would still find yourself growing up in a largely unconscious world" (by unconscious he means spiritually unaware, locked in the world of form). So, apparently, we are destined to find ourselves in emotional pain as an inevitable aspect of the human condition. Yet, if our souls are polished and refined through suffering, are we supposed to embrace tough times with equanimity: as a sign of our willingness to grow spiritually?

Something in me was eager to disagree with Mr. Tolle. His ideas, wise and powerful, still rang hollow when I compared them to my new life, the one without a living son. And now, as I write, I'm fairly sure more than a handful of readers are thinking: life is painful—adapt, show resilience, endure, stay strong. Don't be a whiner, weak or overly sensitive; don't expect the world to get you, understand you, like you, offer patience or a sliver of genuine compassion. Stay realistic—determined and focused, right?

But perhaps we have gone too far with this meritorious, almost quaint line of thinking, and have unwittingly sold out. Exchanging healthy, legitimate needs for rationalizations, generic expectations, and losing propositions. What does the tough-guy mentality deliver in the end; what does *real strength* look like up close?

For whatever reason, we tend to expect unique human beings to behave like an army of glossy-looking clones, while living under a mountain of denial about the reality of the human condition. Sighing, I thought about coffee again, and this time I got up, walked to the kitchen. Lights. Water. Coffee. Cups. Maybe cream. The morning drill in motion, as my mind plowed on—ruminating on the broader issues. Simply put, it seemed that we all could benefit from greater flexibility, encouraging understanding and allowing space for those who prefer compassion and peace instead of violence and aggression.

Look at the negative consequences of bullying, for example, as it intensifies in some school systems. I once worked for a nonprofit organization with a mission to reduce the frequency of bullying in classrooms. The repercussions are serious, and it's yet another glaring symptom of a culture that hasn't quite found its way.

Grinding coffee, filling the coffeemaker with water, my gaze was again drawn outside, as I considered the emotional and mental damage bullying delivers—how it creates lifelong ramifications, leaving behind quiet scars of bruised self-esteem, even lives lost to suicide. While pain and life are an inevitable coupling, not everyone is equipped with an arsenal of internal resources—able to roll with the punches, brush off negative comments, ignore ill-treatment—so why not dedicate ourselves to peaceful change on a global scale?

Clearly, we shouldn't toss aside our gracious, wise, and loving qualities, jumping to label them as unrealistic, noncompetitive, non-aggressive, naïve, feminine, or unhelpful.

This picture is skewed and, intuitively, we know it.

Listening to the steady drip of coffee, I pulled a sand-colored cup from the cupboard.

Such a phenomenon, to take hold, would require a concerted, sustained effort on the part of many; we would need to reach a tipping point so global dynamics might positively impact world societies. Possible, probable, or neither?

I could only pose the question.

But I believed what Saint Francis of Assisi told us: "A single sunbeam is enough to drive away many shadows."

Hearing footsteps, I knew my morning reverie was coming to a close, but something important was weaving its way into the light of awareness. I was seeking God in a way never imagined. Not through rigid religious definitions that always make someone right, someone wrong—ideas that seem to encourage senseless destruction and utter havoc, as generation upon generation commits nearly every kind of violence in the name of "their" God, the one adamantly claimed to represent universal truth—but by studying, ever more deeply, my spiritual roots in a largely "unconscious world."

Tolle's terminology, but I knew what he meant. When we are unconscious, we only see a generic, self-serving world; we let the ends justify the means. And since we're not fully tuned in to *this* moment, we aren't *here*. Rather, we run spiritually blind, carelessly closed to the true nature of existence. Unawakened, we stare at the rose without *seeing* it.

I listened to steps on the stairs.

The suffering on the planet pointed to many things, but when we believe the critical answers are external and disconnected from what lies within (undiscovered, unexplored, undervalued), our profound suffering is guaranteed to last.

In *Power vs. Force: The Hidden Determinants of Human Behavior*, the gifted Dr. David R. Hawkins reminded us of something important. "We forget that every heinous crime that man is capable of has been perpetrated in the name of God." Even Pope Francis has echoed that sentiment, noting that some fine people in history haven't believed in God, and some of the "worst deeds were done in His name."

Spirituality, I was coming to believe with greater urgency, needn't be linked to a set of beliefs. Rather, it can transcend the endless bickering, the useless conflict, about specific religions, and since this insightful distinction is where the world—nations, governments, churches, groups, families, and individuals—stumbles time and time again, it was where I wanted to begin. Where there is struggle—where there is strife—unseen possibilities are most assured. Don't knots beg to be released; doesn't tension seek resolution?

≈

The human condition, as reflected by each person, is a big part of the puzzle, of course—a fundamentally mysterious "condition" that preceded Matt's life, mine, and yours. Take for instance Thomas Penson de Quincey (1785–1859), the English essayist, opium addict and alcoholic who penned the infamous *Confessions of an English Opium-Eater* in 1821.

Reportedly, de Quincey had many things going for him, a loving family (his father, a prosperous merchant), good looks, intellectual strength, but sought relief from *something*—physical, mental, or emotional issues that seemed to control him.

In 1804 he turned to opium for relief, a habit that continued until his death. His intake increasing, as de Quincey tried to maneuver ubiquitous obstacles—dark days of self-recrimination that seemed to haunt him from the start. In *Confessions* he wrote about the "burden of the Incommunicable," and the "divine luxuries of opium."

It should be clear by now that addicts did not *create* addiction, nor can they cure it, singlehandedly. That will take systemic change that flows from the very origins of our species, from the fabric of society and societies.

We are each born into the human condition, a state of being as curious as the universe itself, and here, we see the ultimate connectivity of all life. Changing, yet changeless.

Inviting the Bell

"The Way of Heaven is to
benefit others and not to injure.
The Way of the sage is to act
but not to compete."

—LAO TZU

So little is understood about suicide. If we write about it,
the center of our writing is about something unknown,
unexplainable. Start from this shaky place; see where it leads.
—NATALIE GOLDBERG, *OLD FRIEND FROM FAR AWAY*

Outdated Codes

My thoughts, drawn to deeper, more challenging, subjects, didn't eliminate the need for the basics—cooking, for instance, still had to happen. Walking into our kitchen, I would open the pantry door, stare at the cans, the boxes, the miscellaneous, but vivid memories of cooking for Matt would invariably surface.

With zero interest in food, I didn't get far, and now Thanksgiving was approaching. A memory-laden holiday focused primarily on food and family was of no help.

Sunday morning breakfast sounded innocent enough, but was just another emotional landmine. Matt loved homemade sweet rolls, and while that probably sounds nostalgic, it was part of our relationship: one of the ways we celebrated life together. A simple joy, a way to connect, a tradition with personal history. It's funny, the ordinary things we build our lives around—the common ways we nurture the people we love.

In Matt's absence, I realized this more than ever.

Never demanding or difficult to please, I don't recall him saying, "No thanks, I don't like that." He must have, though, because no one likes *everything*. Most, in fact, manage to overdo it, habitually releasing a dark, endless stream of complaints. Mind pollution, ego, confusion, self-centered yapping.

Matt, however, wasn't a complainer—not in comparison to most.

A Phenomenon

Time skittered along, but my culinary resistance continued. I couldn't muster the same creative satisfaction in the kitchen—not even when I dug out a favorite recipe or tried a new one. One winter morning, still in a long, warm robe, I sat down at the kitchen table and wrote down some things I wanted to do again *someday* without reluctance. Without sadness. Though dreamlike, I kept writing—and imagining.

Nothing was too small, too insignificant, to include.

My list grew quickly: sitting by a window to reflect on poignant memories; opening a Christmas or birthday present; gazing at family pictures, at Matt's baby pictures; listening to music he'd loved; remembering his smile, his voice and his laugh, the way he walked; attending church on Christmas Eve; taking a long walk on a brisk fall morning; watching the first snowfall. Remembering Matthew as a happy child—I wrote that in capital letters.

But besides knowing what I wanted to experience again without the sharp edge of pain smothering the moment, I was also learning that *not doing*—shunning plans, schedules, demanding goals—is how an acceptance of loss is forged.

If I pursued senseless, unceasing activity, I could only create an illusion of peace. My acceptance, paper thin, not genuine or lasting. Endless activity, the primary offshoot of a futile game some are tempted to engage in to avoid the intimidating grip of sorrow, was merely another path to exhaustion.

Glancing up, I spotted the bright blue numbers on our microwave: the ever-in-motion time of day. The list I'd begun seemed endless. I put down my pencil.

But moments later, I remembered it was okay to feel like nothing would ever be the same: because it wouldn't. And despite the formidable shadows of vulnerability, guilt, or apathy, I had to let the world go by without me. I'd always expected too much of myself anyway. Yet, no one should try to live up to the image of self created by an "unconscious world"—family, friends, teachers, leaders, organizations, society. We're all a funny blend of who expected what, who assumed what, and who taught us what.

Glancing out the window, I saw squirrels chasing each other. One darting up a tree; one running toward another tree. Squirrels doing what squirrels do, time and time again. Wasn't this a small reflection of the haze of activity, I, like most, lived in? But Holocaust survivor, Viktor Frankl, told us years ago: "Between stimulus and response there is a space. In that space is our power to choose our response. In our response lies our growth and our freedom." He was right. But it takes tremendous courage to "stop doing."

Somewhere along the way, I'd been programmed to stay focused, productive, unless seriously ill. Now, I *knew* it was time to stop. For one thing, I was no longer willing or able to live by outdated external codes. It wasn't good food for the soul. I needed to let what had happened seep deeply into my bones, allowing it to come to rest undisturbed. Of course, I feared the pain of that stark truth settling in; the dark, senseless words, "I will never see Matt again," rolling off my tongue without a shred of resistance. Of course, my natural instinct was to stall, disallowing deep acceptance, pushing it safely aside for the "right time." Only scarcely could I look at this stumbling reality—then, for a passing moment from the far corner of my eye.

Looking down, reading my list—what I hoped to do someday without feeling sad—it occurred to me I was being impractical. Trying on a distant level to will myself through the thick gates of time. But I wasn't going to get through a life-changing event, or soften its blow, with a futile wish list.

I glanced outside again.

Our backyard was home to a southern line of trees stretching skyward with serious enthusiasm. They looked so complete, so sure of themselves, even in the bareness of winter. I, in stark contrast, had never felt more unsure, more unsteady.

Separating the past from the present had generated a swirl of incompatible, competing thoughts: a ferocious internal inconsistency.

The layer of shock that had insulated me was long gone.

Now unprotected from grief's offensive, I was exposed to the elements in every way.

Hearing a jet race across the morning sky, I was struck by my serious disinterest in its destination. Physical transportation, period. Someone going somewhere. Wasn't nearly every activity overrated?

I noticed my breathing, its predictable rhythm, its comforting presence.

Maybe my list could be simplified.

Picking up my pencil, I wrote: just breathe.

There it was: something that offered a genuinely peaceful moment, and it wasn't anything I had to explain to anyone. Uncomplicated, soothing. Even noticing this felt hugely calming—somehow liberating.

Just breathe, I whispered.

Oxygen filled my lungs, I was safe. I was okay, and alive.

Another insight followed.

The highly personal nature of loss didn't yield to succinct explanations to share with others. In other words, it didn't translate well. I *really* was alone, left to contend with an unknown world—indeed, the wrong world—for an indeterminate number of days. As if encumbered by a phenomenon, an uncompromising force that lacked shape or common understanding, if things improved—simultaneously, they worsened.

Essentially, I was at grief's mercy. Such were the contradictions, the complexities, of pain beyond human understanding. Yet, others would ask, and others would wonder, when I didn't have the energy for their wearisome questions. It was a winter morning: all I could do was breathe.

Inviting the Bell

"The Way of Heaven is to
benefit others and not to injure.
The Way of the sage is to act
but not to compete."

—LAO TZU

And now there is merely silence, silence,
silence, saying all we did not know.
—WILLIAM ROSE BENET

The Sound of Nothing

A rather famous castle stands near Alexandria Bay, New York. Constructed at the turn of the century by George Boldt for his wife, Louise, Boldt Castle was a symbol of his love. A multi-millionaire and proprietor of the Waldorf Astoria Hotel in New York City, Boldt had invested 2.5 million in this replica of a Rhineland castle, when Louise died suddenly in January 1904. The enormous project was immediately halted. No longer interested, Boldt abandoned the incomplete structure and, reportedly, never returned. Finally, some 73 years later, the Thousand Islands Bridge Authority acquired the property in 1977, and eventually rehabilitated the structure, which had been left to the forces of nature.

Much speculation has surrounded this story and, in 2001, *Boldt Castle: In Search of the Lost Story* was published. This intriguing tale of affection illustrates the far-reaching consequences of loss.

Without Louise, the castle had lost all meaning, so Boldt deserted his cherished dream. I fully understand his painful decision.

As a symbol of his love, the castle and surrounding buildings were not only stunning physical structures, they were gifts of deep, abiding emotion: his feelings made manifest. And so it is with memories that capture extraordinary moments. I call them "defining memories" because they hold such deep significance, often ushering in major life passages. There is a transformational quality about them—an identifiable symbolism—and many resemble, when placed under a literary microscope, the plot points for a novel.

December 2007 had arrived, and I, too, felt tempted to leave the castle unfinished, to walk away and never look back. Matthew's loss may have transformational power, as inspirational material promised, but what did that mean exactly?

I posed this question during another night of long, empty hours when I'd gotten up, glanced outside to find thick snow cover not in the forecast.

Picking up the remote, I opted for bad television on mute.

Transformational.

Did this mean pretending to forget, feigning smooth and easy renewal, or tenaciously forging on, perplexed by the past and future, but trusting in both nonetheless? Or might I wake up one morning, brand new and significantly improved, or would this hopeful, to-be-anticipated transformation make itself known in other ways—how would I recognize its presence, *know* its true mark? I didn't have a single flimsy clue.

I stared at the screen, wondered why, after a long day, I wasn't fast asleep.

I was getting better, though, at sitting quietly with no agenda, with less internal pressure to stay busy striving toward the next goal: learning how to truly coexist with time, instead of resisting, implicitly or explicitly, its sidewinding pressure—its relentless push and pull.

Reaching for a wool throw draped over my chair, I remembered a book I'd read when deep into my research about the nature—the formidable power—of memories. The 1966 classic by Frances Yates, *The Art of Memory*, explained how the human mind was once portrayed as a theatre of memory places symbolizing seven grades or steps. Its inventor, Giulio Camillo, was born around 1480, and his intricate system of memory was referred to as Camillo's Memory Theatre.

Controversial theories about the potential of human memory were well known in Italy and France, and Yates reviewed them in depth, linking the art of memory to the history of culture. But when Camillo died in Milan in 1544, he hadn't had sufficient time to perfect his Theatre or to publish a complete theory of explanation.

Still, as a historical reference, his ideas are noteworthy. Even fascinating.

I understood the powerful human desire to make the invisible, visible; to capture all things fleeting, ephemeral, thereby linking mortal experience to the divine, the infinite: the lasting. Both castles and memory theatres point to these normal, heartfelt desires; the ones our life memories fuel. Honestly, though, I wasn't willing or able to let love evolve into a dust-covered memory; my son lived on in my mind, heart, and soul: in living color.

"Hi, Mom, it's Matt."

"Hi, son, how are you?"

I would have known his voice anywhere, but Matt liked to identify himself. Maybe there was something about a phone call that prompted him to offer his name. I should have asked. Perhaps I did, but many (most?) of our memories are shadowy, incomplete, and simply unavailable. To believe we can accurately reconstruct the details of our lives is painfully delusional. The conditioned mind, a strong ego, can tempt us to try, but our spiritual dimension, our much wiser inner voice, points firmly to the futility of this task.

Memory Shelf

From out of the blue, Christmas turned up on my calendar, so I sat down to write a poem. So much to say, so very little to say. Still, I wrote a few lines that felt right, made copies, and sent the poem and a holiday picture from 2006 to friends, family. The picture, taken during our last Thanksgiving with Matt, couldn't have been more customary: Matt and I by an enormous Christmas tree in the lobby of the Four Seasons at the Lake of the Ozarks (a convenient place for all of us to meet). Relaxed, smiling, unsuspicious of the throttle of ticking clocks everywhere, the mere seven months remaining.

What title might Matt have chosen for the poem?

"Red Yarn" was about feeling unsteady under the glare of twisted strands of holiday lights—too bright, blinking at speeds unknown. Would he have wanted me to share the poem, our picture? I had no idea. Memories swarmed like the seductive glare of the season. Overwhelmed by their powerful grip, my poem had the shape of sadness at a time when many yearn to feel lighthearted: swept away by the fanciful, the extravagant.

Was it the wrong time to remind others of our loss, to focus on who we were missing the most? Wrapped in layers of dense emotions, I only knew I needed to honor (include) Matt's continuing place in our lives—make his brief, earthly stay visible. And relevant.

As I look back, it seems I wanted those close to us to understand that we would *never* put Matt on a distant memory shelf in some neat, tidy, far-removed way. Perhaps fine for tangible, manmade items—family heirlooms, silver vases, gold watches, ruby pendants—it surely wasn't applicable to human beings. Still naïvely believing in the power of time, I may also have hoped to bring Matt back to life by revealing how I could hardly think of anything else, and maybe, if we all thought about him long and hard enough, maybe, my grief-stricken mind postulated, I would wake up with a start one day to discover Matt, in the flesh, still walking among us.

But this is where "believing" has its painfully obvious limitations.

It's unrealistic to trust a heart, a soul, or a mind consumed by absence, but we don't know it at the time, because we are tunneling in the dark.

Part of me, I think, even wanted others to love Matt the way I did. Couldn't they sense his good traits—kindness, warm sense of humor, intelligence—beneath that reserved exterior, and detect the gentle, well-meaning soul struggling to unearth his personal truth amidst the explicit and implicit rules of existence, myriad expectations, spiritual teachings and sensible ideas abundantly offered to help him solve life's most daunting mysteries? Some did, and I am sure most did not.

Notes to Self

Dennis Apple, pastor, father, who endured the sudden, inexplicable loss of a son, wrote this in *Life After the Death of My Son: What I'm*

Learning: "Few people whose children are all living understand the formidable task that bereaved parents face." Poignantly, he explains: "Our injury is made even worse by people who try to fast-forward us through our grief." I'm not sure how I discovered his book, but after the holidays, I opened to page one. Apple's ability to discuss some of my most difficult emotions was comforting. Noting that closure is a cold word—impractical when coping with the loss of a child of any age—he spoke for many parents.

Grief, and its unwieldy companions, isn't something we can package up, tie a ribbon around one bright summer morning to finalize an inherently awkward process. So why do we love to imagine (and promote) these tidy, very orderly, endings?

A sad kind of nonsense, I'm afraid.

Sitting near a sunny kitchen window with Apple's book, I tried to imagine his young son. As a society, a contemporary culture, we are painfully uncomfortable with loss and grief because we don't want to feel our own mortality: the deafening moment when time-based realities and treasured relationships cease. We are thrust, however, into the gooey guts of life through loss, and maybe everything else is but a shadow of this truth. Still, I was only beginning to understand that this bewildering pandemonium also generates a scattered and imperfect experience, never offering an exact beginning, a precise ending.

We begin to lose our children at conception—certainly, at birth—but this can only be understood when we accept that children belong to life itself (*they are life*), not to their parents. Serving as their temporary, but fortunate, caretakers, and largely caught up in the rapid flow of pulsating days, most fail to see beloved children as impermanent gifts. We expect them to live beyond our years. But expecting something can't make it happen, and so it is with those who *expect* grieving parents to get over their loss—to come away from the depths of their despair, renewed, recovered, smiling, and eager to pick up their steps as though *nothing* had happened. Cured, and over it.

My journal was nearby, so I scribbled a few notes—this, in particular.

When unrealistic expectations are unspoken, mostly insinuated, grief-stricken parents (siblings or other close relatives) may wonder if they are imagining things.

Am I being rushed through this, pushed to the other side before I'm ready, or is it me, my skewed and cheerless perception—primarily?

Another important note to self: do not cater to those who are unable to empathize.

Most people had stopped asking me how things were going; I noticed they definitely stopped short of saying the name of the dearly departed. God forbid we bring up *his* name again, as though avoiding it made some kind of difference—made death a "past event" that no longer impacted shiny, carefree lives. Maybe there was a compelling illusion of control even, a sense of thank God that is over, now the reality of loss can be forgotten again.

No death for me, or those I love. No thanks, we'll pass.

Question for my journal: Why am I being hushed into forgetting, prodded into letting go? *Shh*, are the looks, the non-response and gentle hints. *He's gone, remember?*

Some seemed on the verge of sharing this curious sentiment: We graciously gave you ample time to resume your life, but that window has closed. So no longer are we willing to converse about the son who committed suicide during a serious drug relapse after sporadic periods of recovery. Be advised, if he comes up, we will gaze at you as if we're not quite sure who or what you're talking about.

And please don't expect us to bring up the Matt subject again.

The implicit message, more specifically, seemed to be: We're extremely busy with our own lives; you, too, should get busy with yours. Furthermore, we are prepared to forget the past (almost keen, truth be told), and suggest you too look straight ahead, leaving that difficult, troubling chapter in the dust. A closed book, a tough time, a gut-wrenching saga.

Let's get back to harmless, happy talk—that mindless, sheltered existence we adoringly call reality.

Those exact words, never spoken, but as 2008 ushered in a cold, blustery January, it was apparent that after 180 days, some people felt enough time had elapsed. Things should get back to *normal*—and I should let go, get on with it. Whatever "it" was. Naïvely, it took awhile to fully absorb this implicit message—to believe anyone could be this formulaic, so sadly demanding, superficial, and egocentric.

Unfortunately, I must admit to a share of weak moments when I instructed myself to deal with my grief once and for all so others wouldn't feel uncomfortable or inadequate.

Cover up those unsightly, forlorn feelings, right?

A hypothetical question felt like a non-answer, so staring out the window for another impromptu meditation with nature, I pushed deeper. I wanted to find a better perspective on this. As a grieving mother, a perpetual student of society, and someone who believed the human condition deserved our attention and genuine concern, I felt troubled by these dynamics. It was the dead of winter. My son was gone and very few understood the nonlinear resonance of grief.

How had we created an artificial world that believed in time, above nearly everything else, a world that also justified an acceptable timeframe for loss, grief, and bereavement? How long had it been like this—how had others coped with this strange lack of empathy, and compassionate awareness? Even more disconcerting, what could I possibly do about it? Six months was nothing. I was too new at this to figure out much of anything—to spot even a shockingly bright light in a dense morning fog.

Personal Truth

A few weeks later I sat down to watch the national news. The content was predictable: violence, tragedy, politics, controversy, and tossed in at the close, a brief story of goodwill or survival to balance the "hard news." To end on a high note or to compensate for the overall harshness of the broadcast. Television personalities, with an air of certainty and time as their master, seem to bow to whatever story is deemed timely, pressing, or urgent.

Reaching for the remote, I clicked the power button, opted for the welcoming hush of silence.

Sometimes I craved the sound of nothing; it was often better than anything else, and I was beginning to see how important it was to ignore our cultural devotion to time, even though many seemed wedded to it—an entrenched dynamic that skews our perspective, that causes us to flounder, to suffer, to run harder and faster, all to no avail. Likewise, in rushing through the intricacies of grief, a powerful catalyst for spiritual realization, we miss a golden opportunity. When we bury painful feelings—disavow, or run from them—we also resist the deep stir of grief. Surrender becomes even more unlikely. And maybe, just maybe, it goes like this because the world keeps whispering, *There is no time.*

But doesn't this sound counterproductive?

Why mask the face of grief by generating complications stemming from unresolved, unexplored feelings that linger at the sidelines, waiting to be acknowledged? If we fail to grant ourselves permission to ignore social feedback and implicit expectations, we may not even detect a latent desire to explore, more fully, our spiritual dimension.

The silence in the room seemed to applaud, but was I strong enough to follow my own instincts, to let this arduous process reveal itself to me gradually?

I was living in a weakened, vulnerable state; it was tempting to want to please others to avoid feeling selfish, confused, or even utterly hopeless. Could I muster the courage to serve my spiritual growth, instead of superficial, time-laden expectations?

Glancing at Noah, his gentle brown eyes meeting mine, I caught yet another wave of worry. Was I dealing with grief in the *right* way? Society (including inner circles) has a way of dropping *big* expectations on us, regardless of personal circumstances, and rarely are we (civilizations, entrenched systems of organization, cultures and societies) flexible. We're not even prepared to allow for a variety of personalized responses to something as natural as death. *Not really.*

Worst of all, by not understanding or appreciating our spiritual significance, we tend to perpetuate our suffering by adhering to unspoken rules without meaningful reflection. We forget how to be discriminating in our assumptions—to carefully examine society's intricate web of influence in light of legitimate human needs.

We go along, don't we?

We get in line and follow, instead of exploring the profound truths that emanate from within: that spring from our intuition. So I guess it's not that surprising how rare it is to encounter our eternal essence: the self that only can be discovered and experienced beyond the heavy gates of time.

Walking to a nearby window, I noticed the absence of visible stars in a distant January sky. *Thick clouds and time, both, mere camouflage.* This minuscule flicker of awareness was easily absorbed, however, by the next thought, and the next. My tentative sense of place, a flimsy piece of debris—empty can, broken twig, shard of glass—or maybe a child's sand castle. Within minutes, the insistent tide of grief tossed me back out to sea.

Luckily, before my insight was totally lost, I sat down at my desk to jot down lines of poetry that came to me like a succinct description of Matt's life on a figurative, spiritual level. Even more intuitively, the title emerged, and only later did the poignant truth of the last line hit me: We are *all* barely touching the earth.

A mortal presence: ephemeral, unexplained—an awakening never guaranteed. Most of us, heads down and blindly rowing through time, much too certain that we *know*.

GLIDE

Still a boy he ran along the tracks:
a whistle blew
something was coming
the roar of an engine
the rattle of tracks and steel

running faster, he hoped to beat
the train somehow—his spirit
on fire against a power he
could not name

and with each heavy breath his legs
rowed through time,

feet barely touching the earth.

Inviting the Bell

"The Way of Heaven is to
benefit others and not to injure.
The Way of the sage is to act
but not to compete."

—LAO TZU

Part II
What Time Reveals

*Know the whole world is nothing when it is compared
to knowing your own inner mystery of life.*

—OSHO

Anna, the author's grandmother, the author and her young son, Matthew, are enjoying a Christmas Eve visit and birthday cake—a shared celebration for the author and her beloved grandmother.

Matthew with his sister, Erin, on Christmas Day.

Easter Morning

In the isolation of grief—self-imposed and otherwise—I'd connected more deeply with aspects of what felt like eternity. A necessary isolation, you could say. Purposeful. And seemingly part of the universal plan for our spiritual evolution—the stark, overpowering contrast of life and death allowing something much greater to shine through: to emerge.

We *need* all of this—my soul journey a mirror image of a more universal one—but a swirl of competing forces still played war games in my head. Life was unpredictable. And uncomfortable. And despite the persistent collision course between the past, present, and future, Easter approached. An unwavering linear calendar confirmed it; sequential days, months, and years, offering no alternative. An invincible pattern that marched on quite oblivious to human proclivities. Its certainty, annoying, and most unpersuasive even as it pointed toward a lovely holiday honoring renewal, optimism, and beginnings.

I wasn't remotely certain about such concepts in 2008. How does one tiptoe forward feeling traumatized by the past, tricked by the present, uncertain about the future?

Despite the illusory nature of time—a mystifying dynamic that seemed contradictory, if not beyond true comprehension—it was master of all. Sometimes, to assuage the unpleasant sensation of confinement to a suffocating tunnel called past, one severed from the forward motion of humanity, I tried to concentrate on especially poignant memories. Scanning for the tiniest details like a miner panning for gold, I searched for something ephemeral in an expression, and there, swam freely in the memory's depth, granting it a powerful immediacy, long expired.

There wouldn't be an opportunity to build on these memories—a stopping point had intervened—but I could linger on the warmth of a particular smile, dwell on a knowing glance that captured something essential, even timeless, or relive bright waves of laughter that were carefree, as if beautifully innocent and utterly complete. Then, as if someone whispered time's up, I worked to convince myself that the dogged push of time had swept it all—warm laughter, eyes conveying love, understanding, and appreciation—aside.

This, however, only led to a massive drain of psychic energy. So I was never sure if deep remembering helped me contend with the vagaries of time, or simply flattened me to the ground. Regardless, Easter arrived. A rush of memories dared me to come closer, to face the details of days that evolved into a last visit with Matt.

The waterfall of time was again in charge, so I finally peered inward—reluctantly.

Conflicting Signs

Spring 2007, Easter weekend. I opened the front door and there was Matt. With a big smile, he dropped his duffel bag, wrapped his arms around me—happiness flooded the room. I hadn't seen him since Christmas, when we'd traveled back to the Black Hills to rendezvous with family members for the holidays. In a rented cabin on Deer Mountain, just north of Deadwood, South Dakota, and within walking distance of decent ski slopes, it was a memorable (and joyful) trip.

Matt, however, had ordered a drink or two during family dinners—nothing excessive, but alcohol in any amount sparked my immediate concern. Recovering addicts are at risk when any *substance* is involved, and while he probably just wanted to enjoy the holidays like everyone else, his history was unique. Matt's challenges were about life and death. The usual concerns, work and housing issues, health and exercise, financial matters and saving money, buying a car, relationships or religion, were only partially relevant to him.

Later, when alone, I'd asked Matt about this.

Asked, specifically, how drinking, even socially, supported his plan for recovery—his goal to stay clean, free of drugs. But immediately, Matt's defense mechanisms kicked in, as he rushed to explain how good he was doing (didn't I *see* that?), and how a few beers were no big deal. Maybe I should quit worrying so much, he added, as his tone grew more hostile, his logic more deadly. Familiar alarms sounded in my head and, sadly, I knew, on some level, that we'd lost him all over again. Rationalizing, being dishonest with himself, with me or anyone who would listen, was never a hopeful sign. Discouraged, I took some deep breaths, wondered what to say or do, but when he reverted to tough guy mode—my life, just leave me the hell alone—talking to Matt was futile. After staying clean for a few months, as usual he was trying to deny the dangerous ramifications of behavior that would never support his recovery.

Post-holidays, Matt was headed for relapse, hell-bent, in fact. While we are all capable of deluding ourselves about troubling personal traits and patterns, many addicts specialize in this—believing what they choose, shunning the rest. And Matt desperately wanted to believe he had the self-control, the emotional strength, to live exactly the way he wanted to live ("like everyone else") and *still* recover.

The disconcerting contradiction his thinking revealed was obvious, but addiction and sound reasoning are unlikely partners. Addicts devise their own logic: mostly, whatever they want to believe in the moment. And telling people "not to worry" is standard cover for a dubious sense of self, for wanting to do "whatever" without interference. Sadly, for Matt, it also translated to feigned bravado that was actually arrogance and unpersuasive pride. What he seemed to want to say was, I *wish* there was nothing to worry about, but for now please let me keep pretending that somehow I can survive this disquieting path by repeatedly telling myself there is nothing to worry about.

Self-absorbed thinking can be extremely glossy and darkly convenient, can't it?

So when Matt made the seven-hour drive to Indianapolis on Good Friday, April 6, 2007, I wanted to feel justifiably hopeful, but the inevitable relapse, the one I'd anticipated after Christmas, had occurred.

And now, after a subsequent relapse in late winter, he insisted that he'd reversed course in time. *Knew* the steps to take; *knew* he could do it this time. We (John and me) sat around our kitchen table listening to him explain in a subdued tone how he'd suffered from loneliness and depression—a cold, gray winter—but was feeling better as the days warmed. As spring approached. The three apple trees from the Easter before also had made it through the winter: were greening, showing signs of life.

Matt was encouraged. We should be, too, he insisted.

But my usual optimism—a mother's hope—showed only meager signs of life, and sagged noticeably when I looked closely at my son. Thin. Draped eyes that conveyed a new and noticeable weariness. Skin with a dull, gray hue. Matt looked older than his 27 years—much older than he'd looked at Christmas, in fact, only three months prior. The ugly roller coaster of relapse, recovery was taking its toll; long-term recovery sounded more and more like a dream—remote, at best.

What should we do? What could we do? What was Matt willing to do; what hadn't he tried or discovered? What kind of treatment program did he need now and where would he find it, how would he finance it? Would something considerably more dreadful have to happen to spark a lasting recovery? Was even the smallest miracle too much to expect?

Matt agreed, without argument or excuses, to attend an Easter Vigil that night at the Catholic Church just north of our home and, as usual, seemed happy to be sharing the weekend with us. Matt's apparent joy, at times like this, was one of his more authentic traits: an endearing quality I will always miss. Part of him found easy contentment in conversation, nature, pets, card games, family dinners, watching a movie that made us laugh, or just reminiscing about "good times." In the throes of addiction that part of our relationship was usually lost, or badly minimized, so it was especially meaningful when the sun broke through the thick haze of difficult times.

Then, life felt right, and it didn't feel wrong (naïve) to hope for more days like this.

On Christmas Eve, during the winter gathering I mentioned, I recall Matt pulling me aside during a family card game to say, "Mom, I just love it when everybody is together like this." Those few words coming so spontaneously from him had meant a great deal. And, now, with his voice silenced, they ring ever louder in my memory.

Faraway Look

The Saturday after Good Friday was a raw day draped in somber hues. It was the first weekend in April, but Easter was early, and our weather seemed resistant, unprepared. Matt, in contrast, was eager to get moving, said he had energy to burn.

I made banana pancakes for breakfast, and we shared our ideas for the day. Matt offered to rake the backyard.

Our massive oaks dropped plenty of twigs and small branches in winter. Still scattered everywhere, John and Matt grabbed warm jackets and gloves, headed outside. Later, when I glanced at them from the kitchen window, they were stuffing yard debris into the chiminea. Flames, red and orange, darted from the top. Sparks flew.

Signs of life.

Noticing the little things helped. Besides offering respite from a persistent stream of worry and doubt, they somehow had the ability to speak the loudest.

Staying warm by the blaze in their summer lawn chairs, they talked, laughed like old friends. Seizing the moment, I grabbed a jacket, a camera. After convincing them to endure a few pictures, John stood up, took the camera. "Stand by Matt," he said.

Not the greatest picture—Matt's ongoing battle was apparent; we both looked cold—its poignancy stretches beyond time, expectations. Matt in his chair, me standing behind him with my arms around his shoulders, my chin resting on his head—the beige ball cap. Purely instinctive, but he was with us—a small miracle, after all—and something within me seemed to whisper: *dwell on the gratitude of his presence.* I'm glad I didn't know it would be the last picture taken of us.

An ordinary moment on the day before Easter, it's a picture I return to often. Maybe I'm still trying to envision a different aftermath, one arriving less than three months later. None of us knew what the future held, but the noticeable dreariness of the day seemed to point in all the wrong directions. Brittle leaves, dusty brown and lifeless, blew aimlessly around the yard, and the entire scene, except for the short-lived, well-contained fire, was devoid of color. Spring was nowhere in sight.

Trying to shrug off a random sense of dread, a nagging, open-ended fear, I went back inside. The future was a perpetual question mark where Matt was concerned, and while I had hoped spring and Easter would bring a sense of renewal, the faraway look in Matt's eyes told a different story. The residual influence of meth produced a restless energy in him, and I asked myself how many times he could walk this deadly path without giving up. For that matter, how many times could I summon the faith to believe in a better day: to brush aside yet another cold, gray morning?

Maybe I had been as weary as Matt, as I sought the courage to accept uncertainty—in this context, a reality that can overwhelm. But hugging him good-bye Monday morning, I remembered his apple trees were coming back to life. *Wasn't that a good sign?*

Though lovely symbols of growth and rejuvenation, as things turned out, they weren't reliable indicators of anything. Apple trees Matt was once proud of, that's all. Someone took his picture by them after they were planted. Well-staked and putting on new leaves, he was beaming—showing them off with an outstretched arm.

Look, the trees are alive, growing! Sometimes things do go right.

But the oddest aspect of our parting—a final parting—that unforgettable morning in early April, was this: he hugged me at the door, started to walk to his car (engine idling), and then turned around, walked back. A second hug. A reluctance. *Something unspoken.*

He'd never done this before.

Had he sensed, subconsciously, the end was imminent, or had he just hated to leave? Was Matt longing for a greater sense of security around an uncertain future? More than likely he didn't have the precise words (or couldn't share them) for what he was feeling; maybe he was hesitant to return to the farm, the questionable (dangerous) influence of old friends. Vague trepidation he might never return, or grateful for the time we'd spent together?

I'll never know what prompted his unusual display of affection. I could only guess as I waved good-bye and closed the door. *When he called from the road, it might come up.* Later, when he did call, Matt sounded lonely, a bit down, but that wasn't unusual for him after a visit. Otherwise, we didn't talk about his departure, if anything special was on his mind. Perhaps I should have asked, but I didn't want to embarrass him—or probe too deeply. That usually didn't go well. Should I have stopped him from leaving, been able to sense that something horrific was in the offing?

Outwitting time, and perhaps the inevitable, is never in the cards.

A Silent Presence

Now, a year later, it was the first Easter without Matt. I sat down at my desk to send a couple of cards. One to Erin, one to my mother. From habit, I usually dated cards in the upper right corner. But I changed my mind this time, and merely wrote: *Easter morning.*

On an intuitive level, I knew dates were irrelevant, and it felt liberating to focus on the day—the moment—itself. There was such lovely poetry in Easter morning: lilies, spring blossoms, greening trees and lawns, straw baskets and hats, pastels and white shoes. My usual reference to the calendar felt beside the point. A specific year according to the gods of time but, simultaneously, much more. It was *every* Easter wrapped into one.

The hint of colored eggs in the cool grass with a spring wind blowing long hair in my eyes. A chocolate bunny wrapped in shiny foil; a yellow and pink straw basket with plastic grass and tiny chocolate eggs. A girl's white purse, just enough room inside for a tissue or a piece of gum; shiny new shoes to wear with a pink dress. A hat with blue ribbon that I didn't want to wear to church. Or anywhere. White gloves for small hands.

Easter, all of this and more.

Family dinners with siblings and cousins, aunts and uncles, my grandmother. White tablecloths, white candles, heaping bowls of green beans and sweet potatoes, sliced ham. An Easter lily perched nearby. Lemon pie. Maybe banana cream or apple. Blueberry or pecan possibly in the mix, a fluffy coconut cake, strawberry shortcake.

Funny, isn't it, how desserts are the best part of special meals?

∽

Easter 2006, another curiously haunting day, also looms large in my memory, almost as clearly as Easter 2007, the visit that was his last. Matt had finally completed a long-term treatment program, one he spoke highly of, while serving two more years (about seven in all, of an 11-year sentence for a felony conviction that involved acquiring some $220 for drugs—regarding the exact amount, there are those things we *want* to forget—plus a possession charge when paroled), and was quietly enthused, as usual, about recovery: another chance to get it right. While away, he'd grown a long, rather thick mustache, not his usual style, and seemed in pretty good spirits—looked rested and content, though slightly tentative.

Out in the world again; how will I manage this time?

I took in his newish blue jeans, a long-sleeved, Gap Athletic, white shirt, and scuffed cowboy boots. I could *almost* envision good days ahead. Predictable, safe, hopeful.

We'd driven to Hannibal, Missouri, from Indianapolis to meet Matt at a riverside park for an Easter picnic. Mark Twain country, and a gift without price or measure to spend time with him outside of an institutional setting, so we braved the day with smiles and optimism, despite the blustery wind that almost blew away our red-and-white checkered tablecloth. We held it down with whatever we could find.

Yet somewhere in the background, the familiar pulse of worry rubbed the shine from the day—even as I reminded myself it was *okay* to feel relaxed, happy, even encouraged. That despite my son's history, the terrifying odds that stood firmly in his path, I wanted to remain present and enjoy the moment, even against the weight of accumulated sorrow, legitimate trepidation. But on that breezy afternoon of guarded promise, a coveted Easter reunion, our valiant smiles took enormous courage: the kind that must be otherworldly. There we were: sanguine souls with our heads down in a ferocious storm, believing the next clear day wasn't far away.

Then again, facing something so frightening and worrisome, maybe we could scarcely breathe. Our proximity to death was completely unknown, yet the future sat there with us at our picnic table. A silent presence that dared not speak on that partly sunny day on the banks of the Mississippi River in the imposing shadow of Tom Sawyer and Huck Finn. Perhaps Mark Twain's keen understanding of human nature—his literary ghost—offered inspiration for this poem about that unforgettable day of troubling mixed messages.

GRAY EDGES

A stretch of green-brown water,
waves bouncing against the river's

shoreline, stood watch over our
spring picnic, one that came as a

gift after a long absence, yet the
blustery afternoon, all dressed in

undertones of gray, felt wistful,
and I had to wonder if the stretch

of time behind him stood a chance
as a lasting passage, a lifeline,

or was it yet another devilish facet
of a treacherous slow ending.

Three Easters in a row, 2006, Hannibal and the picnic, 2007, last visit home, and by 2008 cards that simply said Easter morning—a breezy delicate dawn that cradled thousands of moments, millions of beginnings.

It had been a treacherous slow ending for Matt, for us, but we are all on that slippery slide; we are all part of something that encompasses every dawn and every sunset without distinction. Like a planetary magic trick time conceals, and time reveals. Or as Shakespeare might put it, "All the world's a stage, and all the men and women merely players."

Inviting the Bell

"The Way of Heaven is to
benefit others and not to injure.
The Way of the sage is to act
but not to compete."

—LAO TZU

Looking for God is like seeking a path in a field of snow;
if there is no path and you are looking for one,
walk across it and there is your path.

—THOMAS MERTON

Persistent Rain

The death of my son generated a powerful waterfall that spilled into all aspects of my life—its influence not to be contained. Close relationships were no exception. Matt's sudden absence a burning emptiness—individually, collectively—in all of us; a void that sought expression in various and sometimes daring ways. Other than my ex-husband, my daughter and I shared the longest history with Matt, and as Erin's 30th birthday approached, I began to understand how often I thought of her as half of my favorite pair: the Matt and Erin pair.

Digging into old photo albums one Sunday morning, the powerful realization hit me. Daughter and son as joyful young children, teens, and then adults. Like one word, their names rolled off my tongue, forever intertwined. So many experiences had involved *both*—a younger brother with his older sister, the older sister with a younger brother. A family unit, a special and unique combination, not one or the other, alone or divided.

Sitting in a crowded church pew a few hours later on a brusque winter day, I found myself dwelling on this during the sermon. Maybe my reflection was counted as private prayer, perhaps not, but either way I remembered how both of them had arrived in mid-February, missing Valentine's Day by a couple of days on either side. Friends and family brought me chocolate candy in heart-shaped boxes. Winter babies, they were Aquarians, according to astrological charts, and weighing in at or a little under seven pounds, both were in good health—and cherished.

Almost exactly two years apart, we chose strong names for them. Names that felt right, not contrived or trendy. Erin and Matt were born when I was in my mid-twenties; the typical American family—one boy, one girl—just like that. Described as strong-willed and bright by those who spent time with them as children (day care providers, babysitters, preschool teachers, friends and family), of course I had no inkling that my beautiful young son would, one day, experience daunting challenges. Like good friends who sometimes annoyed each other, Matt and Erin laughed and teased, sang and danced, listened to stories, and learned new words from children's books with playful illustrations.

Playing with abandon, that enchanting innocence of childhood so apparent, they loved the usual things: swimming, sledding, making cookies, decorating the lower branches of Christmas trees. Another favorite: making elaborate tents with sheets and blankets. Both hugged, cared for dolls in buggies; both enjoyed weekends at the family farm.

And when it came to drawing, painting, coloring, creating "people" out of Play-Doh—it was a joy to see those early learning skills develop.

Watching them discover the world reopened the windows of my childhood, as well. I love author Elizabeth Lawrence's (1904–1985) description of such memories: "There is a garden in every childhood, an enchanted place where colors are brighter, the air softer, and the morning more fragrant than ever again." *Than ever again.*

Before becoming a parent, I knew I wanted to raise spirited children with a sparkle in their eye, a spring in their step, a smile on their face. The things we are taught to believe are indicators of joy, intelligence, and kindness. But life, miraculous and mysterious, was also a high-challenge endeavor; I wanted them to feel certain of themselves, determined and confident. In other words, I encouraged them to grow strong wings of their own.

I believed that domineering, overbearing parents raised passive, insecure children who lived to please and obey, somehow unable to fully experience (or commit to) their unique life path: to discover their truest selves, their God-given potential, their deepest spiritual yearnings. Whenever practical, I gave them options to help them grow in self-awareness.

This meant offering simple and safe decision-making opportunities: what color socks or shorts to wear; what games to play; what to fix for lunch or snacks; what to watch on TV; what to read; what toys to buy; what songs to sing. Things relevant to the world of children. I believed it was better to offer them alternatives—within an appropriate range of acceptable choices—than to constantly proclaim, "My way is the only (or best) way."

No one grows much in a dull, lifeless dictatorship, and I wanted their childhood to be creative and happy; them thriving in a stimulating environment that encouraged learning and self-respect. Erin and Matt responded well. They were engaged, joyful, curious. We took neighborhood walks with pets or friends, went to the park when the trees budded in spring, returning frequently on good-weather days, and at least once a year, traveled to my hometown in South Dakota so Matt and Erin could spend quality time with my family—sample my world as a girl, the place I'd grown up connected to the prairie in lasting ways.

After story hour at the library, we rummaged through the shelves, checking out books by the armload (Dr. Seuss, a major favorite). One Christmas, I arranged, like gifts, their growing collection of holiday books under the tree. Erin, to my surprise, continued the tradition for many years. Well-worn books, perhaps, had become as important to her as bright ribbons and bows atop *new* gifts.

And, of course, we went for ice cream, discovered bakeries, rode bikes, and spoiled our pets, usually a cat. Dancer, a black and white male, liked to trail behind us when we went for a walk. Matt and Erin loved learning programs like *Mr. Rogers' Neighborhood* and *Sesame Street*, often imitating their favorite characters.

We talked about those less fortunate—we cared, and connected as a family. Could it be more complicated than that? I had no reason to suspect otherwise. Nothing unusual, perplexing, or troubling presented itself. Pediatrician visits were uneventful—no emotional, physical, or mental issues surfaced. Matt spent a few days in the hospital with complications from an ear infection right after his first birthday, but otherwise, they were content, growing, and seemingly well-adjusted.

The priest closed the mass, and the pews emptied. Our Lady of Mount Carmel Catholic Church was a warm, spirited place. Father Richard had a beautiful voice (he'd recorded a CD), and the outreach center (food pantry, special clinics) was called Matthew 25.

As we'd filed out in a slow, quiet shuffle, I'd watched parishioners greet one another, heard low, respectful voices but, in the moment, was also wondering if my memories of Matt and Erin's childhood were too glossy, too selective.

As a young mother many miles from her original family, surely I'd felt overwhelmed and uncertain at times and, surely, as they'd grown, I'd worried about each step forward. Would they be safe yet courageous—assertive but not aggressive—and would they find contentment in nature, in healthy relationships, in what the world could reasonably offer? There must have been a number of days when I grew tired or felt perplexed by life itself.

We know so very little in our twenties, don't we?

Walking toward the large parking lot, spotting my car amidst a sea of vehicles, I heard soothing church bells—a glorious sound— spotted children everywhere. Some held hands with adults or siblings, others trailed behind or led the way. With a layer of fresh snow on the ground, it was slow going. Infants and very young children were all bundled up, held close by a parent, a grandparent.

What would their lives be like?

What devilish snags would they encounter; would lucky breaks emerge when needed the most; what sort of gut-wrenching losses would they endure?

Getting in my car, putting on my seat belt, and exiting the parking lot behind a trail of slow-moving vehicles, I hoped they would discover their inherent spirituality. It wouldn't matter if they followed a specific religion, dogma and teachings shrouded in many shades of political and historical lore, but it would matter if they discovered their inner worlds, their spiritual essences. God, as I see it, is not only an all-encompassing force beyond our full mortal appreciation and understanding, but is also inherent to the spirit within.

Ralph Waldo Emerson made this wise (and progressive) suggestion: "Make your own Bible. Select and collect all the words and sentences that in all your readings have been to you like the blast of a trumpet." Even Pope Francis has chimed in, noting that "one can be spiritual but not religious."

Following what others have proclaimed can be helpful to a point, but blind allegiance can also leave many mired in a futile search for answers on an external level. Words are only words until we develop the capacity, the spiritual awareness, to internalize and actualize their message. This, I've learned, requires looking within long enough (deeply enough) to put it all together in a way that is unique yet universal: an ever-evolving process that can sound confusing or paradoxical until grasped on an almost primal level.

Sacred Territory

Parenting is neither a perfect art, nor a perfect science, and parents, the entire world over, are imperfect beings—learning under pressure, on the job. During my short drive home, I thought more about the children at church. Some sat quiet, subdued; several were fidgety, restless, and a few cried. One young boy with longish hair pulled at his mother's brown corduroy jacket with pleading eyes. So many stories, so many hopeful beginnings.

I could still hear the church music. The small choir bustling with instruments, music, and microphones. Obviously, perfection wasn't the goal when raising and loving a child. Most of us, consciously or otherwise, emulate our parents in ways we admired or agreed with, but we also try to do it our own way, don't we? As the choir sang, I'd remembered with loving clarity my grandmother perched at her old player piano. Fascinated by her wrinkled fingers on the keys, the calm joy she expressed when playing, I liked whatever tune Anna came up with. But I was a quiet, cooperative, child, especially after six years in a Catholic school. Navy blue plaid jumpers, white blouses. Mass every morning.

Instinctively, I kept a low profile: Don't upset the nuns! I would have been seriously embarrassed if negative attention had come my way. I paid attention, earned good grades, followed directions, raised my hand, said my prayers, walked in a straight line, and tried not to whisper in the halls.

Was I looking for the safest route to the next grade? Without a doubt.

In junior and senior high, I read profusely, spent time with friends, and stayed on the honor roll. Getting in trouble, breaking rules, or taking careless risks, wasn't part of my world, and that suited me fine. Had I been slightly too cooperative: compliant, eager to get along, pleasant—like most females of my era? Possibly.

Growing up in a hectic household with five children and silly, sparring parents, I dreamt of like-minded adults in a happier setting. We enjoyed plenty of good times, but bickering that seemed largely habitual can't help but communicate an overall unwillingness to tow the family boat in a unified, purposeful, constructive direction. That's not to say I wasn't well cared for during my growing-up years, because I truly was, but it felt like the adults weren't connecting all that well.

Then again, my main point of comparison was my grandmother's quiet, solitary life. Anna's dependable kindness, undivided attention, and compassionate demeanor felt very natural to me. Of course, she'd matured fully, had something *real* and *substantive* to give; plus, she wasn't raising children, holding down jobs, making mortgage and car payments.

Things were smooth-sailing with her and, understandably, the emotional pull was strong. "No worries" could have been her mantra— to an impressionable young girl, Anna was contentment personified.

Pulling in our driveway, I opened the garage, drove in, but sat in the warm car a few more seconds. I was trying to figure *something* out, and didn't want to lose the trail.

When I became a mother in the late 1970s, a curious mix of childhood influences came to life in me, but children, I believe, are meant to stretch us. Erin and Matt were eager to push the limits. Free-thinkers, and not nearly as concerned as I'd been about staying out of trouble, reciting prayers, or living up to the expectations of others, I wouldn't have had it any other way. They were energetic seekers, seemingly unafraid to discover their own answers, even if that meant an unconventional or contrarian approach.

But with Matthew gone and strangely absent, my certainty, that morning after church, felt more like uncertainty.

I headed inside, closed the garage, and Noah, with his usual heartwarming enthusiasm, greeted me at the door.

Looking around for John, I found him in the kitchen working on lunch.

"How was church?" he asked, chopping onion, green pepper.

I didn't attend on a "must-go-every-Sunday" basis (God is everywhere, in *everything*, not just in a church), and usually John also went, but today he stayed home to relax a bit. I told him about the little girl in the fuzzy blue coat; how I'd watched her walk to the exit with her mother. My eyes trailed them as others shuffled in pews, gathered up coats, hats, and mittens.

I had some difficulty imagining my daughter's life without a brother. If they already had adult families of their own, this jarring separation might have been easier, more natural. But I'd noticed how Matt lived on in our conversations. Spoken or unspoken, he was with us: in memory, in spirit. Maybe things weren't so terribly final, our group identity merely shifting in space, in time, in essence.

On better days, I could nearly say the word *family* without feeling awash in emotional turmoil. Usually, though, the unassuming word pierced my awareness with something painfully perplexing, and while the significant others in my life had changed, the three of us, a poetic trio—Erin, Matt, Mom—hadn't. *That* was the definition of family I'd wanted to believe was solidly in place, until *my* death.

Relaxing at an antique table (I loved the history it quietly conveyed), I surveyed the winter scene just beyond the kitchen: sun-brightened patches of snow, squirrels searching for food, birds skittering about to stay warm. I visualized the church doors, parishioners pouring forth in waves like brave soldiers off to battle, released anew.

What issues were they facing; how many had also lost a child, children?

I hadn't anticipated the need to grieve for my children's child-hood … again. Hadn't I done this, the years slipping by, merging, like melted butter, one into the next? Yes, but a deeper kind of letting go was required now, and yet another reason why Matt's absence felt so enormous. Losing a child forces us to revisit a sacred territory: a place many of us are never able to give up completely, until (or unless) there is no choice offered.

Not bravely, but most cautiously, I meandered through miles of heart-shaped memories of angelic faces, tiny hands and feet, trusting smiles, first words and steps.

Good Intentions

Matthew's 28th birthday rolled around without him; Erin drove to Indianapolis for the weekend. When they were young, and into their teens, we celebrated many of their birthdays together, but this year, we were more like lost souls.

I had arranged for a morning mass in Matt's memory, but after much indecision, we opted to stay home. Sounds awful, doesn't it?

The simple truth is that we couldn't face seeing his name on the bulletin; didn't want to hear his name spoken from the altar. Too soon, I thought, with pangs of guilt. We didn't trust our emotions, though, and maybe we weren't ready to face Matthew's death in a public setting. Coming to understand, only in hindsight, our unexpected hesitation, I was glad we hadn't pushed ourselves to do something we weren't comfortable with.

Matt, in particular, would have accepted our misgivings without undue analysis. His heart was generally compassionate, uncomplicated. But living in a foreign reality, such that we were, even seemingly easy things turned into a maze of contradiction and confusion. Grief is when *nothing* feels right, and there's no place to hide.

Even my keen sense of timing was off. A dedicated mass had sounded fine while planning it, but that feeling hadn't endured.

Waving good-bye to Erin from the driveway—her birthday visit coming to a close—I was glad we had at least ventured into the kitchen to stir up an elegant-looking red velvet cake. As though starting over, we put a single candle on top, and the red tulips I'd picked up at the florist for her were a pleasant contrast to February snow. I smiled, just picturing the jolly-looking snowman she'd built in the backyard.

And not making it to church was put aside, as I considered Erin's challenge: the cumbersome days ahead. Grateful for her warm presence in our lives—her reassuring smile, our shared history—I knew Matt's sudden loss had impacted her life in ways she, too, was only beginning to understand.

Innocence Relinquished

Everyone feels the pain of loss differently. If I doubted this, being married while coping with significant loss took care of that. Our personal histories were unremarkable, but like all couples, far from identical. And, of course, we had unique relationships with Matthew. Beyond labels and time, however, we were committed to the same things.

A simple but meaningful lifestyle; an enduring relationship built on shared priorities; contributing to the well-being of those we loved; caring about the planet, critical social issues, and whatever else felt relevant. After Matt's death, though, we found ourselves in somewhat new terrain. Challenges weren't uncommon given Matt's history, but intense sorrow altered our landscape, and instantly exceeded accumulated experience. Likewise, our coping mechanisms weren't identical, so we had to gradually tease out the best ways to support each other once the heaviness of grief set in.

Countless other variables came into sharp focus.

For instance, we, as a concept, as a reality, had to evolve into something new: a "we" that didn't include Matthew, in the physical sense, as part of our lives. A deeply personal journey, obviously, yet one we were also on together. Not by choice, nor design, but we made a lifetime commitment when Matt was here, body and soul, and sensed that while death wasn't something we'd expected or felt prepared for, it was ours to grapple with. Given the enormous, tangled complications of Matt's fight to overcome addiction, we'd developed a strong, flexible foundation that definitely helped. Admittedly, though, grief pushed us to evolve in ways never imagined.

Did we, for instance, pressure ourselves to "feel better" for each other's benefit? Of course. And though we could dream of keeping an identical calendar, managing unique emotions and needs at the same time, that wasn't realistic given the strenuous situation thrust upon us. Fortunately, we didn't over-react, believed in patience to see us through the harrowing stretch ahead. Amazing what a little common sense can offer.

Marriage, regardless of context or history, is all about learning. Ideally, it's also about becoming spiritual partners. Not all couples know there is something beyond traditional, stereotypical roles that often fail to deliver long-lasting or rewarding results. Questioning habitual patterns, superficial expectations gleaned from popular media outlets, cultural influences, or family exposure when young and impressionable is important. So much of what we pick up along the way is oddly reminiscent of a cute, but utterly useless, fairy tale.

Happily ever after gets most people in trouble, and false notions of happiness, possibly the most misused, overused ideal we encounter, can defeat us before we begin.

"The world," reminds Eckhart Tolle in various video programs, "isn't here to make you happy," and relationships are supposed to "wake us up"—to our spiritual identities. Though he speaks from a spiritual perspective, I see the practical aspects of his message. What about his definition of love (*The Power of Now*) posted on many blogs? Pointing to God as the one eternal life form supporting all others, he asks: "What is love? To feel the presence of that One Life deep within yourself and within all creatures." So, essentially, "all love is the love of God." In other words, only by looking within can we value or understand relationships. He also suggests: "To end the misery that has afflicted the human condition for thousands of years," we must begin with ourselves by taking full responsibility for our inner state. Not an entirely new observation, but still worthwhile.

We weren't the first couple to be hurled into extraordinarily hard times by tragedy and emotional upheaval. The more people we talked to about loss, an inevitable cornerstone of mortality, the more we understood that similar experiences were *everywhere*. Though details varied, the essence—the core of the experience—was analogous. Seemingly, the depth of life has little to do with personal details. If loss is a universal experience, and of course it is, then it must be trying to lead us all to the same place.

Life is loss; loss is life. Inseparable components like yin and yang, night and day, hot and cold; imagine polar opposites that seamlessly meld to form the vast universal whole.

I see this now, but when grief was the arrow aimed directly at us, it felt as personal as the first day of kindergarten, and while a broader, more enlightened perspective flickered in our awareness, it was mostly as a distant promise. And telling ourselves we weren't the first to bury a son, that many have been through much worse, missed the mark entirely.

The "everyone has to go sometime" comments, like generic mandates and overworked sentiments that felt distancing, not comforting, challenged us to go beyond them. In many ways grief held us prisoner, allowing in only a sliver of light, a particle of nourishment, a drop of water. We were forced inward to survive. And while those peering in—sometimes awkwardly, or critically—from the outside felt oddly baffled by the complexity of the process, its duration and demands, I was fortunate to be with a spouse who understood the pressing, fundamental need for space and time. We both did.

John had known Matt since his sixth grade year. With a strong history of relationship, they had weathered many of the growing-up years together. I'm sure that helped John to appreciate my unenviable position: an unwilling, unhappy, exhausted traveler; a mother who tirelessly believed in her son's ability to conquer the complex issues that plagued him, persistently searching for creative, progressive answers in countless directions.

When we revisited the emotional wreckage, we tirelessly asked ourselves what went wrong. Had a life course gone amiss, a young life unduly lost, or had Matt's destiny pre-determined a brief, 27-year path? Of course we aren't meant to know these things—*can never know*—but such useless musings seemed to beg for a place of perpetual life in my psyche, living on like a cold, persistent rain.

But as the spiritual realm became more apparent—vital, rewarding, relevant—I began to understand, on a God-fearing level, that, like the enchanting innocence of childhood, nothing lasted. I knew life was fragile, fleeting before Matt died, but I didn't *know* it from very close range—a difference, largely inexpressible.

Thoughts can be as empty as barren land, but living through hardship connects us to our soul like a laser. We must know pain firsthand. Innocence must be relinquished to grow spiritually.

Inviting the Bell

"The Way of Heaven is to
benefit others and not to injure.
The Way of the sage is to act
but not to compete."

—LAO TZU

We are only just beginning to understand the power of love because we are just beginning to understand the weakness of force and aggression.

—B.F. SKINNER, *WALDEN TWO*

Saving Things

We drove to the Missouri cemetery on Memorial Day. I arranged pictures from our visit into a collage. The calendar—I was still sporadically hitched to that dreary, rusty wagon called time—pointed to 2010, but Picasso's perspective, "the hidden harmony is better than the obvious," pointed elsewhere. Specifically to a non-linear universe with little bearing on sequential explanations or traditional expectations.

So when I shared the collage with family members in memory of a three-year journey beyond Matt's physical presence, I included Picasso's keen observation. I loved how it captured the ongoing integration of loss into the fabric of daily routines. Perfect, because sketchy elements of harmony were apparent in the pictures I selected. Even the tombstone spoke of life and death without division. Engraved with a sheaf of wheat, a cross, and a famous quote ("Blessed are the pure in heart, for they will see God," Matthew 5:8) that resonated with a timeless message, it seemed to reflect the twisting river of sparkling energy we are born into and depart from, never knowing precisely why.

And couldn't that quote be interpreted to mean … for they will see God … within?

In the collage there was a picture of me standing by the arch-shaped stone, a similar one of John, and there were pictures of Matt—alive, engaged, smiling. A stately oak tree behind his grave brought the photos into peaceful synergy; the vibrant green suggesting a gracious outpouring of life—a dynamic force rooted in quiet repose. And I hadn't overlooked the contrasting realities that quietly emanated from the dance of weaving branches. Life and death *could* coexist as elements of a mysterious whole: as facets of the same.

After enlarging pictures of the tree, I framed them, hung them on the west wall of my writing study to remind me of the power of life to bring us closer to ourselves through time's poetic unraveling—the mystifying yet inevitable process that hopefully leads to awakening and spiritual realization. For me, to an intense spiritual encounter that pushed me to grow ever-deepening spiritual roots.

The collage, that my subconscious seemed to create, also confirmed that my spiritual journey had intensified—in ways I hadn't pieced together before. I had reasons to be hopeful, after all. But … it was only with this poignant realization that I decided to finish writing this book. It had been on hold, because I couldn't muster the stamina to proceed, and I absolutely needed more time to glance at the other side, the ground around me still shifting.

Life anchors had vanished; points of reference had disappeared like a summer sun; and time hadn't magically healed all wounds, as many had promised or assumed. So it wasn't like, "wow, that's all behind me now, time to move on." *Not at all.*

Rather, I felt greatly subdued by everything I'd experienced, and couldn't understand why so much uncertainty persisted.

In fact, when I studied the collage, the array of pictures fitting together almost artfully, I felt oddly aware that I had no idea what the next day would bring. I was free-floating to the next destination in a vague, unstructured kind of way, while hoping to sustain a hard-earned, still emergent spiritual path.

Frequently wondering when this arduous transition might complete itself, show signs of consistent relief, at least, I still delved into painful questions almost daily. Irrationally, I held up an invisible yardstick to measure my progress, to see how I was doing against spoken, unspoken expectations, but a strange inner vacancy held firm—one laced with fruitless, time-based questions—even as I hoped for something more illuminating.

Did *aftermath* have an end point? Would *acceptance* arrive with a bang, a whimper, or at all? What did life-after-loss mean, precisely?

I reminded myself that Matt's absence would only gradually become integral to a new self-definition—one I'd never known. Caught up in a fluid process without parameters, it would never come to an end like the flu, a troubling dream, a hail storm. Life integration was the proper term, the wisest perspective, but the murky process stalled without notice, so I was reluctant to trust those rare days that felt less tenuous.

It remained alarmingly easy to get seriously lost in dark swirls of self-criticism, fear, frustration.

Everyone wants me to forget my son.

I'd accurately sensed that some people were watching to see if the worst was over, as they anxiously tried to decide if I'd returned to my "old self" yet, or to my "normal self."

How could anyone remain unchanged after what I'd been through? Such a person would have to be made of stone.

What was so great about my old self anyway?

I knew from my work with nonprofit organizations, and life experience, of course, that everyone resists change. Change of any kind or magnitude, and for any reason, shakes us up, forces us to look within to figure things out, to grow. Logically, as I changed, others were forced to square off with their own mortality, and that's what they wanted to avoid, bottom-line. It's almost childlike how much we resist change, clinging to worn-out roles and expectations as though they *permanently* define us.

Maybe we want to believe we can prevent the light of change from ever touching our personal worlds. Yet, cherished comfort zones are destined to disappear and, without a doubt, life always ends (in the physical sense).

Driving to the post office, I mailed the collage to those sharing the highlights of our journey, and knew in that instant that Leonardo da Vinci was right: *While I thought I was learning how to live, I have been learning how to die.* Clearly, we are on Earth to live and learn, but one fragile day after another, we simultaneously must learn how to die: to let go gracefully, to trust the infinite power that created humanity, to accept the dire brevity of existence. It sounded harsh, sounded dreadful. But as I drove the short distance home, my insight only deepened, despite my efforts to look the other way.

Cottonwoods and Geese

In August 2008 we moved back to South Dakota. We'd lived in Indianapolis for five years, but I was seeking the solace of my roots. So when the opportunity to move came via John's career, we chose a small college town on the eastern side of the state—fairly close to the Twin Cities.

We'd both grown up in small towns, and a break from city life sounded appealing, timely. Still, moving invariably has a few drawbacks. Hard to leave behind a yard, a garden that had been a labor of love, for instance.

What would grow, what would die … once we left?

What plants might the new owners decide to uproot?

We had hung feeders to attract a variety of birds; tried in vain to outsmart determined squirrels before they emptied them; kept the bird bath clean and filled; listened for the easy poetry of wind chimes. In the heart of summer, I loved how clematis vines climbed our north fence like colorful curtains of purple, blue, and white. Tiger lilies near the back of our yard flourished in just the right amount of sun and shade, and towering sunflowers I'd planted on a whim stunned us with their massive faces.

I loved how they leaned into the sun.

Moving west only a year after Matt's death, I worried about the demands of a new yard: would I have the energy to create beauty again, to water massive evergreens that lined the north side, to hang feeders for different kinds of birds—those native to eastern Dakota? Luckily, goldfinch (what a brilliant yellow!) lived in both areas, along with blue jays and cardinals.

Nature, with its persistence, has a way of drawing us out, even when it feels unlikely. Granted, it was at a snail's pace but, eventually, I took an interest in our new yard. And, now, I'm still learning not to get overly ambitious when the comforting warmth of spring arrives. After a long, dark, extremely cold winter, bright colors of renewal are very tempting, but invariably, the hot, dry, windy days turn into *real* work.

But taking care of a yard was one thing—avoiding stressful thinking, quite another. Easily, without warning, I'd slip into a futile search for answers I would never have, and once in this mode, with steely resolve, simply had to push through a row of days that felt blank, yet blinding. Plumbing the depths of my soul for *something* to assuage my angst, I wondered if I was hoping to discover unarguable reasons to end my fruitless seeking.

Possibly.

Had I fully accepted the unknown? *Of course not.*

My heart still wanted to know.

Tackling a stack of dishes or a pile of laundry, walking Noah down a quiet sidewalk, or maneuvering my way through the busy aisles of a grocery store, new theories sprang to mind. Sifting through apples or oranges, I would think: Was it the time of his birth, or the karma Matt brought into this funny world? A deadly meeting of cultural influences or the way Matt's brain was wired? Bad luck, or an ending set in motion eons ago, when the universe took its first breath—maybe a condition that science, the medical community, hadn't identified yet?

Maybe someday there would be something to prevent *anyone* from becoming addicted to whatever they were overly drawn to: television, food, sugar, gaming, drama, violence, alcohol, drugs, shopping, negative thought patterns, risk-taking, sports, travel, sex, or whatever you might wish to include.

Strangely, this relentless stream of powdery questions beckoned with the promise of something more. Vague, ephemeral. On an ordinary autumn day in mid-October, when I was strongly aware of that comfortable feeling of being home again, one tough question, in particular, took root. Was there an exact moment when this outcome could have been prevented? Only an omniscient being could give a definitive answer, but I gave full rein to my thoughts anyway. Sitting by a giant cottonwood, golden with color on the shoreline of the Missouri River, maybe, I'd mused, it was okay to dip once more into the dark well of time: my return home providing a bit of a safety net.

Perhaps special insights were built into this return trip.

I was open, listening.

A few feet away, a middle-aged woman with short legs and a yellow lab took in the shoreline; they jogged together with abandon. The scene: inviting, almost idyllic.

What was she thinking?

But my eyes were drawn to the glorious stretch of water in front of me. To the river I'd grown up with when life felt fresh, endless— before invisible days weaved their way into this moment. Matt's life and death tucked into mine in a mysterious yet powerful way. With the lure of familiar surroundings, the Missouri's peaceful blueness seemed to effortlessly open distant doors to the past.

Beginning with Matt's infancy, I considered the days one by one as if "real answers" would suddenly make themselves known to me. If I looked hard enough, long enough; if I could manifest the perfect memory—objective, complete—with a rare ability to discern the precise meaning of each second of his life. Then, only then, would I know why he had been lost to this unfathomable world.

A divorce (albeit amicable) when he was still young? Probably not. Many cope with divorced parents, including myself, without becoming drug addicts.

Perhaps it was the educational, personal challenges he faced; a quick, determined mind—Einstein, at 16, was disruptive in school, dropped out—that resisted structure. Maybe, as some say, the soul chooses the circumstances it needs to develop spiritually. That, in fact, we *dream* our entire lives beforehand. If true, we manifest our destinies, pre-birth, right?

What an interesting premise.

Author Robert Moss, *Dreamgates: Exploring the Worlds of Soul, Imagination, and Life Beyond Death*, claims: "Dreaming, the souls of unborn children choose their parents and rehearse for the lives that lie ahead." Browsing through his book, one eye a wee bit skeptical, I'd admitted that anything, after all, is entirely *possible*.

Geese, preparing to land, glided closer to the water. I turned to watch. Using expert radar systems, they made it look so easy. Carefree perfection came to mind. Nature, a seamless presence under the steely gaze of stars and sun silently aligned with universal prerogatives. Never wondering, refusing, or complaining.

As they landed, I remembered the Walt Whitman quote: "Let your soul stand cool and composed before a million universes." I wanted to bring that kind of knowing presence into the world. The clarity it suggested was most appealing. But as I continued to soak up the warmth of a soothing autumn day, a rather futuristic concern wormed its way into my awareness.

Short of creating a memorial foundation like so many others, how would I keep Matt's memory alive? What *new* place would I find for him that felt creative, appropriate, not weepy, forlorn, or uncomfortable? Writing this book was, of course, one way to broaden the lens of loss. By bringing death into a more timeless light, the sting of physical absence wasn't the *only thing*. We are all losing life—a matter of degree, timing only—so inching across painful landmines, enduring the unspoken, the misunderstood, and the unwanted requires a persistent kind of strength. Finally we learn that life never plays favorites: the universal playing field dependably leveled one way or another.

Yet, this book, and nearly all books, has a definable lifespan. Some classics survive the ravages of time but, realistically, most books are born, mature, and pass into a quiet, ordinary past. With the sad, ever-shorter attention span of our frenzied culture, a book's lifespan can resemble that of a tomato—so I once read. Even if this one earned a blessedly respectable following, questions of "what next" were inevitable.

What else could transform a stream of sorrow and spiritual searching into something constructive? Speeches I should write and deliver, articles I should compose, or nonprofit causes that needed greater involvement and support—innovative organizations with the potential to make critical differences?

A couple of fishing boats, one elaborate and expensive-looking, one basic and several years old, eased their way down stream. Both seemed to know where they were headed. My eyes trailed their steady path until they became tiny dots in the distance. The geese, taking off for chalky blue skies, eased into perfect flight formation. I envied their quiet, noble beauty, their natural contentment, and wondered, in terms of memorial projects, if I could create something this inspiring in Matthew's memory.

Human needs were limitless. Since I'd worked with nonprofits for a long time, it was easy to conjure up viable options. Everything from designing a nonprofit to help children develop and sustain creative interests, to forming an organization that supported spiritual exploration for those in the throes of grief. What about innovative programming around suicide, loss, and all forms of addiction? Would I target children, as that is often where nascent problems are detected, and therefore the best opportunity for positive impact, or was it better to focus on youth—cultural influences so pronounced during those years?

What about the plethora of treatment centers, slow-moving legislation, the antiquated legal system? Mental health systems, mostly overburdened, had to be considered. Since addicts are often self-medicating, how might we better detect mental health, or related issues as prevention, before deeper problems manifest?

What pressing needs exist for educational systems that want to offer a more varied experience, a stimulating environment that meets the unique abilities of each student? What about expanded counseling programs in school systems?

Imagining the number of legitimate (and worthy) needs made my head spin.

Compelling artwork that captured the human struggle—the spirit in continual motion as it labored to survive and thrive—also interested me. I believed Matthew's journey, his long personal struggle, was also humanity's—in its many guises and forms, the seen and the unseen. Sometimes it takes art to capture connections of this magnitude.

Or maybe a special summer garden in Matt's memory was a better way to go.

Clouds were starting to collect in a seamless stretch of blue. The cottonwood tree was also coming to life, its imposing branches swaying to a hidden heartbeat.

I packed up my book, blanket with some reluctance. Hoping for an epiphany of sorts, it hadn't happened. I would have to wait for "the" idea to surface as an intuitive nudge. Surely there was some way to make a difference in the pool of human needs linked, one way or another, to this story of life and loss. Opening the car door, it also occurred to me that I would continue to grow in ways not yet obvious; maybe one day I would choose to dedicate my career to spiritual pursuits—to finding innovative ways to share an evolved, enlightened perspective.

I tried to envision myself opting for a life of prayer, introspection, but it was too soon. Barely glancing at the other side of this gritty path, I was only beginning to learn how to shift my internal gaze beyond the steely bars of time. I still lacked the certainty of stately cottonwoods, the stunning precision of the swift-moving geese.

Cool and Composed

When Matt was in grade school, he didn't like nuts (walnuts or pecans) in cookies, so one evening, about to toss damp clothes in the dryer, I spotted a bag of walnuts. An odd place for such things, but I got his logic. If you want chocolate chip cookies to emerge from the oven without nuts, one simply needs a creative hiding place. Of course the memory stuck—an endearing, youthful antic.

In contrast, my efforts to align Matt's boyhood scheme with incarceration—monthly road trips to spend just a few hours with him in guarded visiting rooms—felt futile: a perilous, ill-advised attempt to merge night and day, sun and moon. Never had I anticipated venturing inside the imposing walls of a prison to visit anyone, but like everything else weaved into this experience—unworn tennis shoes, a dark green coat, blue jeans, a favorite plaid shirt … all things of Matt's I had kept—it was impossible to unearth the logic behind any of it.

Did I *really* think he was returning?

Why was I saving his mortal belongings?

Nonsensical. Surreal. But intrinsic to the journey beyond a personalized sense of self. Saving things gets us through the days we barely understand. With any spiritual mission, the path isn't always apparent, but living from faith delivers adventure, *knowing* a higher power will one day connect the dots, effortlessly, in ways we can't envision.

As Joseph Campbell explained, "If you can see your path laid out in front of you step by step, you know it's not your path. Your own path you make with every step you take. That's why it's your path."

⤳

One evening, I watched Dr. Sanjay Gupta interview Edward Kennedy's son, Patrick, on CNN. "Coming Clean" focused on familiar topics. Kennedy talked openly about rehab, estimating he'd been through some six programs; he discussed the shame of addiction, as well. Mentioning his impending marriage and ongoing efforts to fund research for brain pathologies that include chemical dependency, Kennedy apparently believes addiction is a mental health disease—a disease of the brain, a neurological disorder.

After 25 years of substance abuse, he didn't specify how long he'd been clean. *Wise.* Addicts experiencing extended periods of sobriety, as mentioned earlier, can grow falsely confident: a common juncture where addicts tend to falter yet again.

Dr. Gupta asked about enablers—who would Kennedy point to? Since he'd worked in the political arena, I could see how there might be a long list of possibilities. So Kennedy apparently dropped his political ambitions to generate a lifestyle that better supported his long-term recovery: one more deeply grounded in love, connectedness.

I was encouraged to hear Kennedy share information that countered the myths and faulty stereotypes that fed this age-old issue. Taking notes during the program, I thought: *I really hope he makes it.* Experienced, dedicated leadership in this complicated terrain is so important. When the diagnosis is incorrect—when we fail to consider the roots of addiction (in its many forms) from an enlightened yet realistic perspective—we shouldn't expect meaningful change to magically manifest.

Addiction is a global issue (a symptom of something deeper, perhaps) that impacts the majority of lives one way or another. Here's another way to look at it: a deadly cocktail of habitual (or obsessive) behaviors, a belief in glamorized values and shallow lifestyles, and counterproductive personality traits that block individuals from experiencing their depth as human beings—*in the spiritual sense.*

Like my photo collage, or the blissful feel of a comforting autumn day on the shore of the Missouri, I hope we, *the world,* can piece together a healthier picture where most aren't drawn to a*nything* artificial … where more are drawn to nature and simple, safe, constructive pursuits, all while standing cool and composed—knowing, aware, calm—before a million universes. Maybe then superficial perceptions will yield to something deeper, more insightful, truthful, and complete.

We *all* must be dreamers of a new day. And one way to do this is to remember that a "good question is never answered. It is not a bolt to be tightened into place but a seed to be planted and to bear more seed toward the hope of greening the landscape of idea" (poet John Ciardi, 1916–1986).

Inviting the Bell

"The Way of Heaven is to
benefit others and not to injure.
The Way of the sage is to act
but not to compete."

—LAO TZU

The ultimate value of life depends upon awareness and the power of contemplation rather than upon mere survival.
—ARISTOTLE

The Way of the Sage

*B*efore Matthew's death I'd spent very little time in cemeteries. Like foreign countries or distant, tree-covered islands, a sense of mystery surrounded them, yet I had little desire to venture beyond their imposing gates. Trepidation, of course. Final good-byes, talk of eternity and the everlasting, loomed large against the dreamlike aura of "today." And what about excruciating crash landings caused by senseless tragedy, disease, or suicide? Fiercely sad realities we mourn and honor, but without undue delay, push from our minds. The discomfort manifested mostly nameless, yet quietly intrusive.

I guess you could say that, like most, I kept cemeteries in the background until events mandated otherwise. There were exceptions, however. My grandmother was buried in my hometown so whenever I went home, I visited her grave. Almost a century old when she died, Anna and nature were earnest, enviable companions. I took

Matt and Erin to see her when they were children; she lived in Mary House (residential care facility) by then, but Anna smiled at us like we were sparkling lights in a strange and confusing world. Matt, clinging to my side or safely perched on my lap, only peeked at her. Genuinely mystified, and quite shy as a boy, he didn't know what to make of this frail old woman—faded blue eyes, cloud-white hair—sharing a lively grin with family members and caretakers.

We hadn't spent much time with her because we lived several states away, and Matt hadn't seen anyone quite so elderly. I understood his uncertainty, his caution. Peering at him from her metal wheelchair, leaning toward him like an old tree about to topple over, Anna frightened him.

Otherwise, in terms of cemetery visits, my aunt died, at 38, from melanoma, the same year I graduated from high school. Her oldest son, my cousin, died a few years later in a car accident, as did my nephew, as mentioned earlier but, overall, cemeteries weren't a big part of my life, not until I buried my own son. After that, they jumped out at me from every corner and highway, as though silently beckoning me to step closer: to confront the unknown, the power of unpredictable endings, the disconcerting close of sun-drenched days. Once we began visiting Matthew's grave once or twice a year, cemeteries were no longer something I could avoid or even separate from my next breath.

Rather, these subdued, somber places, where light and dark danced close like mysterious friends, became integral to my life, and I envied people who lived near those they had lost. What an emotional luxury to simply drop by whenever the spirit moved me—when intense thoughts of Matt urged me to spend time with him, even if only graveside. Instead, we tried for a spring or early summer visit, a return trip in the fall.

Given the miles, it was an imperfect solution, but the best we could manage.

On Mother's Day 2011, staring at the sand-colored stone and reading my son's name, I gently asked the ever-listening God within what happened. Where had he gone, after all, and what sort of prayer was *right* after nearly four years—what was left to say, to do? But it seemed like too much thinking, too much logic, so I opted for the comfort of silence—noticing how I wanted to stay, wanted to leave, at the same time.

Will this ever get easier, more natural or normal—more comfortable?

I glanced around. John and Noah were out of the car, walking toward me with Noah pulling on his leash, per usual. His energetic schnauzer personality such a stark contrast to the peaceful country setting—the smallest, most private cemetery I'd ever experienced. I couldn't decide if his joyful being was a blessing or an inappropriate distraction. This, after all, was a narrow opening, a dot of time to meditate on Heaven and Earth, endings and guarded beginnings, life and death.

Huge, heavy things, that weighed on my soul.

We had the cemetery to ourselves, and Noah finally paused to rest. The silence was deafening; the perfect spring weather was soothing: a warm day with a brilliant sun and sky. But what was it about death that made everything seem *less than*—not quite right, not quite whole—no matter how lovely otherwise? I presumed it was a gap within that represented Matthew's absence. In the spiritual sense, he hadn't gone anywhere, but I wasn't done relinquishing my expectation of a physical presence. Now it seems much easier to be satisfied with spirit, since it's the only aspect of life that truly defies death. But time hadn't released its unwelcome grip on me, in sum. Its force, something we squirm against endlessly, until we begin to peer deeply into its purpose.

We'd parked just off the gravel road outside the cemetery gates, and walking back to the car with Noah, off-leash and trailing, I reached for two shrubs on the floorboard of the back seat. Little Princess Spirea, a "tough, adaptable plant" flowering in clusters of pink in late spring (with full sun) was winter hardy to −30 degrees, according to the tags. John grabbed gardening gloves, a small shovel and jug of water, Miracle Grow for outdoor planting.

Unsure if perennials were permitted on the grounds, we were more than willing to take the chance: we had very little to lose.

"Will be a miracle if they make it a week in this rock-hard ground," I said. "But … maybe."

John nodded, kept working, as I sifted through more thoughts, let them flap about like laundry on a clothesline. It took courage to dwell there, to allow tangled emotions to penetrate without automatic resistance.

Later, trickling water around each plant—a healthy green promising new life—Matt's absence pierced my awareness with a poignancy I was never eager to experience, never prepared for. With a deep breath, I looked upward: anything to deeply allow the feeling. We're always weaving past, present, and future into "this moment," a constant, necessary process of reorganization. Trying "not to remember" never works. Remembering deeply, part of our very soul.

With the shrubs finally tucked in place, I got a picture.

We hoped they would survive, but if not, a picture would suffice.

I also wanted to spend time with Matt's grandparents buried several feet north. John and Noah went for a walk, so I gathered up some extra flowers for their graves. I'd loved Kathleen and Lindell, but *something* felt different as I stood before their names.

I don't know exactly how to describe this curious sense of internal expansion. But not only was I beginning to let go of Matthew as "my son," I was also letting go of *myself*: the largely unimportant, personalized self I'd believed was "me."

You know—the temporary, manmade self we create, sustain, and/or defend. Human existence via the heavily conditioned mind, as some describe it.

But something else—nearly imperceptible—was emerging.

A spiritual dimension beckoned: more strongly, more noticeably.

Sensing the moment's importance, I realized my pain had finally lessened enough to glance back more fully, more deeply, at an earlier time. A time when I was a carefree new mother with living in-laws, a young daughter and son and their father. We met in college, during our undergraduate years. I was a freshman at Stephens; Charles was a sophomore at the University of Missouri. Different academic and social worlds flourished on the two campuses, just blocks apart in a midsized college town in central Missouri. Mizzou men traditionally dated Stephens women, because my alma mater enrolled just a handful of males.

We compared notes, like people do.

I learned his father was from Martin, a small town in my home state. Not only that—sort of surprising to meet someone in Missouri with a family tie to South Dakota—we were both raised as Catholic

Democrats in quiet, rural areas. Our attraction was mutual, but like many first marriages, we grew apart, and after about seven years, I enrolled in graduate school, decided to venture down a new path. Well before that day, of course, I'd known his industrious, warm-hearted parents well. Gazing at their shared headstone under a big shade tree, vivid memories came to life—as I slowly opened that dusty door.

Remembering how happy Kathleen had been when I joined their family, I was glad she and Lindell had been spared the death of a grandchild: an experience no one "needs." She loved having some help in her busy kitchen. After five sons, no daughters, at last she had someone to talk to, plus another set of willing hands to share her workload.

I was always amazed at how much she could cook and/or bake in a single day—*a single day*—and the joyful intensity with which she worked. I'd grown up in a family of five children too, but keeping six men, plus friends who stopped by to hunt or help out on the farm, fed was (no exaggeration) an impressive work of art.

Like a high-flying, big-city chef, Kathleen assembled dishes so fast—it looked *easy* to my naïve eyes—that I felt inept in her big, welcoming kitchen.

Anyone walking through the door of their brick ranch home was offered a chair at the table. As part of her wizardry, there was always enough of whatever she had prepared. I learned a lot about cooking under pressure in her kitchen. My mother also had mastered this aspect of family life, but on the McCartney farm, generous, holiday-type meals were the norm. Everyone worked hard to keep the growing farm and ranch operation running smoothly (or *reasonably* well), and hefty, male appetites followed.

"I take my share of shortcuts," Kathleen admitted with a smile, whenever I marveled at her culinary prowess. One Sunday afternoon, for instance, I watched her open a can of sweet potatoes for a pumpkin pie. "Will taste the same as pumpkin when all the spices are added. No one will guess."

Resourceful, I'd thought, and wise.

Why make a big deal out of a silly pie when she could adjust the recipe with a little imagination and creativity? The nearest store was 15 minutes north on a narrow, curvy country blacktop; it wasn't even a real grocery store. Rather, it was (still is) a small gas station called the Derby with a convenience store and a deli where Matt picked up sandwiches for lunch when rushed to complete a project, or feeling lonely, perhaps. Farming, ranching were mostly solitary pursuits, so stopping by the Derby for lunch and easy conversation made sense.

Vaguely, I remembered a kind young woman from the reception line at Matt's prayer service. In a calm, sad voice, her words measured, she told me how much she'd enjoyed seeing Matt whenever he stopped in for lunch.

"He always had a smile," she said, "but didn't like mustard on his sandwiches."

Powerful memories converged in my soul like a rushing mountain stream. Transfixed, I stared at engraved names on a rectangular stone that was showing some wear. Reading the engraved dates (year of birth, year of death) over and over again like someone who still couldn't grasp the brevity of life, the power and sharpness of death, I winced.

Kathleen died in May 1994, after a fateful heart attack. Lindell, in February 2006—also from heart failure. Neither suffered in sterile hospital rooms, or lingered in lonely nursing homes, and by any measure, their earthly days were well-lived. Work, family, relaxation, plenty of friends. They loved to fly to Las Vegas for a few days in winter: to try their luck, see some shows, soak up some glorious sun.

About to turn away—John and Noah, only headstones away—I took another picture. *Erin might want one.* Strangely, this sent me sailing back in time again. Matt and Erin, as children, shimmered in my memory: bright smiles, warm hearts, inquisitive minds.

The first of many grandchildren for Kathleen and Lindell.

Cell phone back in my pocket, I thanked them for everything, and glancing at the open cemetery gate—*you can go now*—detected a rare inner peace. Finding my children's grandparents lodged in my heart, like old friends, was a nice surprise. And consoling.

I hadn't forgotten their friendly, accepting natures—how they made *everyone* feel so welcome. A deeper, ever more inclusive sense of compassion was settling into place like an important puzzle piece. I recalled Buddha's message: "In separateness lies the world's greatest misery, in compassion lies the world's true strength."

Powerful words that resonated with clarity, truth, and vast hopefulness. I was grateful for this compelling insight: the gift of grace emanating from my soul.

Later, I ran across a quote by Henri J.M. Nouwen that beautifully captured the moment: "The spiritual life does not remove us from the world but leads us deeper into it."

❧

We loaded up, tucked ourselves back in the car, but … sat quietly for a few minutes. The only sound, the idling engine, occasional bird song.

We could see Matt's headstone from the road.

John glanced over at me: "We'll be back soon."

"And maybe the spirea will make it," I said.

I knew it would be difficult to leave, but on such a gentle spring day, I could have sat for hours in the shade of the tree behind Matt's grave, pretending he could see me—hear me. How wonderful it would have been to ask about his day: his recovery, his projects or plans, his dogs (the black labs that strangely disappeared during hunting season a year or so after his death).

But wishing didn't bring me greater peace. And only delivered a sharp emptiness: a deeply uncomfortable feeling I now knew intimately, as though etched into the fabric of my soul.

With a long look back, we returned to the country blacktop. Not another car in sight. I wanted to stop across the road where Matt had lived to check on his apple trees, the ones we gave him in Hannibal during our Easter picnic by the Mississippi. Now more than five years old, they were small, scruffy looking, because they hadn't been pruned, watered, or fertilized.

John parked just off the road; I got out, walked closer.

White blossoms with hints of pink. Frail, yet, strong; delicate, yet, empowered. Trees blooming from sheer determination, right?

The wind picked up, tossing branches and leaves around almost wistfully. I waited for a calm moment to get a picture—memories to tuck away until our next visit—and there it was again, that hard stab of melancholy. Yes, the trees had survived, but Matt hadn't, and their sad appearance reminded me of the years that had disappeared since I last saw him. Lost years that had run right by me as I watched from the sidelines, dazed and crumpled. The dwarf apple trees, trying so hard to bloom, looked exactly like I felt.

I loved them for their truth: the unmistakable story they told.

A sizable amount of hope was tucked in my heart the morning we picked them out at an Indianapolis nursery.

"These look great," I'd said, "water, sunlight, maybe real apples in a few years."

Pulling into Hannibal to meet Matt (trees in tow) that breezy, spring day, literature came to mind—Mark Twain stories we all seem to know, love. And, now, looking intently at weaving branches, I recalled how happy Matt was when we gave him the trees. We joked about calling them Easter trees. They would grow; he would grow: a team intent on survival. Besides, Matt wanted to put down roots on the family farm with something of his own; young fruit trees seemed inspirational. Life would be better in the days ahead … surely.

Is it good we can't foresee the future? Without a doubt.

Readers who believe parents are responsible for everything that goes right or wrong in their children's lives may dare to presume that a similar scenario could never happen in their lives, that things would inevitably turn out much rosier, and assuredly, less tragic. Conjecture of this ilk, I'm afraid, is easy, dreamy, prideful thinking. Hubris … comes to mind. Some well-intentioned professionals (gifted, concerned) also have tidy-sounding terms for the serious, deadly problems people face. The problems we faced.

But mere words fall flat in an uncertain, rocky terrain that no one, when honest, fully understands. The variables are unique in every situation, *never textbook*, and I have yet to meet a perfect child, parent, or family. And I've never heard of a perfect system, society, culture, or organization. Our world is as confused as the individuals who comprise it, and living with a complicated situation is never remotely the same as analyzing it: dicing it up into convenient, manageable pieces. Until you've lived with an addict, loved and buried an addict, one who may happen to be your son, it's largely impossible to grasp the totality of the dynamics. As the brilliant saying goes, until it happens to you, *it hasn't happened.*

Hard core addiction isn't an ordinary problem, but the steepest mountain, the deepest ocean, rolled into one. No cure, no best way— no method that works every time. A word that means something different to everyone. There is only trial and error, doing the best you can under miserable, life-altering conditions you never envisioned. You pray, seek advice, and try to follow it. You hope, pray some more.

One day, you believe; the next, you doubt. Hints of progress vanish like morning fog, and you want to give up—you can't. It's your son, and you love him. *You love him.* He wants to give up; you pray he doesn't. He wants help, but where to turn: *this time.*

You look again. You all try, one more time.

But the dawn only delivers another debilitating cycle of relapse and questionable recovery. Surely *this* is that illusive, coveted turning point. *Your son has to hit bottom.* Once a man, someone part of Matt's journey, told me it was helpful to say "no" to kids. Hearing that, a potent feeling of futility washed over me. Did he think his advice was a revelation, that we could impact Matt's world with a simple "no" when addicts leap over that two-letter word like a micro-puddle in the street after a brief spring shower?

Superficial mandates, blame, and assumption-making are tempting dead ends leading nowhere—certainly not to viable solutions or useful insights with true creative power.

I glanced overhead, but silence prevailed. No jets, no birds or distractions. Just a light breeze against the apple trees. My thoughts picked up speed. Matt had to hit bottom; we understood that (we thought). But how many times—*how many ways*—would this tricky marker have to come into deadly focus? Was suicide hitting bottom?

❧

I feel deeply for anyone grappling with something larger than life—a painful situation with no sign of lasting resolution. If a form of addiction, it's one of the most dangerous and complicated diseases you'll encounter. You'll need all the endurance and strength you can muster for an indefinite period of time. Even then, as I know too well, you may not witness, or enjoy, a truly favorable—in mortal terms—outcome.

There will be sleepless nights, emergency phone calls, police and parole officers, court hearings, visits to rehab centers, jails, and possibly prisons. You'll quietly wonder exactly how much more you can take in this effort to care: in this mission of mercy and patience, this exercise of faith and trust. When such things happen, be kind to yourself; definitely, be compassionate when you meet others feverishly coping with the intricacies of life and death. Be *more* compassionate, period. Offer a sincere helping hand instead of a snicker, a snide or sarcastic comment.

Life is imperfect, we all know that. So why do so many feel the need to quietly, but insistently, mask challenging issues? My guess ...?

The unspoken rules of a "polite society" based on false, superficial distinctions and feigned concern contribute greatly. Yet, our fragile web of life, the vast interconnections, also depends on our ability to *know* deep compassion for one another. Not pity—brittle, breakable like china—with its haughty ring of superiority, but empathy, genuine caring. The difference is always perceived. One says, poor you, that would *never* happen to me, to us, but empathy is connection, understanding, and equality. *I am here for you.*

We are all learning how to live, to die, one earthly second at a time.

Pema Chödrön says this: "True compassion does not come from wanting to help out those less fortunate than ourselves but from realizing our kinship with all beings."

Interestingly, on another level, there is research that now suggests narcissists' lack of empathy is tied to less gray matter in the left anterior insula, a region of the brain linked to empathy. A fascinating premise that may shed light on a variety of significant issues.

Noah watched me from the car, head out the window and, suddenly, he barked, as if to remind me we had a long drive ahead of us. After another glance at Matt's Easter trees, I spotted the old pump from a well that once stored water for the family farm house until rural water arrived. Nearly buried from view by purple iris, peonies about to burst, weeds and tall uneven grasses, how long had it been since I'd seen it? Had I ever seen it, tucked away south of their country driveway? Probably some 25 years ago.

Now, it was an old rusty piece of metal merging with unkempt surroundings, blending naturally with persistent flowers. I took another picture—Erin was artistic, liked to draw, paint, and I thought she might appreciate the history. The pump, how it hid from the world, also might ignite her imagination—become the catalyst for a new painting.

Walking to the car, I considered its symbolism.

Just another obsolete item on the farm, a poignant reminder of days once filled with the bustle of family life, or had the pump been silenced by time—the ceaseless tides of change the universe demands? Inevitably, there is a bigger story framing the details that we latch onto prematurely as "the story." Layers of truth, rings of reality—a dynamic mix of priorities, perspectives, and possibilities.

Was I witnessing the end of an era with Matt's death here on the farm; had he found himself at the unlucky juncture of past and future: a pivotal moment representing the end of a family story (his grandparents, generations dating back to 1853), not just the close of a single life? Of all the grandchildren, Matt (I'd almost named him Paul, but another Paul McCartney, like the famous musician and rock star of Beatles fame, didn't seem like the best idea) was the only one with a possible future on the land. No one else signaled a lasting interest.

A rural area with predictable isolation, work with considerable challenge, wasn't for everyone. With the big picture in focus, it seemed likely that *more* than a personal death had occurred. The reassuring phrase, to everything there is a season, floated in the spring air. Nothing lasts forever. Not apple trees, wells or pump handles, or the people we love. The story will end: as expected or significantly otherwise. Acrimony is never the way to go. It dilutes, sadly misshapes, the noble human journey by separating us from the deep sacredness of each breath, and then, we lose sight of the brevity—the miracle—of *today*.

"Trees look a little tired," I said, glancing at the brick house, as we drove away.

A dark, dust-covered car approached from the north, the driver waved, we waved, but seconds later, only silence and rubber tires against blacktop, the steady whir of an engine, Noah resting on his striped red blanket in the back seat. Windows open, we listened for a red-winged blackbird, relished the smell of fresh air, its absolute freedom as it connected with our weary, time-bound faces.

Maybe we would spot a stunning blue heron in flight.

It was the way of the sage. To perceive deeply, to acknowledge the divine oneness of the universe, our inherent, ever-changing role as imperfect life custodians. The life that we are … in countless forms. Temporary yet timeless. And when I am fully aware, not absorbed, or sidetracked, by the dictates of mind, time, or circumstance, I not only see beyond this paradox: I see into it.

Inviting the Bell

"The Way of Heaven is to
benefit others and not to injure.
The Way of the sage is to act
but not to compete."

—LAO TZU

Out of suffering have emerged the strongest souls;
the most massive characters are seared with scars.
—KHALIL GIBRAN

Parting Ways with Someday

Loss, as you've gathered, made me to want to reinvent parts of my life, and Matt's. I yearned for the impossible. Opportunities to begin anew, to strike roller-coaster passages that sprang to life unbidden, asking so much of me. In short, I wanted to tinker with time. Surely, I'd unwisely rationalize, if I could only *fix* or *alter* pivotal pieces leading from A to Z, sharp endings along the way could be softened, even eliminated.

Matt's father, step-father, and I would be the wisest people on the planet; the world, a veritable paradise of contentment, peace, fairness, love, and goodwill.

Matt would be one of those "super amazing" kids who *never, ever* disappoints. I could hear the proverbial, curiously glowing terms some parents rattle off when speaking about their offspring: the son, the daughter, who is decidedly and abundantly wonderful.

Now I can't help but cringe when I hear these trite descriptions: quick, tidy labels that fundamentally dishonor the inevitable complexity of human life.

Who is wonderful, who isn't, and why; does it matter, and how so? We can be strangely eager with meaningless distinctions. Slightly too quick with popularized, mainstream adjectives without real knowledge, true understanding.

In 2012 Andrew Solomon (award-winning author, psychiatrist) published a landmark study of parents and children that also considered the common labels we affix to others. Matt, not unlike Solomon, endured negative—harsh, stereotypical—labels.

If not spoken aloud, they were inferred.

From Solomon, in *Far From the Tree: Parents, Children, and the Search for Identity*, we learn a great deal about the complexity of parent-child relationships, especially when extreme challenges manifest. From the first of some 700 pages: "Parenthood abruptly catapults us into a permanent relationship with a stranger, and the more alien the stranger, the stronger the whiff of negativity." What an insightful perspective; yet we assume that if a child is *our* child, we should be able to understand him or her ... almost by osmosis.

Maybe, but probably not.

And while Matt never felt "alien" to me, nor was there a "whiff of negativity"—we were kindred spirits in some ways—I relied on unconditional love to transcend a lack of perfect, or complete, understanding. The beloved Bengali poet Rabindranath Tagore aptly wrote, "Say of him what you please, but I know my child's failing. I do not love him because he is good, but because he is my little child."

Yes, yes, of course.

❧

A couple of weeks before the four-year anniversary of Matt's suicide, I walked into my office, opened the blinds—the sky looked calm, bright, endless—and sat at my desk with my morning coffee. I wanted to dwell on something that had been on my mind in a fuzzy kind of way. So far, I'd only managed a jumble of meager questions about how to honor his memory this time. Nothing felt right.

All I could manage to focus on was the pressure, the presence, of time. How had four years elapsed, blinding me with their somber hues; how had June 24 turned up on my calendar so soon, and yet again? Trying to find my way through this quandary, I picked up a pen, scribbled vague notes.

"Feeling blank," I began, continuing with: *Out of ideas to remember Matt that aren't trite or predictable. Still stuck between past and future, the synergy of merging moments—each, a small emotional collision. What more could be done, said, with time defiantly inching along: insisting on sunny days, wild winter winds and snowstorms, joyful springs that shouted something about the invincible nature of life itself, while dragging me along—a road weary individual who didn't fully understand the mission.*

Stopping, I took a deep breath, put down my pen. My journal-like notes felt true, but sadly useless. Getting thoughts on paper nearly always helped me sift through thickets of converging emotions—the dilemma at hand—but I wasn't getting anywhere. Only rarely had I dipped into the dark pool of resentment, but as I scanned my hasty notes, I sensed it was wise and important to "go there"—diving in without reservation.

Maybe I had every right to resent death: how it whisks us from Earth with utter control, dubious compassion, and too often, without any warning. An invisible, inevitable intruder most of us ponder for years on end.

When will it happen, how? Will I be ready? Who will live longer? And what, if anything, happens next?

Strangely, this indulgence in negative emotions steered me in the right direction. As a safe outlet for my human misgivings around an imperfect existence and the inability to save my son from serious challenges, complex issues lacking long-term solutions, or loss of life, once more, I came face to face with the bleak gray ghost of hardship. There, I was reminded that grief, the world's teacher in disguise, has a powerful agenda of its own.

Landscape of Years

After the initial 11-year sentence came down, we went to meet with Matt's attorney so he could explain, politely, professionally, what we had witnessed. Assuring us Matt would never serve the entire sentence, he suggested, "Maybe three years."

I remember—shock palpable, undoubtedly etched on my face— thinking: people have committed far worse crimes and never served an hour, a day, a month, a year. Matt was barely 19 that gut-wrenching day in court, and 11 years, isn't that a lifetime?

An eternity.

If he lived through it, he would be a young man by then, well beyond his teens. How would he build a reasonably "normal" life with a record—how many, I wondered, manage that magical, death-defying, most unlikely, feat.

Leaving the law firm (feeling glad I hadn't become a lawyer, how did they cope with the stress and challenges of the criminal justice system?) in a numbed state of disbelief, we found our car. What would this harsh, mind-bending experience do to Matt? Who might he be after a few months, a year or two, in confinement? Would he, in fact, become alien to me, to us?

Before his court date and formal sentencing, Matt served a fair amount of time in the county jail, because no one recommended making bail. So we'd endured those dreadful phone visits behind glass already. But ... a *prison?* At his age, no less.

Granted, many people have served time and survived, even prospered when released. Actor/comedian Tim Allen, for instance, served 28 months of an eight-year sentence for cocaine possession. Reportedly, before the arrest, Allen had been active as a narcotics dealer, and during his stay at Sandstone Federal Correctional Institution in the early 1980s, turned to his passion for comedy. Few arrests and convictions evolve into such glamorous storybook endings, however. Allen's father was killed in a car accident when Tim was 11, but despite it all, he's enjoyed a fruitful career: starring roles in *The Santa Claus* trilogy, *Galaxy Quest*, popular sitcoms.

Good for him.

I'm glad when someone makes it beyond the rocky shores of the legal system. Glad when anyone lives to see a better day.

A multitude of celebrities have openly battled drug addiction and alcoholism. Many have come and gone from rehab, probation, or incarceration, often courting disaster, but somehow prevailing. Others didn't quite make it to the other side. Many names light up on that fluctuating continuum between "clean" and "in recovery."

If you care to study a long and growing list of names, Wikipedia publishes one, but here are a few I recognized: Robert Downey Jr., Johnny Cash, Joe Walsh, Keith Urban, Betty Ford, George Jones, Craig Ferguson, Judy Garland, John Belushi, Eric Clapton, Stevie Ray Vaughn, Keith Whitley, Elton John, Robin Williams, Charlie Sheen, Aaron Sorkin, Fergie, Eminem, Maureen McCormick, Etta James, Richard Dreyfuss, and Mel Gibson. It seems surprising *not to* find a celebrity on the list.

Driving home that day, I mostly recall the waves of nausea that rolled through me. Not knowing where this story would end, I assumed I'd have to live on a steady diet of hope—believing Matt would miraculously conquer his trials and tribulations, and one day enjoy a "long, prosperous life"—the kind everyone talks about with an assuming gleam in their eyes. At least there was a chance he'd get long-term treatment—the kind he couldn't slip away from, giving up on himself or the program, or be dismissed from for mistakes, omissions, or for not manifesting the required symptoms. When it comes to symptoms or diagnosis, eligibility is another significant hurdle for many recovery and rehab programs.

Luckily, I was just a passenger in our car that bright, sun-drenched afternoon, because I had to close my eyes against the searing pain of debilitating sorrow. My son would be gone for some time, isolated from society, friends and family, while enduring a life I couldn't imagine. Complete strangers would surround him—who would they be, would they harm him? The rush of fear only a mother's heart can know almost stopped its beating.

And how was Matt handling the prospect of serving a great deal of time behind bars? Should I expect panic, despair, shock, or would he act brave and contrite, determined not to reveal his innermost feelings? Maybe Matt would calmly pretend to accept his fate, not knowing what else to do.

Collect phone calls were allowed from the inside (unless the privilege had been lost), but we weren't allowed to call him, and there were strict visiting hours to abide by.

Still, we wanted to see him, and talk to him: encourage him not to lose heart.

Time would pass; parole would happen.

But no matter what Matt said or did in a public setting, or even by phone, as a mother, I knew an 11-year sentence had to feel overwhelming, maybe like the end of the world. Somewhere in the recesses of my mind flickered the understandable worry that he might do something rash, even attempt to take his own life.

Realistically, when looking out on a vast—seemingly endless—landscape of time, how might a frightened 19-year-old weigh the gravity of his new reality?

An unbearable weight around his neck.

A tenuous sense of relief, being distanced from troubling temptations.

Or a dire situation that couldn't be measured or fully comprehended.

Somehow, we arrived back in our driveway. I looked around—the yard, the house, the "family things" Matt was leaving behind for a dark foreign world of steel, concrete, strangers, and possibly, *probably*, a steady diet of fear. How would he not *become* these years? How would I not *become* this painful reality?

As spiritual masters explain, we are all connected—all one.

The year was 1999.

I'd written my first book the year before, and felt certain the process kept me alive by giving my soul room to breathe during difficult days. The book, a search for everything uplifting in a place of some adversity, the prairie's heritage, after all, contained wisdom I would need myself. *More than ever before.* Even as Matt's journey seemed fraught with risk, difficulty, and pain, I also had to unearth the stamina, desire, and energy to launch a first book. I remember digging deep within to stay focused on the project at hand, while wondering, simultaneously, if Matt would ever find his spiritual dimension when drawn to the empty promise of drugs.

Might wisdom ever come to grace *his* life?

At the time I wasn't familiar with the work of Ursula K. Le Guin, or her thoughts on unanswerable questions and not trying to answer them during especially trying times.

Walking in the house after his sentencing, I asked myself a tough question: Were there valid and objective reasons to stay involved, to keep hoping to make a difference in Matt's life? Of course by now you know I wasn't the type to give up—to turn away—just because the reasons seemed nebulous, distant, or difficult to discern.

Besides, Matt was *so* young. Even if this was his challenge, his learning experience, his issue, everyone needs meaningful support, love, and understanding; and who among us doesn't have more to learn? I was certain I did—and hopefully, always would.

More than an Ending

The four-year anniversary of Matt's death would be marked by a 6:30 a.m. Mass at our church back in Indianapolis. I hadn't figured out much, otherwise, and was still unsure what to share about the spiritual journey I, and Matt, in spirit, seemed to be on. But my desire to create a tribute with creative depth had only grown stronger.

Time had not stood still—neither could I.

Fortuitously, a picture I hadn't seen in a couple of years found its way into my hands. Matt with his fishing pole—calm, smiling, radiating contentment. Seemingly fulfilled by the simple wonders of a carefree afternoon in late spring. Studying the details—his hat, boots, blue jeans, tan shirt—my mind resisted the hidden eventuality. Taken a short time before his death, not far from where he drew a final breath, it captured something vital, pure. I loved it.

Matt at his best—finding joy, sustenance, in his routine surroundings, in nature, in something that wasn't illegal or dangerous.

Tucking the picture in an envelope, I drove to a photo shop for copies. The scene captivated me.

A small pond surrounded by a green meadow, towering lush trees in the background, abundant sunshine, a peaceful sky, and no trace of what the future concealed.

Not the slightest hint.

But life is always ready to surprise us, to complicate things, isn't it? When I picked up the copies, they were noticeably blurry. Self-doubt clouded my eyes. Was it a sure sign from the gods—the wrong picture, a bad idea, time to forget? Tears pushed to the surface as I stuffed the copies back in the envelope, rushed out the door.

Aware of my overreaction, time pushed me for answers—insisting I *not* allow June 24 to slip away like Matt: like all the other forgettable and free-flowing dates on a calendar. Why does the blinding power of routine impair our vision, so we *see* so very little?

I didn't want this habitual blurriness of perception to steal what was memorable about Matt. Besides, what is a day in time, if not something to be remembered in a special way?

Though this intriguing question felt relevant then, I would come to see how this kind of high-pressure remembering was another way we keep life and loss firmly separated. As in *that* happened *then*, when everything happens simultaneously: life and loss, mysterious partners in a vast, incomprehensible universe. While this "truth" was embedded within my eternal self, I hadn't *experienced* the insight directly—not yet.

The day wore on.

I continued to puzzle about "what to do" … when nothing came, I resigned myself to a day of quiet reflection that only a handful of people might also recall for its significance. It would have to be okay; I wouldn't force the wrong idea into existence.

Nothing was better than the wrong thing, because something contrived and artificial would in no way honor Matt's memory. Honestly, though, wasn't I letting myself down, allowing the date to come and go without special notice?

That night, tired and unable to concentrate on any of the wonderful books teetering on my nightstand, I turned off my light early. Would I dream about Matt; might a nightmare jar me awake deep in the night with an unsettling vision of the afterlife? Maybe in living color. Maybe in stark black and white, or as a parade of abstract scenes lacking a concrete reference to anything known.

Gingerly, I closed my eyes.

I'd been reading, in my usual style, in no real hurry, several books at a time.

Titles like: *Life After Death: The Burden of Proof* by Deepak Chopra; *Heaven is for Real* by Todd Burpo; and *Heaven: Our Enduring Fascination with the Afterlife* by Lisa Miller. Chopra, a physician and author I've appreciated for many years, wrote: "When all images have disappeared at the subtle level, the dying person arrives at eternity. Eternity is the source of the soul."

I craved knowledge about the afterlife.

Where had Matt's spirit gone?

Reaching beyond conventional explanations, I explored various schools of thought, as books about the afterlife jumped out at me from bookstore shelves. *Here, read this. And this.* But imagining Matt in a faraway place called eternity wasn't much comfort, I had to admit. "Eternity gives you more freedom than the mind can conceive," writes Chopra. He adds, however, that this amazing possibility makes us uneasy, because we are all used to living within established boundaries. Explaining further: "At the end of the journey there are no loved ones, no physical destinations, no memories of the material plane."

Maybe, with death, souls return to eternal alignment with a divine force we are simply incapable of perceiving as mortals. Resistance is futile, perhaps?

That night, not surprisingly, I did dream about Matt. Whenever I dwell on something, it often shows up in my dreams. He was an energetic boy of seven or so and wanted to go out for pizza; the dream came to mind as soon as I woke up, earlier than usual.

Curiously, the insight that followed came like a script from a higher dimension.

I couldn't have missed the message if I'd tried—it was that insistent.

Like a startling edict, "life is more than an ending" rose from an inner wilderness with the precision of Shakespeare, and while it sounds obvious *(of course life is more than an ending)*, to someone grieving her son's absence, it felt like a monumental revelation.

Daylight hadn't quite arrived, but I'd never felt more awake.

I knew the dream, the message, were somehow intertwined. A soothing memory from Matt's childhood (pizza night) was a good reminder of the simple, yet dazzling moments that comprise a life *before* it ends. Regardless of the duration, in days or years, each life: rare, luminous, inimitable. That was the point: *maybe the only one.* Before the dream, I'd been stuck on endings, Matthew's ending. The closing of a parent-child relationship—of an assumed future, of his clash with the hush of night, alone, terrified.

My insight may seem implausible; common knowledge, right? But knowing Matt's life comprised *many* moments was essentially an intellectual understanding before that morning—not an emotional, spiritual insight felt and experienced with deep clarity. The difference, far-reaching and profound. This was that sudden rush of knowing: that sharp (welcome) realization that comes after a long time of not knowing. In that instant, dawn sneaking in behind drawn curtains, I *knew* a peaceful space that settled in easily. As if a door opening into something vast, it felt timeless, limitless: an internal space I've heard others describe. Within that sacred sphere, as encountered, was the son I'd known.

Matthew in his many incarnations. An infant. A boy. A teenager, young adult, and then, as a young man. It was all there, all known simultaneously, as if for the first time. T.S. Eliot famously wrote: "We shall not cease from exploration, and the end of all our exploring will

be to arrive where we started and know the place for the first time."
And Rumi says, "This place is a dream / Only a sleeper considers it
real / Then death comes like dawn / and you wake up laughing at /
what you thought was your grief."

This possibility, also from Rumi, resonated with sweet urgency:
"Out beyond ideas of wrongdoing and rightdoing there is a field, I'll
meet you there."

Had I encountered the field he so eloquently described?

Human Suffering

We were visiting my husband's parents when Matt committed the
felony that resulted in that startling 11-year sentence. With everything
going on, we'd put off time away; even this break was very brief: a long
weekend. Despite the nature of recovery—its jumbled essence—Matt
had been doing reasonably well. *So it seemed.* Guarantees never existed,
however. Even leaving town for a few days was a small leap of faith.
In hindsight, how Matt seemed to be doing wasn't the best yardstick.

Addiction, the behavior it fuels, is seldom predictable or trust-
worthy. Few addicts can even trust themselves. If you could pin down
a dissipating cloud, maybe you could also pin down addiction and its
impact. Matt was always starting a treatment program; always doing
just enough to convince us, *himself,* that lasting, substantive change
was imminent. But I often sensed his deep reluctance to make even
the slimmest promise about the next hour, let alone, an ambiguous
futuristic destination.

He'd been told, *ad infinitum,* by professionals and otherwise,
that there was no cure—no total recovery to be courted, achieved,
or expected.

Still, human beings, regardless of context, crave certainty—even if largely imagined. Matt, however, seemed to translate the unpredictability of life (including powerful waves of self-doubt) into a sinking hopelessness: a private cry of despair. Fighting something he could never really understand must have felt frightening, nearly impossible, and his self-esteem suffered. Of course. How could it not? So now you have an increasingly unwieldy dynamic that exacerbates the entire picture.

Matt had been steadily employed that summer, and was also attending group treatment sessions because of misdemeanors that resulted in probation. But a felony was difficult to envision. We had seen intermittent progress (enough to indicate growth) but, in the end, just as we all stumble through loss, grief, and hardship—weaving a unique, personalized process—we stumbled through the complex challenges of Matt's reality.

To claim otherwise would be nonsensical, untrue.

Life, under tolerable circumstances, is *still* an enormous journey—a vast experience never truly mastered—so try, if you will, to imagine your days riddled by a violent inner struggle to survive the private hell of drugs and addiction. A struggle you probably don't understand any better than anyone else. Yet, indirectly, we look to addicts as though they should have the answers: as if they should simply shape up. While their behavior, seemingly, trial and error, may stand in stark contrast to conventional logic, I have also detected an unfair, unrealistic attitude of … addicts know how to change, but merely refuse to do so.

Seriously?

Does anyone *really* know what leads to lasting change?

I saw, felt, my son's pain, anguish, and though he tried to hide it, intuitively, I knew lasting answers were as distant and reclusive as the sun's warmth on a stark winter day. Despite potentially useful treatment programs, plentiful admonishments, streams of advice, and well-meaning individuals offering support and direction, on a deeper level, Matt, *like everyone*, was tragically alone with his problems: with the terrifying mysteries of human existence.

We can place blame at the feet of parents, society, the legal system, friends, families, addicts themselves, even the weather or time of day, but this is a child's dream against the determined grip of addiction. Regardless of logical-sounding opinions about addicts (or anyone in the throes of a supremely thorny problem), we are essentially talking about human suffering. How to understand it; how to end it. Or at least, reduce it.

Matt suffered. Silently, or at times with noticeable frustration and worry—before his sentence was handed down, and after. But does suffering compensate for wrongdoing, making him any less guilty, when in fact he'd broken the law? I don't have the answers. The legal system is what it is—imperfect like the world that created it—and judging what happened will never lead me to a peaceful perspective.

As Einstein reminds us: "Time is an illusion." So for me to know what an appropriate punishment would be is impossible. A dead end. Admittedly, the years Matt served as an incarcerated citizen may have kept him alive longer, but to what extent did the residual impact—or the heavy prospect of having to return—contribute to his suicide?

According to a surveillance video, he threatened an unsuspecting stranger in a car at an ATM with a makeshift weapon. Instant drug money. Youthful desperation fueled by a mind charred by chemical dependency, yet an illegal act *no one* should be subjected to regardless of motivation. As a woman, mother, and parent, I hated that *my son* had done something this terrifying, and every possible emotion, from shock to pain to deep regret to utter disbelief, arose. Though the individual in the car hadn't been physically harmed, *what if?* Dear God, *what if?* And what about the indelible mark on his soul, the pounding fear in his, the other person's, heart? What if Matt had been killed during the exchange or perhaps, worst of all, not felt any remorse, which I know he did?

Life is filled with mistakes, missteps, and trauma, yes, but why hadn't Matt pursued help more diligently, made better decisions, or found a way to prevent this inexcusable act? Didn't he grasp the extremely serious repercussions—realize his waning days on Earth would never be remotely the same after a felony?

Vacuous questions in the context of drug addiction.

Maybe *this* was where Matt hit bottom.

What I want to explain, without the sarcasm, is that during the course of his addiction it was mostly impossible to differentiate one critical marker from the next, pretending to *know* which of them was indeed the proverbial bottom. Such black-and-white thinking, while commonplace, can lead to a false sense of confidence because this ever-changing, undesirable destination floats in the background like an invisible puzzle piece. And since thorny issues like addiction are only supposed to improve *after* this inauspicious target has been attained (so the theory goes), what happens when an addict, his friends, family, his therapist and probation officer, believe that the latest relapse, or associated behavior, was indeed the proverbial bottom? Things can't get any worse then, can they?

They can. And they do.

It's all relative. It's also a particularly dangerous, ill-advised guessing game, because when people *believe* the bottom has been reached, expectations rise for a sudden, nearly magical metamorphosis: everyone anxiously wanting to believe *in something*. And some addicts let their guard down, feeling that, now (and inevitably), things will improve.

Yet, addiction is never totally conquered, because there is no known cure—besides significant and enduring personal growth.

So when "the bottom" has been declared or assumed, things still seem to evolve. New lows are experienced. Hopes are dashed once more, while everyone murmurs: must *not* have been the bottom after all. *Not yet.*

And that's when you sadly wonder—worry, imagine—how much worse things will need to get before the illusive bottom is reached.

Highest Intentions

After my morning insight on the 4-year anniversary of Matt's death, I knew how I wanted to convey appreciation for the life that left in such haste: a brief message with the fishing picture. I made the copies myself this time. They were in much better focus, as were my thoughts. Interesting how life circumstances slow us down when things aren't quite right—how obstacles mysteriously arise when we're in doubt. Consciously, or otherwise.

The deeper message: calming deep breaths are a wise reaction to stalled plans.

The German architect, Van der Rohe, wrote the obvious: "God is in the details." And since I was beginning to accept that Matt's life could never be understood—not by mere mortals—I included his quote with the joyful picture. A poignant reminder that rushing to judgment usually will be premature. Only the universe, the one, magnanimous source that everything flows from, can possibly know the true story. Even as I write, sharing what I feel I understand "today" about the precious life expression named Matthew, it can only offer a sketch, a tiny snapshot: an educated guess, at best.

Deeper truths come gradually with spiritual growth—with an ongoing commitment to awakening, ever more intensely and fully, to the unseen.

I also wrote four short lines to go with the picture, but only when people thanked me for the "lovely poem," did I catch the poetry in my own message. I'd written that Matt, looking happy and content, told the story of a beautiful day: that life is always more than an ending. The note, the picture, became a celebration of what had been—instead of what was lost. Somehow it lifted the spirits of others, made them smile by encouraging them to remember Matt's life, in sum, instead of primarily as a shocking ending we had despaired over and, painfully, wished away.

❧

Another powerful dream, stunning in its accuracy, was weaved into this perilous journey. While we were away—the night Matt committed the felony—I was jarred from sleep in the middle of the night by a frightening scenario. Too vividly, it spoke of death, and my panic felt stark, urgent—not something I could brush aside as *only* a dream. A paralyzing fear welled up in me, as I recounted the eerie details in my sleepy mind.

Hoping to extract the scene in its entirety before it faded, I woke up John and flipped on a lamp.

"It was extremely real," I said rapidly. "I found Matt in a cabinet, door closed—curled up, no longer breathing." The black cabinet in my dream was small, looked like the same one that was part of our living room entertainment center, a place we stored photos, CDs, videos. Barely had I finished describing the dream, when I reached for the phone.

I had to find Matt.

About two in the morning, not surprisingly, there was no answer. The phone rang and rang. I hung up, tried back. But the endless ringing sounded hollow, lifeless. Taking deep breaths, I reminded myself the only thing I knew for sure was that Matt wasn't home, or wasn't picking up. Not every troubling dream is prophetic—*most aren't*—so closing my eyes, I tried to calm down, tried to sleep. I was several states away. Nothing could be done until morning—when I could reach him (this was pre-cell phone era.) Regardless, I was scared, worried about Matt's well-being.

Something was wrong.

If death comes in stages, what happened that night was a defining moment, because I was never able to reach Matt, and as soon as we were back home, police officers arrived to ask if we knew of his whereabouts. Of course they found him, arrested him and, later, he called from the county jail. But had Matt, figuratively speaking, *died* the night of the felony, the same night as my disconcerting dream?

In many respects, yes. In representative terms, yes.

Heartbroken doesn't begin to describe the blow that felt surreal, yet fatalistic, in its glaring power. Knowing things could always get worse, it still felt like we had tried in vain to prevent Matt's problems from escalating. Futility roared in my brain, and then, with no idea where his arrest would lead, hope and optimism vanished like flimsy themes from a fairy tale—as distant as reliable knowledge of next week's weather.

Endings—final, searing—really do seem to come in indiscernible phases, in big and small waves of decline, and a milestone we had long feared, worked tirelessly to prevent, had materialized anyway. What I didn't know was that I would bury my son nine years later, and four years after that, would struggle over what to share with friends and family in his memory.

If we could clearly foresee the future, the present would likely confuse us, incapacitate us, with anticipated, and undeniable, terror. Yet, Matt's 27 years are extended, invisibly so, by anyone reading this book. Those still searching for a spiritual path—a way beyond the mundane, the gut-wrenching, the less-than-poetic side of life.

I haven't entirely given up my desire to tinker with time either, to alter history so our collective family story might have a happy ending, even though I understand that *happy* is an abstract concept of superficial distinction. What, then, is a proper wish for the future—the story within the story? My best, most honorable, guess: *stop looking to time for anything*. Strive to transcend its artificial limitations by consistently fueling your spiritual growth; seek deeper understanding, and greater awareness of everything "beyond self."

Increasingly, I am focusing my energies in that direction—staying steadily intent on spiritual discoveries to see what the unknown will reveal—about life and death, about our world—when probed. Most have noticed our cultural obsession with time, with shiny dates all in a row on something called a calendar.

It's uncanny the extent to which we are influenced, if not controlled, by its insidious nature. But curiously, when I don't create a firm dividing line between life and loss—death hiding in the background as the enemy of all life forms—time loses its grip on me. Another world opens: a timeless dimension that points to everything visible as illusion, as mirage. The internal spiritual climb, I believe, is stimulated and enabled by the external world, allowing us to experience our only real purpose, but to grasp this we must reverse our perspectives—release time-based expectations, explanations.

Time, generally an organizing tool, keeps us focused on plenty of the wrong things (superficial pursuits, worry, judgment, excessive competition), and can block a deeper understanding of the spiritual dimension that, while concealed, is inherent to my next breath, and yours. Though we are never "finished" or "complete," paradoxically, we needn't cradle our expectations in the hazy light of the future, as if *someday* were real. And time our master.

After making it through the 4-year anniversary, I decided to let go of that hazy light—to part ways with *someday*, so I could meet each day, each second, with less hesitation and greater peace. Understanding that *yesterday* would also need to be transcended, I added that challenge to my spiritual practice.

Diligently, but not always comfortably.

Jack Kornfield, Buddhist monk, clinical psychologist, author, and teacher, explains: "No matter what situation we find ourselves in, we can always set our compass to our highest intentions in the present moment."

He's right, wouldn't you admit?

Very little, in the spiritual sense, is impossible in the present moment. The world of spirit is the door beyond time. Persistently, it calls me (all of us) to discover my "highest intentions"—to avoid a shallow lifestyle with death as the chilling centerpiece, with life and loss as deadly foes: inseparable, disturbing realities. They work in tandem for a reason; a reason each person must discover firsthand.

As my awareness expands, I peer ever more intently through the veil of time, daring to inch my way beyond a murky trail of human suffering. In moments of deep silence—vast, comforting—I also sense I am intrinsic to a captivating fantasy, a sacred play of infinite energy.

Aren't we all just riding some incredible wave?

Inviting the Bell

"The Way of Heaven is to
benefit others and not to injure.
The Way of the sage is to act
but not to compete."

—LAO TZU

Subtle Signs Revisited

*A*s a young girl not even old enough for school, I sat across
from my grandmother at her small wooden table in a cozy
kitchen nook—window facing east, a bulletin board dotted with
pictures, snippets of information she'd saved, on the same wall. As
we sipped from cups of pale tea, my inquiring eyes were drawn there.
Scattered photos, black-and-white and held fast by shiny silver tacks,
portrayed mostly somber faces, dark clothing.

I wondered why these strangers were important to Anna.

But everything in her home, *everything about her*, provoked my
girlhood wondering. Her book of poetry by Tennyson; her well-worn
rosary beads; her head of thinning white hair. Even the dusty front
porch where buzzing wasps loved to hide on hot summer days.

Naïvely, I believed her soothing companionship would never end.
That sitting together, without agenda or timeframe, would be a lasting

pastime, just like stooping low to gather black walnuts that dropped in the fall from a towering tree in the center of her front yard. What more did I need to know, or do?

Yet, the days wore on, and I encountered a much bigger reality—learning, as we must, that frustration, confusion, uncertainty, even searing pain, meld in mosaic-like fashion to enable and support this temporary, earthly framework. A young man, gone in a heart-stopping second, when Anna died only two days shy of 99, right before her Christmas Eve birthday—a birth date we shared, celebrating with cake, presents, and piano music until she, too, was gone. What a curious discrepancy.

Does someone dispense time as an award for good behavior? No. Yet, the mind drifts and wanders, and on some unanswerable level, we wonder why one life is too short, the other, gracefully long. But besides years lived (mostly relevant if you allow time to shape your perceptions), there was another big difference between these deaths. I expected one good-bye, because of Anna's age. Sudden loss, though, is when the web of life collapses without warning. Like a bell chiming loudly, much too late in the day, after everyone has fallen asleep, the disconcerting experience feels alien to us.

And so the deeper mysteries call out.

When I began writing this book I wondered what was left to say, to do, after a sudden death. When everyone had returned to schedules, routines, and responsibilities that were insistently framed by calendars and clocks, not by the stirring passion of grief—and I felt alone like never before. Is that where the conversation ends, I'd wondered.

Seemed like it, even though I knew that wasn't possible, or desirable.

Glancing back through the funny tunnel of time, I see myself wading through the haze of years following death feeling perplexed about everything. Clearly, my need to understand hadn't vanished with a funeral. Rather, it had grown stronger, more urgent. Matthew's suicide was an emotional and spiritual earthquake that shook me like a rag doll, dropped me back at the beginning of my remembered history.

So today, when I sat down to write, I wasn't terribly surprised when Anna's familiar face materialized—her blessed memory enmeshed with my intense spiritual voyage.

It was a new year, only day three. The winter sun delivered reassuring warmth. Time to begin anew, I thought: fly high and free, like the skein of honking geese overhead. But free of what, I mused, with a thoughtful sigh—the cursor blinking in its insistent, slightly annoying manner.

Dig deeper.

Ponder, more fully, more intently, the deeper mysteries of absence.

There's still more to this story.

Since writing is like meditation, I sat quietly at the keyboard, waiting for a solid nudge from the universe. Something about my grandmother was seeking expression, but I felt impatient, uncertain.

Finally, I edged my fingers to the keyboard.

Trust the process.

With a touch of compassion, I told myself that spiritual books weren't written without a gutsy plunge into the darkness: a willingness to dance until dawn with unknown forces. Only my intuition could rescue me, so I closed my eyes, waited, and waited, and finally, there was Anna at her upright piano—creased hands sailing back and forth as she played "When Irish Eyes Are Smiling." First published in 1912, here's the chorus:

> *When Irish Eyes Are Smiling, sure 'tis like a morn in spring.*
> *In the lilt of Irish laughter you can hear the angels sing,*
> *When Irish hearts are happy all the world seems bright and gay,*
> *And When Irish Eyes Are Smiling, sure, they steal your heart*
> *away.*

She played by ear, something I could never do, and since McCormick was her maiden name, she definitely had Irish eyes. So did my son. His paternal grandmother, Kathleen, was a McDermott before marrying Lindell McCartney, so they contributed to Matthew's Irish eyes, as well. But looking up the first verse, the last line was a tough one.

> *With such power in your smile, sure a stone you'd beguile,*
> *And there's never a teardrop should fall,*
> *When your sweet lilting laughter's like some fairy song*
> *And your eyes sparkle bright as can be.*
> *You should laugh all the while and all other times smile,*
> *So now smile a smile for me.*

All I could do was wonder if my coffee was cold, as I resisted my own tears. Reaching for it (yes, cold), I went to the kitchen for a warm-up. Scarcely mid-morning, I wanted to keep working. Sustained stillness was the surest way to immerse myself in any creative work— plunging in, staying submerged—so this wasn't an opportune moment to drift off or dabble in another project. Poetry, a short story, an essay, even a novel from years ago that could use some serious attention, a blog post. All other pursuits could easily send me careening off track. As dedicated writers know, it doesn't take much.

Promptly returning to the keyboard, I focused on one thing: this project was launched as a process of discovery because I'd wanted, *needed*, to know what was important about life in the face (the triumph?) of death: what still mattered on a deeply personal level. So I posed the question: who was that girl, so content to spend time with her grandmother—blissful hours that seemed, in hindsight, more like a spiritual retreat? I hadn't unearthed the essential connection between the girl with the sweet smile, thick dark hair falling in soft waves, and the woman navigating life while writing about the mysteries of grief. One thing was clear, though: this odd riddle had profound spiritual underpinnings.

I was a serious fan of the hypnotically calm yet effervescent teacher Eckhart Tolle, but I'd also made a point of looping back to old favorites. Thoreau, Whitman, Buddha, Ghandi, Pema Chödrön, Deepak Chopra, Thich Nhat Hanh, Thomas Moore, Emerson, Kahlil Gibran, and Joseph Campbell. Increasingly, though, newer (to me) spiritual voices were showing up in my life: Neale Donald Walsch, Michael Beckwith, Elizabeth Lesser, Wayne Dyer, Marianne Williamson, Ram Dass, Shakti Gawain, Jack Kornfield, Michael Singer, Jon Kabat-Zinn, Paulo Coelho, Thomas Merton, David R. Hawkins, and so on.

This morning, right at daybreak, I'd heard the unmistakable hoot of an owl. Waiting, there it was again!

I'd listened closely, figured he (or she) was happily perched on a sky-high branch on a backyard evergreen. Our neighborhood was visited by owls frequently in the winter, but it was always a treat to hear one. I'd gotten up, walked to my office to peer out against the darkness. Though unlikely given my limited vantage point, I hoped to catch a glimpse of those piercing eyes hiding in thick branches.

Stealthy, glorious owls, often hidden from view, could be compared to spirituality—heard within via the still voice of knowing, yet sometimes difficult to see, experience, or explain. Increasingly, I wanted my spiritual growth to manifest externally. If there were a deeper purpose in Matt's life and loss, this must be it, and not only for my benefit, but for others, as well. Feeling certain my journey was universal in nature, I still wanted to share it in ways that were helpful, tenable, and illuminating. But my thoughts weren't flowing. I couldn't seem to get beyond Matt's Irish eyes when seen through the warm light of my grandmother's memory. Leaving the demanding keyboard behind, I turned my attention to yoga. Even working through my basic routine, shifted my emotions, settled my mind.

Discoveries and Discrepancies

My attraction to yoga is a good mystery, because I'd never imagined myself rolling out a mat, stretching into odd positions, or meditating—not formally, anyway. The whole idea had never really appealed to me, probably because I hadn't grown up around it.

My husband, however, gave me a beginner's instruction book; he knew the basics, at least, and though he had never been serious about it, enjoyed exploring it.

That was in 1993, or thereabouts, and since I liked to challenge myself, I gave it a try. With no clue what I was doing, I'd rarely felt like such a beginner. But something about the poses—the benefits for mind, body—aroused my curiosity.

Slightly.

Never keen on formal exercise programs, I wasn't a health nut, was leery of anything that made such enticing promises. Besides, some poses were awkward, if not difficult or even impossible, and those that weren't seemed way too easy.

What exactly was yoga doing for me?

Still, I stayed with it for a few months, hoping to improve or see tangible results. I was in decent shape, so losing weight wasn't my goal, but yoga can slow the aging process or, supposedly, reduce the negative effects of aging. I had noticed how relaxed I felt—like my entire body was breathing—after a basic, thirty-minute routine.

Nonetheless, yoga fell by the wayside.

I was busy working as a development consultant to nonprofits, writing grants, giving workshops, and was thinking about writing for publication. Maybe books for children or young readers, some articles or short stories. In my wildest dreams, a novel, a collection of essays. All of this because I'd had quite an epiphany one night when I couldn't fall asleep.

Wondering, like we all do, if I'd found my real purpose in life, it occurred to me how much I loved books—learning, connection, insights, companionship, inspiration—and setting words on paper, and with a faint flicker of awareness, I detected a desire to write. Where had this notion been hiding? If detected before, apparently I had laughed it off as too remote, dreamy, or impractical—a silly idea brushed aside in favor of more pressing demands. Didn't good writers need major blocks of time in a reflective space to generate publishable work?

But ... what if it were simpler than that?

What if I just needed the courage to wrap my arms around my love of writing?

Whatever the reason, as is often true of sleepless nights, I had uncovered something I couldn't easily ignore: my desire to write had been acknowledged, rescued from an early grave. Within a day or two, I was on fire: emotionally, intellectually, and spiritually. An urgent desire to visit the library propelled me further.

How-to books might help me to actualize my insight.

Even if a steep learning curve came with it, something within pressed for expression. I couldn't stuff this delightful genie back in the bottle. Still, the intensity of my realization caught me unprepared, unguarded and, on some level, subdued, even humbled.

Why hadn't I figured this out long ago?

While walking, doing dishes, or working in a small backyard garden, where had this powerful desire been hiding? A potent dream untapped, almost shadow-like.

I'd taken expository writing at Stephens College in the late 1970s— taught then by the now prolific author, William Least Heat-Moon—and, for a time, seriously mulled over a major in journalism. But that was a conventional educational decision, not a choice of passion; I hadn't yet tapped the deeper, soul connection between myself and writing.

Even years later, while working on a graduate degree in sociology, writing was a skill I wanted and needed, but not as an artistic endeavor, nor as a career.

But, finally, about the time Matt was in the sixth grade, I *knew* I wanted to write.

❧

Almost "getting by" in school, Matt still seemed reluctant to grab on to the customary demands of life, accepting them as his own. Though he loved to spend time with friends and family, school, as mentioned before, didn't interest him. And he truly had a saint for a teacher that year. She had worked with kids like Matt, she told me—understood them, felt confident she could engage him academically.

I hoped, prayed, and supported her efforts.

In fact, I'd moved home to South Dakota, as Matt approached the fifth grade, hoping a small school system might benefit him. The fourth grade hadn't gone well, so I tried to enroll Matt in a rather expensive Catholic school with a strong reputation for working wonders (miracles?) with disenchanted students. Previously a student in an award-winning public school, Matt sometimes irritated and annoyed personnel, and that, as you may imagine, led to meetings with the principal more frequently than I care to recall.

Infractions were relatively minor, but his efforts to effectively engage concerned me greatly. Helpful clues were few in that era, but I looked for viable options, and a private school seemed like a good idea. My son wasn't thriving in the academic environment he was in, and we both suffered from the ongoing turmoil. Sensing deep frustration in Matt, I hoped a new school would be the answer. But it was not to be. I'd explained all of this to him and he was agreeable, but when he sat down with a group of kids for the required admittance test, he wouldn't return to the testing room after the first break. It was a rather lengthy exam (darken the correct circles), and he didn't have the greatest attention span but, for inexplicable reasons, Matt refused to complete it.

I was extremely discouraged; if this wasn't going to work out, then what?

The nun in charge told me they would be in touch, but due to heavy enrollment, they eventually decided Matt would need to see a counselor for an evaluation before a final decision could be reached. I agreed: *good idea*. What could the future possibly hold if the fourth grade was an obstacle, such a staggering mountain to climb? Still, none of it made a great deal of sense. At home, he listened, was cooperative and easy to get along with. When school personnel described Matt, it sounded like someone I'd never met.

The discrepancy was troubling, and when I queried Matthew—do you like school, is it difficult, are the kids mean to you, is there a bully in your class; is something wrong, son, how can I help you?—he offered little, as if bewildered by the situation himself. A heavy sigh, sad shrug of the shoulders, or a perplexed, I-don't-know look were typical.

He was also a pro at trying to change the subject, asking, for instance, if he could go spend a little time with his friends.

When I engaged his father around these issues, he, also, felt at a loss.

"It's a phase … he'll outgrow it."

I wanted, tried hard, to believe it.

Personnel at the Catholic school said he'd scored quite well on the portion of the test he completed. A hopeful sign, sheer luck, nothing at all? The counselor evaluating Matt didn't identify anything unusual or deeply revealing, offered few suggestions, and when I explained I was considering a move home to a smaller community, she agreed, this could be helpful. And for the fifth and sixth grades, it did seem to help.

He got better grades, kept a paper route, made lasting friends.

But I sensed he was still disconnected from the process, unable to find satisfaction or joy within the traditional educational system. Since I'd never raised a son before—his father hadn't *loved* school like I had—I wanted to stay open to other realities.

We aren't, *shouldn't be*, all the same.

Maybe, I reasoned, Matt was our late bloomer, or resisting the structure, the sameness of school activities, because he was a deep thinker. A free spirit.

I had studied innovative school systems in college, was a little free-spirited myself. I loved the Montessori concept of letting students advance at a comfortable, natural pace. Staying in step with individual abilities and interests sounded like a wise way to respect different learning styles, unique proclivities. Cookie-cutter kids made no sense to me.

The gifted, revolutionary Steve Jobs is a strong case in point.

The world stage depends on innovation for our survival—creative voices generating novel ideas and solving problems, people suggesting a more peaceful approach to life, something besides the status quo and blind, we've-always-done-it-that-way conformity. Fortunately, for other students and families, more progressive educational programs and philosophies are surfacing.

Wisdom Inspired by Learning Differences (W.I.L.D.), for one, is a mentoring program that partners a young student (elementary/middle school) with learning differences with a college student who has experienced comparable challenges. Sounds promising, doesn't it? It's important to ensure that kids have positive role models that speak directly to their unique needs, perceived challenges.

Recently, I also heard a Colorado principal on PBS.

He explained how a zero-tolerance policy, like spanking or suspension, no longer matched social values, so they were taking a more effective approach.

Likewise, I've been impressed by the president of the National Education Association. As recently as December 2014, Lily Eskelsen Garcia spoke to business leaders in Detroit about taking public education off the assembly line to focus on the whole child. I caught a late September interview with her (also 2014) on MSNBC's Morning Joe and, wisely, she spoke about the pitfalls of standardized testing, factory school reforms, toxic testing regimes, and "stopping stupid." Getting beyond scores and labels seems very important.

Also encouraging, a *New York Times* (May 13, 2014) article: "Exercising the Mind to Treat Attention Deficits" by Daniel Goleman.

"Mindfulness seems to flex the brain circuitry for sustaining attention, an indicator of cognitive control, according to research by Wendy Hasenkamp and Lawrence Barsalou at Emory University."

Thus, mindfulness training combined with cognitive therapy may become a viable option, one perhaps comparable to various medications.

There is also the controversial work of Seth Farber, Ph.D.

In 2014, he published *The Spiritual Gift of Madness: The Failure of Psychiatry and the Rise of the Mad Pride Movement*.

I also stumbled across a book called *The Edison Trait: Saving the Spirit of Your Free-Thinking Child in a Conforming World* (Times Books, 1997).

I haven't read it yet, but the title has great appeal. I wish the book had existed in the 1980s, when I'd looked everywhere for insights into Matt's limited interest in school. But maybe it's not all that mysterious.

Can we seriously expect every child, every teen, to respond to (or benefit from) traditional school systems? Of course not.

A Return to Yoga

Late summer 2003, after serving an initial five (of 11) years, Matt was paroled. We had made countless trips to visit him, but how else would I have experienced the inside of a prison, seen Matt living as one of many—dressed in a plain gray uniform? The same slacks, shirt, tennis shoes ... day after day. Visiting rooms, though never pleasant, weren't nearly as bad as my fears, however.

The atmosphere was generally quiet, calm.

John and I, after getting through security, would wait for Matt while seated at a small square table.

I usually scanned the faces of strangers in the room and wondered about the weather for our return trip (especially in winter). We would also check out a deck of cards. Once Matt arrived, there would be several hours to fill. Sometimes we stuck a bag of popcorn in the microwave, plugged money into the vending machine for a candy bar or coffee, or simply sat quietly.

When Matt emerged from behind the front desk, for me, it was a memorable moment of gratitude: a sigh of relief in *seeing* that he was okay.

Sitting there, the three of us, we talked and talked, smiled and laughed, worried and prayed, and always, I would study Matt's eyes. Peering into his soul, I hoped for a real glimpse of his emotional state—not the one he projected publicly.

Was he holding up, being hurt—physically, psychologically, spiritually—or to what extent? Would he tell me how things were going, or opt to spare me the painful details: the unspoken demands of life within fences, gates, loudspeakers, inspections, and heavy clanging bars? I could never forget his visible joy upon seeing us, his noticeable sadness as we said good-bye—that look of painful resignation, while trying to look impervious.

Matt knew we'd return in a matter of weeks, that weekly phone calls and letters would bridge the gap but, on that day, in that hour, there was only this: another difficult parting. As watchful eyes looked on—we were permitted a single embrace upon arrival, and again on departure—I worried. *We didn't break a rule (new or changed) that might result in a write-up, did we?*

≈

Matt drove to Indianapolis for the Fourth of July in 2006. This followed his March release, and our Easter visit in Hannibal. We played golf, grilled salmon on cedar planks, talked. Catching up on things in person, given his history, wasn't taken for granted. Matt had never looked more comfortable, or content. Tan, relaxed, seemingly happy. It was a long (and hopeful) summer weekend—a gift, a miracle—like we seldom had a chance to enjoy with him.

At 26, perhaps he still has a meaningful life ahead of him.

With a deep breath, I made a valiant effort to keep fear at bay, but when Matt left our driveway that weekend, I got a funny feeling, one I couldn't nail down. Neither the sound of a distant alarm, nor the familiar pulse of worry and foreboding, it was a curious string of random questions that penetrated my awareness instead.

What comes next? How long will this recovery last; could this be the one that sticks? Or will something completely unexpected turn our worlds

upside down again? How will he do for the rest of the summer, into fall?
Still about four years, of 11, left—would Matt serve the entire sentence,
eventually?

Reminding myself not to try to peer too closely into the future, *something* tugged at my inner vision. Looking under the enormous umbrella of time, I would describe it as a vague sense of completion— that the worst of his journey was behind him, that the rest of Matt's story would be *different*. I wasn't thinking about life completion, or final endings, though, merely life passages. In short, while nearly everything pointed to the advent of a new life chapter—the end of something—clouds of caution swept across my internal sky, and a hazy somberness hung at the edge of my awareness.

I detected a gentle warning, in fact.

But what was my intuition hinting at?

Though asking, I also may have resisted the answer; I may have been reluctant to dig too deep. Still floundering around in the concrete world of time, I invested tremendous energy fighting off thoughts of what might happen next. Relapse; a return to prison; a horrific tragedy swallowing Matt's life if I dared to glance away too soon?

I woke up early the next morning, about 5:30.

A restless feeling urged me out of bed and, reaching for my robe, I reluctantly faced the darkness with no idea why I was getting up this early. Walking down the long flight of stairs to the living room, I wondered what I would do now that I was up.

Read, doze in a chair, make coffee, meditate?

Settling into our blue recliner, I flipped on the television.

Assuming nothing good would be on, I surfed channels, explored stations I usually ignored, and there he was: a bald guy, tall and thin and unbelievably flexible, leading a yoga class. Yoga, I mused. *Haven't done that in ages.* But my intuition drew me closer. Feeling spellbound, I watched the entire hour-long program on Oxygen (Oprah channel at the time), and learned that Steve Ross, Los Angeles yoga master, was the instructor.

I loved the high-energy music, at least a dozen students following along and, literally, was captivated by Steve's ability and upbeat, contagious demeanor. I decided to give it a try. It looked difficult: easily surpassing long-forgotten, beginner poses from earlier days.

Still, I was seriously drawn to this energetic and demanding, yet peaceful, world. I had never taken instruction in yoga, but wasn't opposed, even if it happened to flow from a television screen when I would usually be sleeping.

Setting my alarm that night, I urged John to join me in the morning. Secretly, I doubted I would get up in time, and since John wasn't a morning person, I assumed I was on my own. But I did make it up.

The first few weeks were painfully slow. I couldn't keep up, rested between poses, fell over in a heap more times than I can recall.

What a work of art—yoga done well. Funny terms like chair pose, forward fold, and sun salutation were back in my life, and a week or so later, John joined me. We bought a second mat, kept at it. Like my earlier days with yoga, I couldn't believe how peaceful, how relaxed, I felt after each session. Neither could John. We became ardent fans, and I decided to talk to Matt about it. What a positive outlet for him, we thought. Living alone and working on a family farm, surely he had time to do yoga, didn't he?

Next, in customary fashion, I looked for books: *Happy Yoga: 7 Reasons Why There's Nothing to Worry About* by Steve Ross; *Meditations from the Mat: Daily Reflections on the Path of Yoga* also intrigued me. By Rolf Gates and Katrina Kenison, I slowly plowed through 365 daily reflections. Rolf had been an addiction counselor after getting a degree in history, serving in the Army. Yoga, per the authors, was "one path out of the spiritual wilderness, a highway … built by those who came before … trodden by millions over thousands of years." Weren't many people languishing, at least partially, in a spiritual wilderness because they lacked the intentionality of something inspiring, true?

The authors explained that yoga was "profoundly effective self-care," and pointed to *A Course in Miracles*, a book I also wanted to delve into. They described it as a "journey inward." And, sadly, I learned that Rolf's older sister, at 31, had committed suicide. Little did I know how much this would resonate in the upcoming months, and only pages later he wrote about surrendering at 26 to treatment for substance abuse. Willingly, because he felt it was his time to grow, change. Reading on about his spiritual practice, my thoughts naturally drifted to Matt. Encouraged that Gates had turned his life around, I wondered if a sustained practice could give Matt something safe to lean on.

So I tried to interest him in watching a yoga video, in finding a class, or just reading about it. No luck. Matt couldn't visualize himself doing yoga, much less digging deeper into his spirituality. I'm pretty sure he laughed at our efforts to engage him in an ancient art form, especially when John and I demonstrated a few poses. We weren't that good, for one thing, but he couldn't make the mental leap from strange twists and turns on a narrow floor mat, to, hey, this might help me. *This might even save my life.*

The good news: I've never stopped doing yoga, not since the summer of 2006. Same routine, too. The one I learned on television at the crack of dawn. It was something I felt destined, and fortunate, to discover. To rediscover, more accurately. But the timing, how I happened across Steve's class on a channel I never usually watched that very early July morning right after Matt's visit, led me to a disquieting conclusion: change, of some kind, was in the air.

Was I being led back to yoga? Why?

Of course I had no idea how much I would need it as time, like a worn, woolen blanket, unraveled around me.

Inviting the Bell

"The Way of Heaven is to benefit others and not to injure. The Way of the sage is to act but not to compete."

—LAO TZU

We don't know the reasons that propel us on a spiritual journey, but somehow our life compels us to go. Something in us knows that we are not just here to toil at our work. There is a mysterious pull to remember.
—JACK KORNFIELD

More than His Fears

Lately, I have felt consumed by philosophies of loss—the myriad ways we come to view death and its purpose. Biology is one thing, i.e., Darwin's famous survival of the fittest paradigm, but his theory lacks lasting appeal on a spiritual level. Surely there is more to *all of this* than mere survival—although that could be *part* of our mission—so why not consider the soul's perspective? Why not seek enlightenment?

It's a rather intimidating prospect, for starters. One suggesting imposing images of spiritual gurus standing tall like mountains or dancing with the wind, their eyes a calm sea of infinite depth. Men and women with a powerful presence who comprehend life's deepest secrets—and personify them. With such a profile (real or imagined) how can any of us feel entitled, or prepared, to explore such sacred terrain?

Like many, I believed enlightenment was higher than I could (or should) dare to reach: a spotless red apple dangling from the tip of the tree.

Yet, I also believed in Rilke's observation, "the only journey is the journey within," and had noticed how so many of us (knowingly or otherwise) suffer from *avidya*, a lack of spiritual knowledge. That, almost by default, we were willing to pass through life as surface dwellers: operating blindly (carelessly? unmindfully?) because we lacked a serious interest in anything that wasn't easily accessible.

But weren't we missing the point entirely?

I lost a few years believing a religious choice was the salient question, but religion is so easily misused, misapplied, and can become a handy excuse for behavior many would call questionable. Some even insist on rigid belief systems with the potential to obscure reality and stymie genuine spiritual inquiry.

When focusing followers on inflammatory topics that so many *love* to argue about—distracting, unanswerable questions—organized religion can fail to encourage us to discover our true depth, our inherent spirituality. When this occurs, some may never develop a quality of awareness that is deeper than intellectual understanding. There are exceptions, and religion can lead to spirituality, especially if dogmatic views—beliefs, traditions, teachings—aren't overly narrow or limiting.

Matt and Erin were baptized and confirmed in the Catholic Church, and I once said to my adult son during a phone conversation, "Matt, you are a child of God."

Just an ordinary day, but I'd noticed his painful uncertainty: gnawing doubts about the likelihood of long-term recovery. And since I believed he needed faith in a higher power of some kind to conquer drugs or any form of addiction, I thought it might help to remind him that he was *more* than his problems, more than his past, more than others might label him.

Even more than his darkest fears.

Matt grew quiet, laughed softly, like he wasn't so sure, but didn't want to completely negate the idea. In hindsight, I suppose it did sound funny to him. We'd never been the family that had to get to church on all the *right* days, at all the *right* times (the surficial, time-construed realities), but we were reverent, and I had encouraged Matt and Erin to have faith in *something more*: in God (a word, a designation, that sadly invites dissension and discord and resistance, so I use it as a representative term, leaving everyone to their personal sentiments and beliefs), in a force beyond sight and time and mortal expression. As I might state it now, in an unfathomable eternal power of a most benevolent nature.

Maybe Matt had wondered if he could live up to such a lofty designation. Don't we all? I wish we could have that conversation again. And I wish I could have inspired him to seek his spiritual bearings with greater urgency and tenacity, searching within for a lasting peace, for reasons to live and grow that always would be *more* than his troubles. More than what a one-dimensional culture values and rewards.

Then again, who can really judge the spiritual qualities others seek and experience? Within the privacy of his own heart, Matt may have reached for God's light (and found it) in ways I can't begin to fathom. We are so much more than our outer appearances and external perceptions. As Marianne Williamson might suggest, we are all miracle workers in the service of God.

A Return to Love: Reflections on the Principles of A Course in Miracles was part of Christmas 2011, when I bought two copies: one for me, one for my daughter. I'd heard about Williamson's impressive work, but hadn't read her books. Since I was also inching my way through *A Course in Miracles*, the books seemed like a strong combination. Weaving in Williamson's interpretation, I could benefit from both. I'd already learned that a miracle is a shift in perception, as we move from fear to love: as we begin to realize our divine purpose. An intriguing definition, and during the month of December, it's fairly common to speak in terms of miracles.

So one evening, the house quiet, I picked up her book, and there it was, the first line in "The Perfect You" chapter.

"You are a child of God. You were created in a blinding flash of creativity, a primal thought when God extended Himself in love." Williamson's message resonated with striking clarity. I experienced that blissful feeling of reading something I already *knew* as truth. I didn't need to be convinced.

Love is what I most remember about my relationship with Matt. And love is what remains.

A few things were starting to make sense. Glancing at a nearby candle, I saw sleeping pets, our tree (put up at the last minute), and *knew* the only part of Matt that was real was also timeless: because it was love. A changeless force, the source of everything. When distracted by the external world, we miss the obvious: the light within, the spiritual door, the divine power behind our own breath. Love, as our immortal essence, is beyond human destruction, as spiritual and religious leaders have observed for eons.

It was our fifth Christmas without Matthew.

Yet, the present moment was quite lovely, even joyful, and definitely peaceful.

Had some kind of miracle occurred since June 2007, when time crashed around me like a meteor striking Earth—one escaping radar, intuition, the atmosphere's ravenous appetite? Indeed, my perception of loss, or philosophy of loss and the so-called purpose of death, had changed.

I'd moved beyond personal pain, a personalized understanding of loss, to something much deeper. That is not to say my grief had evaporated into time imagined and dreams untold (as I wrote on Christmas cards one year). It hadn't.

Some elements of grief are perpetual. We miss those no longer with us, and will never stop wanting to see them again, speak of them, think of them, while savoring pictures that capture an irreplaceable time yet, paradoxically, the virtual absence of time. Some caring souls—people I so appreciate—have the depth, the innate wisdom, to converse with me about Matt in comforting ways that validate my ongoing relationship with him, and his memory. He will always be part of my life; on a spiritual plane, we are inevitably "one."

Attempts to deny this seem to produce such needless pain and suffering.

Glancing at our tree, LED lights that did their best to add sparkle, I spotted a pale blue ribbon. The ornament it supported was a blue cat with angel wings, a halo sprinkled with gold glitter. Something Matt had created in grade school. My heart raced. Remembering what is gone is comforting, yet never entirely satisfying, either.

Like bodies, temporary, imperfect vehicles that can't save us from the vagaries of time or circumstance, when our memories begin to fly free, they fray at the ends. Yet, every waking second is an ineffable expression of something far more profound. Caught in a windstorm of great force, *only* our earthly duration varies.

Inviting the Bell

"The Way of Heaven is to benefit others and not to injure. The Way of the sage is to act but not to compete."

—LAO TZU

*Our task must be to free ourselves ... by widening our
circle of compassion to embrace all living creatures
and the whole of nature and its beauty.*

—ALBERT EINSTEIN

Where There Is Freedom

*R*aising a child who never quite fits the bright, shiny mold
that society has embedded in our collective consciousness is
challenging. Many of you may know what I mean. Bright, beautiful,
spirited. Things that matter. Yet the child seems mystified by the
drama of life—all degrees of effort, love, faith, and hope. I wished
for a magic wand on more than one occasion. Matt was either fully
tuned in to his surroundings, or largely tuned out.

Fishing, for instance, was something that grew slowly on him. As
our boat motored up the shimmering Missouri River in central South
Dakota, Matt, then in grade school, wasn't the least bit impressed by
the peaceful landscape, the swift-moving fish below. One gorgeous
autumn day, he even decided to take a nap in the boat.

This, after he'd asked me several times why we liked to fish.

"John and I think it's fun to catch walleye. Not bad for dinner either, right?"

"So when will we be done? How long does this take?"

Curiously, I recall his innocent questions so clearly through the veil of years.

"Give it a try, Matt. Let's bait your hook. Worm, minnow? You might get a bite—sound fun?" I'd offer a hopeful smile. John would chime in with a short pep talk, ask Matt if he wanted to give his pole a try. See if it worked any better.

I loved spending time on the water—sunlight dancing on the rocky blue-gray surface, a cool breeze against my face. Catching fish was hardly the point. But, for a young boy, there was no point at all, apparently. When he did show a mild interest in fishing, he was well into his 20s. Maturity, greater internal peace, evolving interests, *much less* social anxiety: who was doing what that was more fun, more adventurous; what was he missing on television; what would the other kids think; why was life so boring?

When Matt had a paper route in the fifth grade, I drove him door to door if the weather was inclement. His lack of enthusiasm was usually palpable, but one afternoon he had a sore throat, a cough, so I suggested a teaspoon of cough syrup before he delivered papers. When I picked him up (snowflakes swirling), he looked sleepy, acted more disinterested than usual. I wondered if his sore throat, his cough, was other than a passing irritation.

"How are you feeling, Matt?" I asked. "Take some cough syrup?"

Studying his eyes, their apparent drowsiness, I could see that he had taken some cough syrup, more like half the bottle. But he offered little, shrugged his shoulders, and tried to change the subject. Most kids do these things, don't they? There can't be a child on the planet who hasn't stepped away from rules or instructions once or twice, so I didn't want to over-react. Now, being familiar with the pioneering work of David Perlmutter, author of the highly acclaimed *Grain Brain*, I'm sure that Matt, like many kids, was consuming many of the wrong foods.

Grains (morning cereal), sugar (he loved orange juice, which can have as much sugar as a Coke), wheat (bread), carbs (he loved pasta). Perlmutter links these silent killers to many ailments, including depression, anxiety, ADHD, and points out that healthy fats and cholesterol are actually what our brains need. I also heard recently that acetaminophen, taken by mothers during pregnancy, may contribute to childhood ADHD. (If personally concerned about this, please seek medical advice; explore the research that is continually evolving.)

Could it be—*could it be*—that most of Matthew's problems stemmed from mind and body chemistry? When he thought I wasn't looking, he would scoop spoonfuls of sugar into his morning cereal. And the cough syrup. These early symptoms may have been one ticket to better understanding his needs. But *Grain Brain* wasn't available then, not until September 2013, and Matt was a child of the 1980s, when conventional wisdom prevailed. "Kids will be kids" type thinking.

I can't help but wonder if Matt continued to shore up his physical chemistry by using increasingly strong options. But once spin-off patterns take root—academic and behavioral issues—other negative cycles are simultaneously launched that readily take on a deadly life of their own.

Dr. Perlmutter spoke in a teleseminar on August 7, 2013, about successfully treating a 4-year-old with dietary changes instead of resorting to medication that often creates new problems. *If only, if only.* Though impossible to know if his recommendations could have altered Matt's life, I hope parents and caregivers stay open to exploring such possibilities—it might save a child's life one day. Medication, too often, seems to lead in all the wrong directions.

For another helpful perspective, Eckhart Tolle has suggested that the hectic nature of contemporary life may be contributing to ADHD. I can see how children are conditioned by social and living environments to have short attention spans. Too much emphasis on doing, going, hurrying, competing, and striving. Impressionable children also absorb vast amounts of questionable information from television, friends, relatives, classrooms; they sense the enormous expectations of others and most must realize that "more" or "faster" or "better" are strongly linked to some generic "success equation." And to the approval of others.

But when my fifth grader drank cough syrup, I wasn't sure what to think. After talking it over with a few people, his teacher included, I was confident this was a foray into the world of youthful discovery. A blip. A curious mind. An experiment. Nonetheless, I sat down with Matt; we talked it over. Primarily, I sought understanding with him, because I've long believed *this* is the most resilient and reliable bridge between people of any age. Compassion, respect, constructive communication, and cooperation: don't they all derive from a fundamental willingness to understand?

When it came to setting limits, for example, I wanted Matt to *understand* what kind of behavior was appropriate and why. I wanted him to truly care: about himself and others, and the world, at large. I wasn't always sure I was getting through to him, however.

Active listening helped; staying open to whatever he might offer was also useful. But Matt wasn't a big talker. Like many boys, he was drawn to high-energy pursuits. Talking, I'm afraid, was sort of like punishment to him: the dreaded conversation about something he didn't want to discuss for more than a fleeting second. And, realistically, I was already up against an insidious male culture of silence—at best, the collective reluctance (there are exceptions, granted) to converse about difficult or uncomfortable personal feelings conveniently relegated to "girl talk."

Culture and society generate an immeasurable *system of sameness* that boys and girls alike must contend with, while seeking a place of ease and comfort within group milieus. You recall how acceptance and likeability were of paramount importance in grade school, middle school, and high school, don't you? Hairstyles to shoes and jeans, best friends and quickly changing cliques, abilities, interests, and class favorites: most kids simply want to be liked. Those blessed with confident, outgoing personalities appear "well-adjusted" and without a care, but *plenty* don't fit the mold that truly, in my estimation, is wearing thin in many contexts.

Social anxiety can be a significant source of stress at any age, but definitely for young people trying to find their way in the world.

Once I drew a picture for Matt to explain satisfactory interaction with kids at school.

I thought the visual might help.

"That's nice, Mom." And moments later, "Can I watch TV now?"

He seemed to understand my explanation, but other things were far more interesting. Matt gravitated to kids he felt comfortable

with—avoided cliques based on group norms, fitting in, and measuring up, and preferred friends more independent in their approach
to social realities. In other words, he liked kids not dedicated to
following the crowd.

Matt had a couple of close friends in the fifth and sixth grades.
We all spent a lot of time together—playing cards or board games,
water or snow skiing, making special meals, or camping out. When
engaged in activities he enjoyed, Matt was your average kid: happy,
content, attentive. I received warm messages from those same friends
when they learned of Matt's death. Eager to share their memories, one
wrote: "A great friend. Blessed to have known him."

Scanning these lighthearted memories, I've searched for *something*
that might predict the future in terms so straightforward anyone could
have seen it, but still, I see a growing boy with a carefree laugh, a
warm smile, a kind eye. I see my young son who didn't mind testing
limits or tradition to search for the authentic, and who didn't seem
eager to adopt or play-along with phony social roles. Nothing else
shines through in a remarkable way.

Blue of a Painted Sky

When Matt was serving time, we learned to accept the blue of a
painted sky. Visits were never outside. In one facility where he spent
the most time, a mural on the wall offered a glimpse of the outside
world. So one day, with Matt, we stood in front of it for a picture;
this was allowed if he made the necessary arrangements beforehand.
But did we want to record such a harsh reality? Yes. In the world of time,
which can never be left behind entirely, it was important to have the
picture, no matter where we were standing, or why.

Besides, as Fyodor Dostoyevsky wisely noted, "I see the sun and if I don't see the sun, I know it's there. And there's a whole life in that, knowing that the sun is there."

Even though the mural wasn't the rich blue of the real sky, we knew, like the sun, that it was there. And, in the end, love knows no boundaries. We felt it in the visiting room, a big open area with tall windows facing east and inviting open sky into our conversations. Families hugging, children talking with an incarcerated parent—laughing or joking, for a few moments, oblivious to who was watching—elderly visitors sipping lukewarm tea or coffee in paper cups from the vending machine, maybe snacking on microwave popcorn, its earthy aroma wafting through rows of identical tables, amidst subdued voices, swirling emotions, created a fantastical experience we almost grew accustomed to. *Almost.* What led these nameless faces—*these struggling human beings*—to this shared destination?

My mind whirred with poignant questions. The dreamlike nature of the place pulling me in, holding me to its mystery for deeper exploration.

Ever-watchful guards—polite, all business—scanned the room. A few would offer a hasty but much appreciated smile. Imagine how much that meant in a prison. *What had brought them to this career choice?* Ushering inmates to and from the visiting room after proper clearance; signing in visitors before and after a visit. Although minimum-security, I expected only the basics from staff. Most human beings, however, regardless of titles or context, sense pain in others. And, in that rectangular room that held quite a few lives, we were all enduring a less-than-optimal experience.

On special occasions we were allowed to bring food in from the "outside."

Food visits were a big deal for Matt.

He looked forward to them for weeks, letting us know the dates, and what he wanted us to bring. One visit, close to Christmas, we packed up a home-cooked turkey dinner; although partially frozen when we arrived, he patiently warmed everything in the small microwave. We appreciated food visits, too, because they offered a thin slice of home: even in a very public setting, an hour or two of "normalcy" was absolutely better than nothing.

Matt was usually setting goals for himself when we sat together for visits—what he had to do to get things back on track, what he thought would be interesting in terms of work. And, of course, what he planned to do to stay clean: to make his recovery a reality. Conversation about family members, pets, or shared interests easily consumed our visit. Matt appreciated our companionship and support a great deal.

Words of encouragement were always welcome.

Rarely, would a loud voice interrupt us.

Maybe an inmate would be escorted from the room, a guest asked to leave, but I only recall a handful of such complications during our many visits. Mostly, a noticeable aura of routine hung in the air. A feeling of confinement, of time remaining. But sometimes we managed to forget our surroundings completely; then a blissful, in-the-now sensation of rising above place, time, and circumstance permeated the room.

Spiritual freedom, that's what it felt like. Especially for Matt, I hope. Freedom from the self he knew behind bars: the self of less-than-desirable labels, like prisoner, inmate, convict, addict, felon. We memorized his inmate number because we needed it often. For mail, for visits. Always visible on his shirts, what, I'd wondered, was it like to be a mere number in the eyes of many. Dehumanizing, demeaning? But Matt seemed to take it in stride; his eyes firmly fixed on the exit sign—the better world he knew awaited him if he stayed clean, complied with every single rule.

If he didn't give up.

As I studied my son's smiling face, eyes with a sparkle—maybe a full or half-beard, sometimes smoothly shaven—I often asked myself, *How does he do it?*

He rarely complained. Stayed intent on the future: on time beyond concrete and steel. And always thanked us for money for food or stamps—he wrote short notes frequently—or for miscellaneous personal items like shampoo. Even phone calls were an investment. Prepaid minutes were expensive, but we liked to talk to Matt on a weekly basis.

Offering a warm interest in his challenging world of sameness, we covered the usual topics: educational opportunities, work projects (offsite, or onsite), treatment options, infractions, or important dates in the offing—a scheduled hearing for a release date, an upcoming visit from an old friend. All things that comprised life in prison.

Health came up frequently. If he had a headache or didn't feel well, just getting an aspirin or a clinic appointment could be a small hurdle. I'd ask about the wisdom teeth that had to be extracted; the moles on his back that a dermatologist had been monitoring. And there were the usual questions: did he get our letter, the photos; was he attending a religious service or meeting with a member of the clergy; what had he read, checked out of the library? Any time for exercise? How's the food been? Playing cards, working in the kitchen? Any luck getting work release; how are group counseling sessions going?

Naturally, a few troubling situations developed—a violation, an "issue." Though infrequent, I dreaded those calls: knew if it was bad news the minute I heard his voice. If headed to the "hole" for several days or weeks that meant isolation with an old paperback … maybe. No windows, no calls—no one to talk to. Hopefully silent prayer: "Now the Lord is the Spirit, and where the Spirit of the Lord is, there is freedom" (2 Corinthians 3:17).

When I heard a frightening loneliness in his voice, or despair over what had happened or might happen, it was difficult to keep breathing. He was on the inside; we were on the outside. Options were nonexistent. I could write him another letter, send another card or picture, or merely hope he felt our support, our love, despite the distance. That a higher power—*the* God, *any* God—would keep him safe. That he wouldn't consider ending his life. *Then or ever.* If he could hold on, make it to the next morning—until things didn't feel quite so dark, empty and hopeless.

If … if … if.

If time behind bars helped Matt, his pain and suffering, and ours, wouldn't be in vain. Rather, it would be the one thing that finally worked. But steps forward felt minuscule—difficult to identify, nearly impossible to discern—against the stern glare of setbacks that suddenly appeared like dense dark clouds dotting the sky's expanse.

Matt saved all the pictures we sent him in basic-looking photo albums he was able to purchase. Browsing through them one day, I was quickly overwhelmed by the passage of time. Like the trickle of a mountain stream you can't catch, time is a wily force that leaves us breathless and perplexed—when we "believe" in it. Granting it power, incredible influence in our lives.

Now, I try to consider alternative perceptions whenever possible. If it weren't for the crazy swagger of time on the planet, what would I be doing, thinking, or wishing? How would my priorities shift, my assumptions, values? Even my hopes, dreams.

Marianne Williamson, *A Return to Love*, wrote about how we view criminals as guilty and seek to punish them, noting that what we do to others, we invariably do to ourselves.

In light of the often-discussed merits of effective rehabilitation, she suggests a transition from "fear to love" to release "infinite possibilities" of healing. Can you conceptualize a world such as this: peaceful, hopeful, enlightened? From a sociological perspective, I assume we would need a massive paradigm shift: a sustained, committed movement away from violence (direct/indirect) in any form, as a popular substitute for healthy, safe interaction, and as a source of "acceptable" entertainment. (Ask yourself how much indirect violence you experience each day via mainstream media outlets, TV, must-see movies, books, video games, sporting events, and so on? Surprised, saddened?)

A concerted global initiative to realize peaceful and progressive cultures, along with greater equity in resources, education, and opportunity, would help. Planetary evolution of this magnitude really suggests a worldwide epidemic of love, one to push us—carry us—beyond the heavy, and largely defining, world of time. With healthier priorities and elevated values, and the elimination of wrongdoing (however you care to define it), could a deeper, gentler view of life purpose evolve?

What we really need is spiritual awareness that enriches all aspects of life, instead of now and then in the isolated context of church, synagogue, or temple during moments of crisis, confusion, or profound suffering. It never hurts to plant the seeds of peace and renewal, time and time again.

As C.G. Jung tells us, "Nature is not matter only, she is also spirit."

Inviting the Bell

"The Way of Heaven is to
benefit others and not to injure.
The Way of the sage is to act
but not to compete."

—LAO TZU

Men do change, and change comes like a little wind that ruffles the curtains at dawn, and it comes like the stealthy perfume of wildflowers hidden in the grass.
—JOHN STEINBECK

Painting the Sun

The morning hours brought subzero temperatures and a howling wind. I stood at the window and observed green trash bins teetering back and forth in driveways and sidewalks in our quiet neighborhood. Empty, with nothing to hold them in place, they rolled around like curious vestiges of yesterday—freed of weight, location, purpose.

Watching them spin about, I remembered it was Matthew's birthday, some 32 years ago. Were clues to the day ahead anywhere in sight; what emotional sustenance could I draw from the natural beauty of my surroundings?

The bare trees and cloudy sky, oddly somber.

Born in the morning on a brisk, winter day, Matthew, meaning "gift from God," had an angelic face. Maybe all infants possess this endearing quality, a peaceful, almost pinkish, glow. A trusting expression, a gentle gaze. But there also was a perplexing moment that I still recall with frightening precision. We'd only been home from the hospital a few days. Matthew was asleep in his cradle (a family heirloom), and I stood gazing at him—like mothers often do. Slightly transfixed as I relished his arrival, I heard from within these strange words of warning: "You won't have him long."

My heart nearly stopped.

Was I imagining things, feeling fearful on a subconscious level? Matthew wasn't ill—*everything was fine*—but the message was unmistakable. Undeniably real.

A deep sense of knowing grabbed me by the throat.

I struggled to push it away.

What could possibly go wrong? When? Why?

This was the last thing the mother of a beautiful newborn wanted to think about. Yet, despite my prolonged efforts to forget this mysterious intuitive message, I never could, and as my son grew up, whenever I sensed Matt's life slipping away one way or another, this disquieting memory surfaced like a faint echo.

Pulling myself from the window, the rodeo of plaintive trash bins, I glanced at a wall calendar, read the date aloud. In the aftermath of death, a fifth birthday, but with no one to make it real, to anchor it, the day was set loose.

Why did I still recognize ghost birthdays anyway?

Because it felt impossible to stop counting, and I didn't understand how the tenth of February, a day, a month, the world of time had created, could slip into "just another day" status. Even as I lived more fully in the world of spirit, looked *beyond* the constraints of time, the human mind clings to dates out of habit and social conditioning: and out of love. Zelda Fitzgerald told us, "Nobody has ever measured, even poets, how much a heart can hold." Yet, I *knew* the traditional counting of lost years was meaningless and unnecessary when viewed from a spiritual dimension—from a place of greater awareness.

Gingerly I'd been stepping away from a personalized sense of self, while sometimes indulging in mental time travel. But now, with a deep Zen-like breath, I reminded myself that "the sun shines not on us but in us." Thank you, John Muir, for clarifying things.

Idaho

At some point, we knew that professional intervention was urgently needed. I researched options for enforced treatment. Matt wasn't living at home, but his lifestyle was less than stellar; plus, he was "scarce" and "preoccupied." Never a good sign. As I studied various programs around the country, I found one in Idaho that sounded like a godsend.

After consulting with references—worried parents who had also been desperate for answers—we felt confident we'd found a viable lifeline. They understood the absolute terror of drugs, and convinced their sons' or daughters' lives were being swallowed by narcotics, a river of grief was sweeping them off their feet. We knew the demoralizing terrain; heard the heartbreak in their voices.

Slow death. Panic, despair, pain. Fear, dread.

One of the most frightening decisions we had to make along this perilous path, I spent weeks on research. We wanted a program we could believe in: a place where Matt would be safe, and hopefully helped. He needed long-term treatment, and local programs, more convenient, more affordable, were short-lived or voluntary. Not nearly enough.

Barely a spring shower in the middle of a 10-year drought.

I have wondered if short-term programs aren't part of the problem. Don't some create a false sense of progress, merely lulling everyone back to sleep?

Collectively, it seems we underreact when problems are surfacing—and possibly still treatable; then overreact, when all is lost. Do we need to reverse our thinking—try long-term treatment (involuntary, voluntary) *first*, when lasting positive change might be more achievable? Of course the price tag is steep. But imagine the *actual cost* when long-term treatment is postponed until "things get really bad" and parents are forced to take action, possibly alienating family members indefinitely when they pursue involuntary options.

Convinced this was something we had to try to save Matt's life, quietly, we made the arrangements and prayed this was the right step. We'd chosen CEDU (pronounced see-doo, closed since 2005, per Wikipedia). If memory serves, Matt was in the Ascent Wilderness Program for teens, a 30-day program that appears to have been reopened by Universal Health Services at a later date (current status unknown, however).

Accompanied by program staff, once safely in Idaho, we received regular updates via phone or fax. He didn't sound angry or fearful but, with the distance, we did our share of parental worrying. Programs to help struggling youth usually get mixed press; we ruled out some because of inconsistent or poor results, or when unable to get solid information on quality, safety. Granted, such organizations are working with difficult (unpredictable, challenging) populations, so reviews will never be perfect, but entrusting your own teen to strangers entails a considerable leap of faith. You want the best possible scenario.

Finally, we were slightly encouraged, thought we had Matt's attention, but a week or so into the program, we were advised that he had been moved to a local hospital because of mononucleosis (likely acquired before his arrival). A program doctor also prescribed an antidepressant, but the results were mixed to negligible.

Before his release, we looked around for a residential school, something of longer duration. But Matt wasn't interested. He had other things on his mind, and even though we tried to convince him he needed intensive treatment over the long term, a teenager rarely believes anything that doesn't fit his immediate priorities. Matt insisted he could quit using drugs (had experimented with several), definitely *had quit*, because of the involuntary trip to Idaho. Perhaps he wanted to believe that; perhaps, he had quit ... briefly.

A Brief Stint

Yet another time we managed to get Matt to agree to an inpatient evaluation at Charter—a local psychiatric hospital and behavioral treatment center. About 24 hours later, he was back at our front door, duffle bag in hand. "They said I could go."

So much for that idea.

I noticed in the *New York Times*, February 17, 2000, that Charter had filed Chapter 11 bankruptcy after once being one of the nation's biggest mental health providers, serving many children. Matt also participated in an outpatient program there one summer, and we went to a few group meetings with him. Probably on probation for a misdemeanor, I believe the program was court ordered or strongly suggested. Seemed reasonably helpful at the time. *This program, this counselor, or maybe Matt's maturity will make a lasting difference, or God on high will shine an unmistakable light on the road less taken. Any road, for that matter.*

But the roller coaster of addiction—trying this or that, listening to *new* voices that spoke of unique or cutting-edge programs, while fearing where this perilous path was leading—rarely paused. The consistent theme running in the background: no one *really* knew what worked, or for how long. Some loved AA's program, for instance, while others found it useless. This was a vicious, confusing circle without escape, and serving time didn't change much of anything for Matt. Most institutions aren't "drug-free," for one thing. A nice thought, but that's probably about it.

Granted, prison may have prevented him from harming himself or someone else along the way but, in terms of impacting the course of addiction, as a disease (or as something that manifested because of personality or biological issues), imprisonment wasn't a solution. I suppose it may "cure" a select few—those ready, able to move on—but it is still very difficult to pinpoint cause and effect. Just a terrifying guessing game with a multitude of variables, known and unknown. By the same token, I fully understand the critical need to protect society from dangerous, life-threatening, addiction-related behavior.

When some experts discuss addiction on television, it sounds unrealistic, like they are talking about someone with a cold or the flu, as they tally up the times someone has been *in treatment*, when there is no magic number. Programs are seldom comparable anyway. A few distinctions: inpatient, outpatient, long-term, short-term, voluntary, involuntary, experienced, well-trained staff, or merely well-meaning volunteers, crowded conditions versus realistic conditions. Resources for addicts, as a rule, are scarce or sketchy or simply unavailable; usually just shy of being enough to make a meaningful difference.

I lost count of how many therapists, programs, or probation officers had the *answers*.

Einstein, however, taught us that "No problem can be solved from the same level of consciousness that created it."

No one is all-knowing; the human mind can only figure out so much.

Plus, addicts didn't *create* addiction. Our world, the vagaries of human nature—all we have done and become since the Stone Age or before—created addiction. So, yes, it is to our advantage to remain receptive to our intuitive sparks, to a deepening connection with a higher intelligence, if we hope to generate effective solutions to the never-ending, deepening problems of our expanding global community.

Then again, addicts have to take full responsibility for their choices— their commitment to personal health and recovery. Matt knew he should never say (or believe) he was "over it," "cured," or anything else resembling finality, but, being human, I am sure he wanted to believe, like everyone, that *real* change was tucked somewhere in the cards of life. As with diets, there is generally the flimsy hope that once the 15, 25, or 50 pounds come off, end of story—even when it is probably nothing more than an enticing pause. We all seem to be part of a repetitive and endless circular story set in the context of "fixing" ourselves.

Memory Collector

In February 2010 I launched an online writing studio: a blog with book suggestions, studio guests, kindred spirit quotes. I wanted to create an online presence that focused on uplifting topics, but otherwise my ideas were unfocused. Things would have to evolve gradually, without undue planning, as I patiently followed the dictates of my heart, intuition. But as the first significant project I had sustainable energy for since Matt's loss, it felt right, even without a detailed strategy. One other thing felt certain: I wanted to honor his life and memory by offering an alternative to heavily glamorized, and endless, media stories.

I didn't rush into this with my readers though; a year passed before I broached the subject. A grief-stricken parent, yes, but first and foremost I wanted to contribute to a saner world and wasn't looking for a public place to unload my sadness.

In fact, I imagined something much larger than self; intended to shine a hopeful light on topics our easily distracted culture tends to avoid because of a dysfunctional craving for novelty, glamour, and excitement. Spirituality and wisdom, art and creativity, books and writing, nature and poetry, meditation and reflection—all in a welcoming, supportive space. Our noticeable global obsession with conflict, contention, and controversy didn't seem particularly healthy.

I also wanted to find kindred spirits: those wanting to cultivate a deeper perspective, and who wanted to connect in a friendly, mindful context. I felt adamant about avoiding acrimonious subjects. *Greatly overworked.* Above all, I intended to nurture a peaceful environment. After coping with excessive turmoil and stress for years, and then a sudden death, I was committed to avoiding toxic mind polarities that initiate an exhausting round of back and forth.

Not everything should be a ridiculous, energy-draining compe-tition. We need ways to look beyond such superficial time traps to survive, and to evolve. Gandhi said, "You must be the change you wish to see in the world." Buddha told us, "Peace comes from within. Do not seek it without."

And I could see how compulsive thinking, as Eckhart Tolle describes it, was linked to planetary suffering. As he's fond of saying, "spiritual awakening is awakening from the dream of thought," so we can transcend it.

Finally, the name for the site surfaced: SunnyRoomStudio, a creative, sunny space for kindred spirits. Simple, yet inspired, with intriguing layers to flesh out.

From my artwork as a girl—the sun I had drawn on the wall—to life isn't always sunny, but if we look within, diligently, honestly, we can forge a stronger connection to our own light, the imagery worked well. I would be drawing the sun again: figuratively, this time.

Still, I wasn't at all sure what came next.

I'd heard of WordPress, but constructing an online site, tweeting or posting to share new blog posts from a sunny room studio, weren't part of my professional background. Becoming fluent in a tricky foreign language surely would have been easier. Gradually, though, I grew comfortable with the fluid demands of technology and virtual friendships. My tentative efforts were met with encouragement; people were surprisingly helpful. But there were other reasons I loved the prospect of sharing a sunny room.

The visual was upbeat, comforting, and I often spotted our sweet pets, Noah and Lola, stretched out in our den in the morning sun. *They sure love that sunny room.* And since it was the heart of winter when this project was conceived, a sunny room of any kind had strong appeal. My sagging winter spirits craved the energy and warmth of sunlight, and when I uncovered this poignant Picasso quote—"some painters transform the sun into a yellow spot, others transform a yellow spot into the sun"—I felt quietly reassured.

Perhaps a sunny studio could, in the literary and spiritual sense, become a welcoming bridge to a new day—a place to bear the weight of sorrow, while simultaneously opening doors of connection, compassion, and creative inspiration. Not wanting to burden others with my grief—its understandable, undeniable place in my psyche—a virtual sunny room could point to the light, at least. Most are walking a challenging path; many reached out. Grateful for any kindness, I was amazed how people I knew only peripherally—a name, a picture, a brief bio on a screen—offered real understanding. Empathy I could feel, caring I could sense, seemed to emanate from knowing the hot fire of grief firsthand—from the depth within, in other words.

I decided to champion those who also wanted to grow in awareness. Creative kindred spirits drawn to personal growth, insights beyond the ordinary, and spirituality. Authors, artists, poets, dreamers. Knowing my pain only could be assuaged by giving to others in ways that felt relevant, I welcomed new voices to my sunny studio when powerful waves of sadness shook my own world.

In other words, I worked through the gloomy days: grappled with a poignant blog post, updated the site, shared a new link on social media, or invited someone I admired from afar to be a studio guest. If I wanted to be a positive force, I had to keep at it. By learning how others have survived difficult experiences, perhaps we can hope to survive ourselves. Swiss philosopher, poet, and critic, Henri Frédéric Amiel (1821–1881) said, "Self-interest is but the survival of the animal in us. Humanity only begins for man with self-surrender."

≈

As I felt stronger, gradually more certain, I began writing about Matt in my sunny studio. Not, I must add, without some trepidation. Precisely, how does one broach the subject of death, of suicide, in a sunny room—a warm, inviting place for kindred spirits to ponder the deeper mysteries from an upbeat, expansive perspective?

Unlike some blogs, I hadn't devoted much space to *my story*, because other things seemed more important. But the silence became unbearable—Matt's life and soul, etched into mine. So I searched, albeit slowly, for my public voice. Quietly at work on this book, sometimes seriously, sometimes not, I turned to my notes for inspiration.

When Matt would have turned 31, I broached the topic in a blog post called "Spiritual Roots." Easing into his death, I explained how I couldn't find the sun for a very long time—my internal sun. *My generally upbeat, positive, inspiring self took a break to delve into a spiritual dimension I didn't know existed.* Not by choice, I wrote.

A deepening spiritual awareness and refinement came via suffering, a lodged-in-the-marrow-of-bone kind of sorrow that writers and poets have described for eons. I wrote about Natalie Goldberg, poet, teacher, author of 12 books, and Zen practitioner, who felt like a friend, even though we'd never met beyond the pages of her books.

In *Wild Mind: Living the Writer's Life*, Goldberg pointed out, "Life is not orderly. No matter how we try to make life so, right in the middle of it we die, lose a leg, fall in love, drop a jar of applesauce." In *Old Friend from Far Away*, the first book I read about the art of memoir, Goldberg helped me understand the urge to share our life stories, pointing to "an ache, a longing, a passing of time that we feel all too strongly."

As I delved into mere slivers of my story, readers were supportive and understanding. Comforted by emails, notes, and comments from those who had also lost a child, a loved one, I took a deep breath. It seemed my thoughts on loss were helpful, inspiring, and even though I hadn't shared the details around Matthew's death, I had revealed a deep sorrow that greatly intensified a lifelong spiritual quest.

When August arrived, I posted "Sun Garden"; in November, "It's Morning Now." A blog post that explained how my early morning thoughts were often of Matthew.

A year later, February of 2012, on another birthday, I wrote "Memory Collector."

Memories, I began, remind me of seashells.

Beautiful remnants of various colors, sizes, shapes. They dot the beach, the sand, and we collect them. Save them. The ones we pick up and take home are empty, clean … the life they held, no longer visible. We marvel at what is left, don't we? And memories are what is left. I explained how I thought I'd understood the power of memories until Matt's death. *Once you experience a profound loss, you begin to look at everything differently, especially memories. Their role is suddenly magnified, nearly overpowering. It seems they seek you out, coming into your awareness with incredible force from out of the blue.*

Through my early posts it became apparent, from comments, messages received, that people needed to talk about death. Needed to put their arms around it, claiming it as their own: a radical truth, not an abstract event, etched into a shared human mystery. But I still wasn't using the word suicide, and wrote around it instead, with words like sudden loss, incomprehensible grief, and troubling absence. It wasn't that I wanted to avoid an obvious reality, but I wasn't fond of popularized, superficial labels and hoped to avoid putting my son in cold-sounding categories leading to instant disregard.

"Oh, you know, another suicide, drug-related."

When a stereotype is affixed to anything, understanding, compassion, even curiosity, become elusive, and sometimes impossible to arouse. Individuals with beating hearts and breathing lungs become generic entities: a statistic, a stick person like we drew in grade school, a less-than-important human life. However in a sunny space—a compassionate, caring environment, although virtual—I could showcase wise, understanding voices to negate runaway levels of indifference.

And not because I believed life should be bright and shiny, always happy and fun. Not at all. But in an era of streaming news alerts, celebrity make-believe, makeovers, and the hype of all-things-irrelevant, I sensed we desperately needed *something else*, not more of the same: senseless noise that alienates, divides and, mostly, distracts.

The power of beauty and light, empathy and compassion, nurtures us—helps all of us to grow, evolve spiritually—and negativity—complaining, criticizing, condemning—is rampant, so why contribute to that old, wearisome framework? Acknowledge reality, of course (denial is not an acceptable substitute), but otherwise, it's unwise, unhealthy, to dwell on what is *wrong* with something, or everything. *Seriously*, it can't be good for us.

There is a "muscular energy in sunlight" that corresponds to "the spiritual energy of wind," according to author Annie Dillard. I also sensed a muscular energy in stepping forward *somehow*.

Still Matt's birthday, I sat down to write. The wind howled on, but a late afternoon sun—beams of western light—landed on my computer screen in a blinding glare. Squinting, I kept at it, blinds wide open. Only eight minutes, twenty seconds, for the powerful rays to strike the window behind me, but … it had felt like forever.

Inviting the Bell

"The Way of Heaven is to
benefit others and not to injure.
The Way of the sage is to act
but not to compete."

—LAO TZU

Dwell on the beauty of life.
Watch the stars, and see yourself running with them.
—MARCUS AURELIUS

Running with the Stars

Another Easter approached. Time still taunted me when I wasn't mindful: *when I allowed it.* Another test was coming. I would be forced to seek clarity against the growing wall of time, once more. This milestone loomed large against history: Easter 2006, apple trees and our Hannibal picnic; Easter 2007, Matt's last visit home. And now, Easter 2012, I braced myself for impact: consciously and otherwise.

It was a vibrant spring morning.

This slow-moving college town in eastern South Dakota had been home for almost four years. From a north window, I surveyed our greening environment, the noticeable brightness outside, and wondered if the Easter lilies I'd planted in our Indiana yard had survived. The ones that bloomed so convincingly the week we lost Matt.

I hoped so. Didn't seem like much to ask.

But a painful and haunting question hummed loudly in the background—pressing me for distant, but crucial, answers.

What now? Time had refused to stop, slow down, or in any way change the reality of death. The sun still appeared each morning. I was intent on finishing this book, working on some poetry, and really enjoying connecting with kindred spirits in beneficial ways via SunnyRoomStudio. We inspired, supported, and learned from each other.

We'd also added a high-energy puppy, a beautiful black and silver schnauzer, to our home. Not yet an avid stargazer, Orion joined us when the famous constellation was most prominent in the late January sky. Holding him in my lap, I tried out different names, but nothing felt right until *Orion* came to me. Would he be a great hunter, we wondered? And would he get along with our beloved 10-year old schnauzer, Noah—our lovely Lola, an 11-year old white cat with gold and gray markings?

Other things were going reasonably well.

My daughter was happily employed, enjoying a new relationship. We'd made a couple of road trips to Dallas-Fort Worth to visit, including a winter trip in 2009 when there was snow, ice, and wind for Christmas. Though negligible, still record-setting for that area.

Tossed from our comfort zones into something inspiring and powerful, John and I felt like a cosmic gift—priceless, expansive, timeless—had come our way. Granted, the price had been steep: the silence and weight of loss excruciating. But undeniably, compared to those who hadn't been through anything of this magnitude, we were much richer for the experience. The stairway to heaven had been made visible. Granted, it was in plain view all along—that untouchable place within, peacefully distant from the ferocious game of life and soaring well above the fray—but it takes an earthquake to deepen our awareness. To push us past the flimsy nature of intellectual understanding to the level of knowing that resonates deeply in our core like a chiming bell. Like the sound and feel of our own breathing, it's unmistakable.

Otherwise, the hopefulness and predictable urgency of spring was upon me, and while I'd survived the rocky road of grief for some five years, "what now?" hung on. Surfacing periodically with added vigor, the question reminded me that I hadn't folded, as feared, when the news of Matthew's death felt like my own; nor, in the weeks and months that followed, when I was ghost-walking through life.

Still, nothing about this remarkable journey felt complete. "Healing," for instance, wasn't a term that resonated with me at any point along the way. So greatly overworked by our culture, the word, in fact, is losing all meaning. Plus, it pointed to something supposedly "attainable" if we did all the "right" things: committed to yet another amorphous goal in a crazy, time-saturated world.

In February 2012, author and public relations expert Gary Stromberg wrote about "drugs, rock 'n' roll and addiction" for CNN Opinion. A catalyst for his piece describing spiritual sickness was the tragic loss of Whitney Houston—headlines that "sent a familiar shiver" through him. The drug conversation, he noted, had gone from "pot, psychedelics, cocaine and heroin" to prescription drugs, and Stromberg felt he'd been "spared a life of darkness and shown a path into the light."

Explaining that "Alcohol and drugs are subtle foes: cunning, baffling and powerful," he mentioned that his saving grace was the journey within "to peel the onion" of his soul where he discovered the real problem. With admirable transparency, Stromberg admitted to being self-centered, shallow, and consumed by fears of "inadequacy, failure, success, intimacy," and anything that threatened well-guarded defenses. There was a time when he could only see "despair and death" in his future. Choosing between life and death should have been easy, but he remembers it as the exact opposite.

When it comes to addiction, an obvious choice is seldom obvious, and perhaps with a mind clouded by "habit energies of the past" (a term Buddhist monk, Thich Nhat Hanh, suggests in *Beyond the Self: Teachings on the Middle Way*), Stromberg explained that "change seemed impossible, unimaginable, incomprehensible and downright insane."

But, fortunately, he made it.

Rare and beautiful and wonderful, because the odds are sadly tipped toward leading a life of "misery, incarceration and death."

But ... *what now?*

Since so few survive this treacherous path, should I dedicate my life to telling Matt's story? Would that help those struggling, looking for the strength to continue a formidable battle with life and death? Or was this a story I should seal away in the vault of memory?

What now?

Would it ease the pain of loss, make a difference, to share my son's tribulations with the swarms of naïve youth and parents who believe drugs (the myriad forms of cultural addiction) are for those "other kids?" Bad, worthless kids.

What now?

Must I transcend this multilayered experience like some kind of modern-day saint or spiritual guru, transcending darkness by turning it into a lovely stream of heavenly light?

What now?

Should I look away, pretend not to care or notice, when a beloved memory begs to be shared, and spiritually unawakened eyes cloud over with: Do we *still* have to hear about him? Shouldn't you be focusing on the living—only the living, remember?

The unstated is often more powerful than the stated.

Death isn't part of our make-believe reality; we keep it safely at bay by not thinking about it—not for long anyway.

But life and loss (don't they see?) are inseparable: one begets, even enhances, the other.

Do I push my son's beloved voice from my mind, refusing to hear its familiar melody, his fervent wish that he, like Gary Stromberg, had chosen life over death, or had foreseen, with a powerful peek into the future, how a party—with friends who were too much like him—would get seriously out of hand that beguiling weekend in late June when the sun was so bright, so encouraging, that the impending catastrophe was somehow overlooked, minimized or, sadly, ignored?

What now?

Should I do volunteer work for worthy, life-saving organizations like the American Foundation for Suicide Prevention? Become an advocate for suicide awareness, helping society move beyond an unnatural, unhealthy culture of silence about something so very important? Or maybe I should help those left behind—when suicide wasn't prevented?

What about the plethora of punishment and incarceration issues?

I had read that Joyce Meyer Ministries donates books (gift bags) to prisoners: outreach with serious merit. Matt read books, one after another, while incarcerated.

Joyce, I believe, lost a brother to drug-related issues; Oprah, a sister. Their global and societal contributions, strong examples of what can be done. Advocacy is so important—I admired anyone engaged along such lines—but it didn't feel like my calling. David Sheff (*Beautiful Boy, Clean*) and Madeline Sharples (*Leaving the Hall Light On*), for instance, have created powerful public profiles to "get the word out." Sheff is adamant about the availability of quality drug treatment options; Sharples creates much needed awareness around effective mental health care and suicide prevention.

Madeline's handsome son also committed suicide when only 27. Paul suffered from a bipolar disorder, the subject of her well-received memoir, but before his death in 1999, he was an accomplished musician. Paul's mother, also an insightful poet, works tirelessly to bring attention to her son's pain, its dire consequences.

"He was such a pack rat," Sharples writes. "He kept everything. He cared about his things, and now he had left them all. I never thought he would leave his things."

What now?

I had also envisioned a special garden for children and youth with a stunning sculpture inscribed with poetry by Tennyson, Tagore, W.S. Merwin, or Whitman. And what about other art forms—inspiring, thought-provoking paintings to honor Matthew's memory and those suffering a similar fate?

What now?

Still gazing from the window at nascent signs of life—a pink rose bush, clematis vine, tulips—I wondered what Matt might suggest. What would grace his universal struggle—inspire others? I pictured my grandmother working in her garden, raking leaves.

What might Anna suggest: prayer, more tea, a little tune on the piano or violin, an afternoon nap, planting another walnut or apple tree? All of the above, perhaps?

Maybe I would keep it simple, just dwell on beauty or run with the stars, as Marcus Aurelius, born April 26, 121, a Roman emperor with an interest in philosophy, advised. (See the epigraph for this chapter for his exact words.) Though he valued harmony and loved mankind, he wasn't sympathetic to all religious beliefs, according to historians.

A proponent and practitioner of Stoic philosophy, his reflections, commonly referred to as *The Meditations*, contributed to his notable legacy. Aurelius didn't believe in an afterlife, however. "Death," he said, "like birth, is a secret of nature." From a noticeably practical stance, he elaborated: "Death is a release from the impressions of the senses, and from desires that make us their puppets, and from the vagaries of the mind, and from the hard service of the flesh."

Circle of Awareness

In Zen-like fashion, I have peered at this mortal walk, this experience of being defeated by greater and greater things, and wondered deeply about the inherent beauty of life, the captivating stars above—so distant and removed from private tribulations—and like the young girl of long ago, have again concluded that life, in its many guises, is always about the basics. Tea and poetry. Nature. Gardens. Music. Prayer. Life and death.

Myriad complications—problems, diversions, opportunities, experiences, and issues—arise in a lifetime, yet the fundamentals remain virtually unchanged.

Aurelius, referred to as "the wise," contemplated precisely the same things we ponder today. Believing death was liberation from human form, Aurelius, before he died March 17, 180, again reminded us that death is nature's secret.

That we *are nature* is the inevitable observation.

We are whatever there is: a mysterious expression of something ineffable, sacred.

I couldn't help but think, poking around in our garden later that afternoon, digging for signs of spring and looking for evidence of renewal, that the impressionable child in me—the one absorbing profound and lasting lessons from the grandmother who shared them with me like precious jewels—had it right. As we talked or sat in silence so long ago, I'd believed that life was all around us.

It was, and it is.

While looking for ways to better understand my son's death—to illuminate the universal, distressing experience of loss—I trusted my intuition. Followed my memories back to the beginning like a faint trail in the dark, and reached for the courage to evolve spiritually, even though I had to dig much deeper than imagined—questioning *everything* in the dense forest of existence.

Because, in the end, we must "know," not "know of."

Fortunately, the sheer force of death pointed me in all the right directions. Prompting me to see beyond the familiar constraints— faulty, narrow, commonplace assumptions—of a time-oriented world, to look instead to the timeless world of spirit, I retraced my steps, only to return to what had once seemed simple and true: because it was.

Our brief time on Earth is a spiritual retreat. A magnificent foray into what is known, yet unknown. The alpha and the omega.

And no one is excluded. We are *all* challenged, through the various life catalysts that show up, to find peace, contentment, and greater spiritual awareness in a world focused on everything *but*.

Inviting the Bell

"The Way of Heaven is to
benefit others and not to injure.
The Way of the sage is to act
but not to compete."

—LAO TZU

Nature's Secret

*L*ittle did I know, as a wide-eyed girl gazing at my grandmother's book of poetry by Lord Alfred Tennyson, that his father was an alcoholic; that one of his brother's was an opium addict. That the sudden death of Tennyson's good friend when he was only 24 inspired him to spend ten years writing over a hundred poems dedicated to Arthur Henry Hallam. Collected and published in 1850 as "In Memoriam" A.H.H. (Epilogue), Tennyson wrote:

Regret is dead, but love is more
Than in the summers that are flown,
For I myself with these have grown
To something greater than before

While the surficial aspects of life are in a state of constant flux, death isn't something we ever grow accustomed to; when it happens, we are stunned into submission, left dazed and bewildered, until we *become* the experience to survive it. But it's a slow, exhausting process because so many of us rely on the heart and mind to comprehend loss, when it is actually the soul that understands.

In fact, loss understood on the level of soul, transforms us.

But now, with nightfall approaching, seamlessly transforming a hectic spring day into a restful evening with a generous, star-filled sky, I went outside and looked up, marveled at the hidden continuity that seemed built into my life story. My grandmother happened to own a book of poetry by Tennyson—one I felt drawn to for reasons unknown—and still to this day, I hold that treasure, like my son's unforgettable spirit, in my mind's eye.

A reminder of all that can ever be known.

Of all that is gentle and right about this ephemeral, planetary spiritual retreat.

I grew up with her beautiful and bountiful apple trees, three in a row. A literal fortress on the west side of her modest home. And without conscious awareness of the symmetry involved, gave Matt three apple trees, when we met him for an Easter picnic in Hannibal. Despite everything he'd been through, everything hanging in the balance, he was excited about growing apples, eager to plant the trees. Now, their spring blossoms are a reminder that nature, like us, continually seeks meaningful expression.

But, in the wake of this experience, *who am I?*

Merely the humble expression of all that I have known: endured or enjoyed. Nothing more, nothing less. Peacefully and mindfully, I am letting go of "what now," replacing it with "what is."

It is the deepening of this moment that I want, not the unspoken pressure to run over it in the pursuit of something futuristic. Only within the depth of each moment can I experience who and what I am, and whether I know it or not, this … this alone … is enough. Each moment has the potential to be "full" and "complete" when I am deeply aware. When I am awake to the spiritual tide of an inner world containing every morning, every darkness. Every unforgettable smile of gratitude, love, and joy. Sinking into "now" is bliss. Letting a golden, comforting silence penetrate every cell, every shadow—every new day, and every sorrow.

The enchanting play of consciousness that we all represent is an animated shadow of something far greater. We begin and end our lives in stunning simplicity, and because of this predictable destiny, the days in-between exist within the sphere of time so we can experience the most profound lessons.

Some we've resisted, repeatedly skimmed over, or yearned to wish away. When haplessly lost in the external world, spiritual growth is unlikely. When we cave in to fear and hostility instead of bravely plowing the hard ground of life and loss, instead of seeking a stronger connection with our innate spiritual selves, darkness prevails. And suffering. But perhaps with the gift of a powerful catalyst, we see past the façade of daily life. Spiritual roots deepen. We transcend suffering—some of the time. I learned how to survive more pain than imagined; learned to surrender after Matt's death by allowing loss to become part of me in every sense of the word—we *are* that ultimate twining.

Yet, I love Matt the same (not in a vague, remembered way, but fully, in this moment), as though he might call, stop by, one day soon.

It sounds paradoxical, because it is.

So what, after all, is left to be said after a sudden death—when everyone departs and you are frightened and alone like never before? Only this: "Your voice, my friend, wanders in my heart like the muffled sound of the sea among the listening pines" (Tagore, *Stray Birds*).

A spiritual voice that seamlessly finds expression within mine—not only in this book, but during each moment. A voice that, one day, will merge with eternity, providing the elegant continuity nature seeks and displays, as if perpetually eager for the next second, the next ray of sunshine, the next apple blossom. And I am comforted by this miracle of life, overwhelmed by its exquisite beauty, soothed by the bright and brilliant love a young mother once knew (and still knows) for her newborn son named Matthew.

An indestructible force that, yes, is nature's secret.

Inviting the Bell

"The Way of Heaven is to benefit others and not to injure. The Way of the sage is to act but not to compete."

—LAO TZU

The holiest of all holidays are those
Kept by ourselves in silence and apart;
The secret anniversaries of the heart.
—HENRY WADSWORTH LONGFELLOW

Coming Together

A Conclusion

During the spring and early summer of 2014, we set aside travel time to visit the small country cemetery where Matt is buried. Had the spirea bushes survived? How were the apple trees doing? But rain and stormy weather kept showing up in the forecast, so we postponed our eight-hour drive to northern Missouri several times.

Finally, though, in early July, the weather sounded promising. Mild temps, and dry. I updated our motel reservation, watered the garden, packed overnight bags. Noah and Orion traveled with us; someone would check on Lola. She was independent, like most cats, but at 13, seemed less comfortable staying alone. Noah, at 12-plus years, traveled well, but Orion, no longer a puppy and well into his second year, was still learning about road trips and restricted mobility. We would be stopping frequently.

And, like always, I wondered what it would feel like to stand at Matt's grave. Trying to release any specific expectations, I wanted to let the visit unfold in its own way.

The day before had been unseasonably cool with a strong wind, overcast sky, and light, intermittent rain. Packing the car the next morning, despite the upbeat forecast, we again felt light rain, but this time we were going, no matter what.

Surely the weather would improve as we drove southeast.

After a hurried stop for coffee and flowers for the grave, we hit the road. But the day stayed cold, gray, and blustery, with more periods of rain across Iowa and south into Missouri. The sun I'd hoped for—yes, counted on—seemed unable to break through thick layers of low-hanging clouds. My cotton sweater didn't feel warm enough when we stopped to exercise the dogs, and my hair blew every direction.

When I was a girl, a teenager and college student, it had been a deep, dark brown, but insistent white strands emerged when I was just a young mother in my 20s. I loved wearing it short, carefree. The powerful Dakota wind was a persistent force (why resist nature's fury?), so I opted for the windblown look. Besides, I had never been interested in high-maintenance hairstyles, trends, or fashion. Oldish blue jeans were my style. At 59, I was even more dedicated to simplicity—to focusing on the substance of life, not shifting superficial elements that come and go like snowflakes.

Slowing, we turned from a winding country blacktop, onto a rough, one-lane gravel road, reaching the secluded cemetery in minutes.

A beautiful spot cradled by nature and silence. The metal gate was closed, and no one was around. I noticed my sense of relief. Because of the distance, we couldn't visit often, so it was a wonderful luxury to have the space to ourselves.

It was already late afternoon and the sky hadn't cleared.

I slipped John's spare jacket over my sweater.

It didn't feel anything like July. The seven-year anniversary of Matt's death, on June 24, was just days before, but now it felt more like late fall.

Still, the great oak trees directly behind Matt's headstone were cloaked in green; the weed-grass mix beneath our feet had been freshly mowed. All was quiet except for wind gusts that effortlessly stirred massive, interlocking branches laden with summer leaves. Sadly, the contrary nature of the dark unsettled sky spoke loudly of Matt's absence.

We pulled some weeds, watered the spirea bushes that, surprisingly, were thriving, and I placed flower stems in thin white tubes near Matt's headstone. Cemetery vases, I guess you could say. The flowers were bright and convincing against the dreariness of the day. Staring at them, their deep red color, their simple beauty, I didn't realize John had walked Noah and Orion to the far end of the cemetery until I heard dogs barking (dogs belonging to someone else) in the distance. I looked back at the headstone.

Then, as if a thick curtain fell around me, *pure silence.*

Deep and abiding, it absorbed all the excruciating emotions I'd known. Devastation, despair and, eventually, the complete, inevitable surrender that life demands from each one of us.

Within that unmitigated silence was Matt's presence.

No separation between us.

While this timeless journey had been a necessary isolation, an experience of becoming ever more deeply aware of all things eternal, *now, at last*, there was union. On a different plane—an invisible one—what I had so loved and admired about Matthew—his humble, most human struggle to understand and overcome his weaknesses, valiant, gut-wrenching efforts to stay alive, goodhearted essence and kind, smiling eyes—was poignantly felt in the silence that held us both.

Suspended like lights against the harsh glare of mortality, at the level of soul, we were, always would be, the one spirit.

Surrender had come slowly. I had crawled back to life.

Unwilling, uncertain, and most assuredly, completely unaware of the possibility of ever finding my son in a space of shared light and profound togetherness, but what I'd come to know, on a timeless and immortal level, *was* this place of union—an infinite destination outside of time, poetically removed from birth and death.

Deliberately connecting with my breath, noticing how powerful it felt to stand there empty of desire and longing, basking in the silence that contained everything I would ever know or need to know, it was no longer the dreaded month of June. Somehow I'd made it to a new day—*a day in July*—and Matt was there. Completely and fully, there. And only because I was also fully there in a transcendent sort of way.

Just like the three apple trees that Matthew and his father planted eight years ago right across the road from where I stood—trees alive, growing, and healthy-looking—a sacred transformation had occurred. A godsend inevitably intended by the world of spirit that is the only *true world* in our midst. I detected a deep sense of personal renewal that transcended time, sorrow, and experience.

It's funny how this works.

I, like most, didn't understand that a deeper awareness was possible until I tapped into the vastness of my spiritual dimension. We don't know what we need to know until we know it; we don't know what is missing until we find it. And we think we are *fully here* (not in the past, not in the future) when we aren't even nearby.

Staying open to all ideas, seeking wisdom from everywhere and anywhere while also trusting experience and intuitive pointers are the shiny, golden keys to the promised land.

Glancing around, I spotted John, Noah, and Orion within a few feet of me. They walked closer. We talked about leaving, remarked that the dreary weather hadn't improved.

Driving north to Des Moines for the night meant three hours in the car, so we had to pull ourselves back to the inevitable necessities of a time-constrained world.

We resisted, of course, but within the sacred hush of another wordless good-bye, I felt a sudden warmth on my back, saw a light dancing at our feet, brightening, like a glorious spotlight, the rugged-looking stone marking Matt's life, the red flowers beside it. Turning slowly westward, looking skyward, there it was—*the afternoon sun.*

Squinting, I shielded my eyes, as thick rolling clouds of blustery, gray-black garlands parted briefly, and sunlight pierced the sky. In the picture I took, I see light and shadow as one. What a captivating moment, this gift of illumination. Tears came to my eyes, but a grateful smile also crossed my face: the journey had mattered.

Standing in the light, *I knew.*

Thich Nhat Hanh tells us, "In the sunlight of awareness, everything becomes sacred."

Despite unbearable circumstances, undesirable eventualities, or raucous debates about the purely intellectual aspects of life and death, like night stars, we are all intense surface lights, sparkling and bright—temporarily, as if for a single, deep breath. Yet, invariably, we do get our moment in the sun and, with persistence or a gentle nudge, find our way to an authentic spiritual freedom.

Somehow, even as a girl, I must have known this.

If the doors of perception were cleansed, everything
would appear to man as it is—infinite.
—WILLIAM BLAKE (1757–1827)

Afterword

Recently, as I penned an essay for the Women's Writing Circle founded by memoirist Susan Weidener, I finally tackled an issue that had been on my mind since the earliest days after Matt's death. Frequently, I encountered the word "healing." Sympathy cards, grief literature, conversations, movies. Intuitively, I sensed its inadequacies: the word's generic, overworked role in our culture. While possibly meaningful in a physical context, it didn't begin to capture the spiritual growth I was seeking or, ultimately, experienced.

When confronted with profound mystery—the fear and intrigue an infinite void ushers in—I wasn't pursuing healing. The notion, in fact, is somewhat misleading, suggesting a linear path, a terminal destination created by a world dominated by time, and its heavy, misdirected expectations. How, after all, could the mystery of life and death be something to heal—and isn't the fierce sadness of loss, at its core, built into that very mystery?

How could it be otherwise?

When I participated with sustained intention in an eternal dance with everything seen and unseen, I intuited a more complete story. Death itself, minus all causal links, is not a disease, a mental problem, or a surgical procedure, and while it leads to despair, anguish, and uncertainty, experiencing the death of a loved one also creates an entry point into unseen forces that offer liberation from our suffering. As noted in my essay, even if this is primarily a matter of semantics, why not choose empowerment over victimization?

Why not listen for the deeper message of loss: the eternal heartbeat of the universe?

The unfathomable void (within, without) ushered in by loss is intrinsic to the web of life: inherent to "what is," not just the stinging absence of "what was." So when looking at the big picture—the yin, the yang, of things—grief and loss are, more precisely, about finding the courage and the determination to come to a more complete understanding of life in its glorious, yet utterly baffling, entirety.

An inexplicable void, in the end, is a troubling invitation—one we are asked to accept by embracing it through surrender and hard-earned understanding. Ultimately, the choice is ours, but to exchange profound spiritual growth for anything less doesn't appeal to me. And if that is "healing," I'm okay with that, because that is a timeless path illuminated by the grace notes of an eternal mystery. One that feels fluid, yet static—that holds the key to everything seen and unseen; one I wish to know as deeply as possible.

Through our mortality we all share the burden of grief, along with its inevitable light. Thus, to speak of healing is to speak of something that impacts humanity as a whole, and despite the seemingly haphazard nature of everything, I sense we are all growing toward something ineffable. Even my awareness feels sacred, undeserved. Letting go of notions of "personal healing" is to embrace a much bigger idea by looking within for a boundless essence that, containing everything, needs no healing at all.

To read my original essay, "An Eternal Heartbeat," please visit susanweidener.com.

Next to ingratitude the most painful thing to bear is gratitude.
—HENRY WARD BEECHER

Acknowledgements

My gratitude to everyone who read early drafts of my manuscript; your interest, patience, time, and keen observations were instrumental in the ongoing development of this book. My appreciation to those sharing relevant material: Loretta Laroche, stress management consultant; poet Edward Hirsch; author Madeline Sharples; Andrew Solomon, Ph.D., professor of Clinical Psychology at Columbia University Medical Center; *Guardian News & Media, Ltd.*, 2014 article. Also, special thanks to Jael Photography (author photo), and Paul C. Jackson for cover art.

A warm thank you to family and friends, beloved pets Noah, Orion, Lola, and Hannah, and the inspiration of countless other people: supportive blog readers in SunnyRoomStudio who have shared key aspects of this journey; Michele DeFilippo and everyone at 1106 Design; and anyone else contributing to this book in big or small ways.

I know of no way to adequately thank the many kindred spirits who generously offered advice, ideas, and wisdom, except to say, *it meant so very much*. And, finally, blessings, love, and gratitude to the beloved son who inspired this journey, this memoir and, sadly, this belated message: I *tried* not to worry, Matthew.

In some respects, this book, indirectly, also gives Matthew an opportunity to help others. For that, I am extremely grateful.

Book Notes

The artist behind the watercolor that graces the cover is Paul C. Jackson of Columbia, Missouri. "Silence of Morning" reflects the intriguing play of earthly shadows and first light—the mysterious nature of life itself. Honored with signature membership, when only 30, by the American Watercolor Society, Jackson is also a Signature member of the National Watercolor Society, and an Honor Member of the Missouri Watercolor Society.

A prolific artist and inspired world traveler, Paul is one of today's most versatile and visible contemporary watercolorists. Whether he's painting landscape, cityscape, portrait, architecture, still life or abstract, his work captivates with genuine emotion, intensity, and finesse. Jackson is the author of *Painting Spectacular Light Effects in Watercolor*, from North Light Books, and *The Wandering Watercolorist*, from Chameleon Press, 2013.

Most of his portfolio of watercolors hangs in private or public collections. Since completing his master of fine arts, Jackson has received top honors in national and international competitions, and has been featured as one of the Master Painters of the World in the *International Artist* magazine. Visit his website at pauljackson.com, or contact him—he enjoys opportunities to collaborate—at pauljacksonart@gmail.com.

• A Word about Capturing Morning Press

I established my own publishing imprint in 2014. My reasons were many. Given the relentless pace of change within traditional publishing avenues, it seems wise to retain the rights to my work. Also, having been a development consultant, I enjoy innovation and project management.

There is something to be said for doing things in your own time frame, at a pace that best accommodates the creative process. Choosing cover art, for instance. A book title. For a deeply personal book like *The Silence of Morning*, I only arrived at the title after trying on many alternatives. It didn't surface until I'd worked on the manuscript for many years, yet fit the book like no other. As if caught in a whirlwind, it instantly returned me to the *very moment* of loss by pointing to a most remarkable truth, revealed in a powerful (and illuminating) context that was never to be forgotten.

On a pragmatic level, marketing is also in my hands with my own imprint. Whether I do it or not, how I do it, or when. Speaking to groups, signings, readings, interviews—all are thankfully, optional. As a quiet, reflective writer, shouldn't words on a page speak for me—isn't that the real point, the challenge, of being an author? Publication, in this era, is about literary choices—carving out a creative space to generate a vision that aligns with authorial priorities and projects, imbuing them with personal meaning, even eloquence.

This book, for instance, could have been edited *(changed)* from perfectly reasonable perspectives, but I wasn't aiming for "literary perfection"—or any arbitrary standard, for that matter.

Is *any life* long enough for that?

Besides, after living through the "silence of morning," and all that followed, many things that are *supposed* to matter ... simply didn't, and don't. A lovely, revitalizing liberation from much societal nonsense, you might say. I was striving, however, for a measure of artistic grace: a memoir remembered and written to the best of my ability that respected the divine proclivities of grief itself. I was also deeply committed to sharing Matthew's story in a way that honored his journey, and mine.

- **Lament**

If you are bereaved, there are many wonderful books to read, to contemplate. One I discovered not long ago, however, deserves special mention—*Lament for a Son* by Nicholas Wolterstorff. Published by Eerdman's in 1987, the author—the father—is (or was) professor emeritus of philosophical theology at Yale. The soft cover is hardly more than 100 pages with abundant white space, but therein you will meet Eric, the beloved son, who died at 25 in a mountain-climbing accident in Austria.

Nicholas notes in a 1997 preface, "If he was worth loving, he is worth grieving over. Grief is existential testimony to the worth of the one loved. That worth abides." He goes on to explain, "I do not try to put it behind me, to get over it, to forget it. I do not try to *dis*-own it." And, finally, "I shall remember Eric. Lament is part of life." But, wonderfully, and joyfully, he specifies that "every lament is a love-song."

- **Memoir (also literary, creative, or narrative nonfiction)**

If you are a writer or a memoirist—curious about the fine art of personal narrative (not biography, autobiography, journalism, or history)—here are a few books (more shared on my website) you might enjoy consulting:

> *The Memoir and the Memoirist: Reading & Writing Personal Narrative*—Thomas Larson
>
> *The SITUATION and the STORY: The Art of Personal Narrative*—Vivian Gornick
>
> *Standing at Water's Edge: Moving Past Fear, Blocks, and Pitfalls to Discover the Power of Creative Immersion*—Anne Paris, Ph.D.
>
> *Still Writing: The Perils and Pleasures of a Creative Life*—Dani Shapiro
>
> *Breaking Ground on Your Memoir*—Linda Joy Myers
>
> *The Gift: Creativity and the Artist in the Modern World*—Lewis Hyde
>
> *The Mindful Writer: Noble Truths of the Writing Life*—Dinty W. Moore
>
> *The Art of Memoir*—Mary Karr

- **The Merits of Memoir and Writing Retreats**

Laura Munson, *This Is Not The Story You Think It Is: A Season of Unlikely Happiness* (2010, memoir), also offers the Haven Writing Retreats in Whitefish, Montana, so I asked her why she believed so strongly in the spoken, and unspoken, merits of the writers' path.

"I hear people say all the time that they're not creative; even if they were, they don't have a unique voice or unique stories to tell. None of that is true. We are all creative beings, in a state of constant creation, choosing the words that come out of our mouths, the couches in our living rooms, the clothes we put on. And no one can do it quite like you. You have a voice. You have stories. They are unique, important.

At Haven Writing Retreats, we help you find that voice, those stories, and give you permission to set it free through the act of writing. You don't have to be a *writer* to attend—just a seeker longing to dig deeper into self-awareness and creative self-expression in a supportive community, with a strong facilitator. Take this powerful stand for yourself. Experience what over 400 people say changed their lives: what is in the top three retreats in the United States. It just might change your life too! Writing, a deeply transformational, therapeutic tool, should be right up there with diet and exercise in the valuable realm of preventative wellness!"

Visit her website at lauramunson.com for retreat details.

Another great resource for retreats and writing instruction is author Susan Pohlman. "I love creating retreat experiences for women. To gather groups of seekers in beautiful settings."

Susan frequently hosts transformational travel retreats in places like Santa Fe and the Italian Riviera—*either location, a journey of discovery and renewal that speaks to the soul and reorients the spirit.*

A wonderful guide, an energetic, spirited leader, she knows Italy well.

I loved her 2010 memoir, *Halfway to Each Other—How a Year in Italy Brought Our Family Home.* I marveled at the courage—the willingness to grow—that graced the pages of her book. If you've ever wondered how an American family found a way to pack up and move to Italy to find a new start (it actually is possible), you'll want to read this memoir.

I was deeply inspired by this couple. On the brink of separation after an 18-year marriage and two beautiful children, they chose not to cave in to their many frustrations, opting instead for a brave and inspiring change of venue: one that worked!

Learn more about Susan's availability (speaking engagements, writing instruction) and upcoming travel retreats, at susanpohlman.com.

I also asked author Shirley Showalter about the world of memoir. "Writing a memoir is like doing archaeology—on yourself. You've got to dig and sift and examine lots of dirt, exposing it to air and sunlight. Then when you have nothing but pieces, you need to locate the structure. It must come from your heart."

For more about Shirley's 2013 memoir, *Blush: A Mennonite Girl Meets a Glittering World*, visit shirleyshowalter.com. Her website includes numerous resources on memoir, including a list of her favorite titles.

- **A Personal Note on Memoir**

To these wise voices I would just add this—if you wish to write memoir, let your most intriguing life questions fuel your journey. Some you will answer while you write, others will linger on. And that's okay. As Rainer Maria Rilke once explained, "Be patient toward all that is unsolved in your heart and try to love the questions themselves, like locked rooms and like books that are now written in a very foreign tongue. Do not now seek the answers, which cannot be given you because you would not be able to live them. And the point is, to live everything. Live the questions now. Perhaps you will then gradually, without noticing it, live along some distant day into the answer."

And to the contrarians out there who don't quite see the merit of a genre that is clearly here to stay, I would recommend the actual writing of a memoir (a strong attempt at least); see if the process changes your opinion. Perhaps the detractor role won't be quite as compelling after digging deep into your own experiences, seeking something of merit to share with others.

Finally, if you want to write memoir for publication ... read memoirs. As many as possible. Style and structure vary a great deal, and we all can learn from the masters of this powerful art form. Many would put Vladimir Nabokov in this category. *Speak, Memory* is a classic that was first published in 1951. Though I haven't read it yet, the book is on my bookshelf, and I have a feeling I will find Nabokov most intriguing now that I have written a memoir myself.

We need memoirs to connect us to others in meaningful ways—to help us grow in empathy and understanding, to learn more about the human condition and how we might contribute to a better world. Only through profound personal connection can we hope to survive the vagaries of existence: the mystery of each breath.

• An Inevitable Direction

As we go about our lives, inevitably, we will face another loss, and another. It can feel like a steady stream of departures is upon us each morning, each evening. We can't change it; we can't pretend it is otherwise. But, perhaps, we can be there for others when death occurs. Not from obligation, but with empathy and love.

"When we honestly ask ourselves which persons in our lives mean the most to us, we often find that it is those who, instead of giving advice, solutions, or cures, have chosen rather to share our pain and touch our wounds with a gentle and tender hand. The friend who can be silent with us in a moment of despair or confusion, who can stay with us in an hour of grief and bereavement, who can tolerate not knowing, not curing, not healing and face with us the reality of our powerlessness, that is the friend who cares."

These gentle words of compassion from Henri J.M. Nouwen, *Out of Solitude*, ring with potential and grace. And trust. Somehow we remember and appreciate those who have been there for us in a deeply spiritual way. Analysis and many words, in general, fall short when emotions run deep. Then, there is a pressing need for the willingness to simply sit in silence in a true spirit of understanding, acceptance, and peace.

Because, in the end, all we are ever doing is easing ourselves into greater self-awareness. Walking on and on until we meet ourselves anew, as if for the first time.

About the Author

The author and her son, Matthew (at 26 years),
November 2006, Thanksgiving weekend.

D.A. (Daisy) Hickman, poet, prose author, and publisher, is also the 2010 founder of SunnyRoomStudio—a creative, sunny space for kindred spirits. There, you'll find her author blog, kindred spirit quotes, and book suggestions (grief literature included). Hickman also features inspiring Studio Guests (other authors, artists).

The author holds a master's in sociology (Iowa State University), and earned her bachelor's in legal studies at Stephens College (Columbia, Missouri). A member of the Academy of American Poets and South Dakota State Poetry Society, Hickman is at work on a poetry collection, *Barely Touching the Earth*, and a new book of literary nonfiction.

For author updates or to subscribe to Hickman's blog, visit SunnyRoomStudio.com or follow her on Facebook and Twitter. Send email to wisdom@sunnyroomstudio.com.

www.ingramcontent.com/pod-product-compliance
Lightning Source LLC
LaVergne TN
LVHW011216080426
835509LV00005B/150